Critical Essays on
W. H. AUDEN

CRITICAL ESSAYS
ON
BRITISH LITERATURE

Zack Bowen, General Editor
University of Miami

Critical Essays on

W. H. AUDEN

edited by

GEORGE W. BAHLKE

G. K. Hall & Co. / New York
Maxwell Macmillan Canada / Toronto
Maxwell Macmillan International / New York   Oxford   Singapore   Sydney

Excerpts from Auden's poems from *W. H. Auden: Collected Poems,* edited by
Edward Mendelson. Copyright © 1976 by Edward Mendelson, William
Meredith, and Monroe K. Spears, Executors of the Estate of W. H. Auden.
Reprinted by permission of Random House, Inc. Lines from "Lapis Lazuli"
are reprinted with the permission of Macmillan Publishing Company from
The Poems of W. B. Yeats: A New Edition, edited by Richard J. Finneran.
Copyright 1940 by Georgie Yeats, renewed 1968 by Bertha Georgie Yeats,
Michael Butler Yeats, and Anne Yeats. Excerpts from "Little Gidding" in
Four Quartets, copyright 1943 by T. S. Eliot and renewed 1971 by Esme
Valerie Eliot, reprinted by permission of Harcourt Brace Jovanovich, Inc.
Excerpts from *Studies in Iconography: Humanistic Thought in the Art of the
Renaissance* by Erwin Panofsky, copyright 1939, 1962, 1967 by Erwin
Panofsky, reprinted by permission of HarperCollins Publishers.

G. K. Hall & Co.
Macmillan Publishing Company
866 Third Avenue
New York, New York 10022

Maxwell Macmillan Canada, Inc.
1200 Eglinton Avenue East
Suite 200
Don Mills, Ontario M3C 3N1

Library of Congress Cataloging-in-Publication Data

Critical essays on W.H. Auden / edited by George W. Bahlke.
  p.   cm. — (Critical essays on British literature)
Includes bibliographical references and index.
ISBN 0-8161-8855-6
1. Auden, W. H. (Wystan Hugh), 1907–1973—Criticism and
interpretation.   I. Bahlke, George W., 1934– .   II. Title: W. H.
Auden.   III. Series.
PR6001.U4Z638   1991
811'.52—dc20   91-15524

The paper used in this publication meets the minimum requirements
of American National Standard for Information Sciences—Permanence
of Paper for Printed Library Materials, ANSI Z39.48-1984. ∞

10 9 8 7 6 5 4 3 2 1

Printed in the United States of America

In Memory of My Mother

Wie hab ich das gefühlt, was Abschied heisst
                    —*Rainer Maria Rilke*

Contents

♦

General Editor's Note

◆

The Critical Essays on British Literature series provides a variety of approaches to both the classical writers of Britain and Ireland, and the best contemporary authors. Formats of the volumes in the series vary with the thematic designs of individual editors, and with the amount and nature of existing reviews, criticism, and scholarship. In general, the series represents the best in published criticism, augmented, where appropriate, by original essays written by recognized authorities. It is hoped that each volume will be unique in developing a new overall perspective on its particular subject.

Both George Bahlke's introduction and selection of essays deal first with various critical assessments of the political and theological aspects of W. H. Auden's work. He traces both sides of the critical debate about Auden's commitment to liberal humanism as he returned to the Anglican church and began to embrace more Christian existentialism in his later poetry. Some of Bahlke's selections treat the poet's considerable involvement with music, as well as his literary criticism. The volume concludes on a biographical note with personal recollections by Christopher Isherwood, Igor Stravinsky, and Stephen Spender.

ZACK BOWEN, General Editor

University of Miami

Publisher's Note

◆

Producing a volume that contains both newly commissioned and reprinted material presents the publisher with the challenge of balancing the desire to achieve stylistic consistency with the need to preserve the integrity of works first published elsewhere. In the Critical Essays series, essays commissioned especially for a particular volume are edited to be consistent with G. K. Hall's house style; reprinted essays appear in the style in which they were first published, with only typographical errors corrected. Consequently, shifts in style from one essay to another are the result of our efforts to be faithful to each text as it was originally published.

A Note on Auden's Texts

◆

The most scholarly and correct editions of W. H. Auden's poetry now available are as follows: W. H. Auden, *Collected Poems,* ed. Edward Mendelson (New York: Random House, 1976); W. H. Auden, *The English Auden: Poems, Essays, and Dramatic Writings, 1927–1939, (EA)* ed. Edward Mendelson (New York: Random House, 1977); and W. H. Auden and Christopher Isherwood, *Plays and Other Dramatic Writings by W. H. Auden, 1928–1938,* ed. Edward Mendelson (Princeton, N.J.: Princeton University Press, 1988). Mendelson included in *Collected Poems* (1976) "all the poems that W. H. Auden wished to preserve, in a text that represents his final revisions" (11). *The English Auden,* the contents of which Mendelson summarizes on pages xx–xxi of his preface, contains the poems through "September 1, 1939" (in *Another Time* [1940]). Most students of Auden's poetry would want to read his 1930s poems, in both their earlier versions, in *The English Auden,* and their revised forms in *Collected Poems.*

 Plays and Other Dramatic Writings, 1928–1938 is the first volume in Princeton University Press's projected complete edition of Auden's works, which will be invaluable to readers of Auden. Mendelson indicates in his preface (ix) that the next volume in this edition "will include Auden's libretti and other dramatic works from 1939" to Auden's death in 1973. Later volumes will offer the complete essays and reviews, as well as the complete poems. Also very helpful to readers of Auden is *W. H. Auden: The Critical Heritage,* ed. John Haffenden (London: Routledge and Kegan Paul, 1983), a collection of chronologically arranged reviews of Auden's individual volumes; Haffenden's long introduction surveys the reception of Auden's poetry from his first volume (*Poems* [1930]) through *Thank You, Fog* (1974), his posthumous volume.

 Other editions of Auden's poetry to which the writers in this collection refer include *The Collected Poetry* (New York: Random House, 1945), *Collected Longer Poems, 1927–1957* (London: Faber and Faber, 1968; New York: Random House, 1969), *Collected Shorter Poems, 1927–1957 (CSP)* (London: Faber and Faber, 1966; New York: Random House, 1966), and *Selected Poems (SP)*, ed. Edward Mendelson (New York: Random House, 1979).

For a bibliography of Auden's works and books about Auden, B. C. Bloomfield and Edward Mendelson, *W. H. Auden: A Bibliography, 1924– 1969* (Charlottesville: University of Virginia Press, 1972) is essential. The annual bibliography of the Modern Language Association should be consulted for critical work on Auden.

Other abbreviations of Auden's titles that appear in parenthetical and end notes in the essays reprinted here include:

AH: About the House (New York: Random House, 1965; London: Faber and Faber, 1966)

CP: The Collected Poetry of W. H. Auden (New York: Random House, 1945)

CW: A Certain World (New York: Random House, 1970; London: Faber and Faber, 1971)

CWW: City without Walls (London: Faber and Faber, 1969; New York: Random House, 1970)

DH: The Dyer's Hand (New York: Random House, 1962; London: Faber and Faber, 1963)

FA: Forewords and Afterwords (New York: Random House, 1973; London: Faber and Faber, 1973)

Critical Essays on

W. H. AUDEN

Introduction

♦

GEORGE W. BAHLKE

Since W. H. Auden's return in 1940 to the Anglican church in which he had been raised, the assessment of his poetry has been very much bound up with the problem of belief. For those liberal or left-wing 1930s intellectuals who regarded Auden as a traitor to what they believed, incorrectly, to be his Marxist orientation in the preceding decade, Auden seemed to have retreated into a private world in which he was merely playing with the counters of twentieth-century Protestant theology. For those writers and critics who were sympathetic to the Christian existentialism in his later poetry, Auden had quite rightly turned his back on what they saw as his liberal humanist position which extended from *Poems* (1930) through *Another Time* (1940).

Randall Jarrell, who had admired Auden's 1930s poetry, wrote two articles in the early 1940s about Auden's career in which he condemned Auden's new poetry as dishonest and frivolous. In the second of these articles, "Freud to Paul: The Stages of Auden's Ideology," Jarrell proposes descriptive tags for each of the three stages that he identifies in Auden's poetry from *Poems* (1930) through *Collected Poetry* (1945). For the third, religious stage, he suggests only one word, *Paul,* adding, ironically, "it is hard to resist [calling it] *Grace Abounding; The Teleological Suspension of Ethics; Waiting for the Spark from Heaven to Fall.*" Jarrell condemns what he takes to be not just Auden's indifference to the human suffering the Second World War had entailed but his "acceptance" of it: "The determinism of Stage I" ["the unrecognized or opposed Necessity that determines men and Man"] has returned, but transfigured by that Christian optimism which, in its avid acceptance of the worst evils of our world as necessarily inseparable from our fleshly existence, is more frightening than the most pessimistic of world views."[1]

Jarrell, in a sense, psychoanalyzes Auden; he tracks down the sexual guilts and anxieties lying behind the three stages of development he defines in the poetry. Auden's commitment to Christianity allowed him to accept responsibility for his fallen condition, "his own guilty depravity," while attributing to God the responsibility for all the rest of the universe. Jarrell, like other writers and intellectuals of the thirties, ultimately accuses Auden of a shocking indifference to political events: "To be able to spend his time feeling guilty over the primary fission of the germ-cell instead of over that primary fission of the atom which produced in a few minutes half a million casualties—what a God-sent mercy this ability is to Auden, what a final expression of the depths and necessities of his being!"[2]

Jarrell's condemnation of what he took to be Auden's irresponsibility had reinforcement and apparent scholarly justification in Joseph Warren Beach's *The Making of the Auden Canon* (1957).[3] The changes Auden made in his poems while preparing them for the publication of *The Collected Poetry* (1945) and *Collected Shorter Poems* (1950) trouble Beach because he believes them to be revisions that allowed the "unregenerate" poetry of the thirties to be assimilated with the "pious" poems Auden wrote following his return to the Church (marked for most readers by *The Double Man* [1941], *New Year Letter* in the English edition).[4] In tracing and commenting on these changes in his book, Beach ultimately finds Auden to be "dishonest," in spite of his admiration for Auden's extraordinary intelligence and wide-ranging reading, his "earnest effort to be an educated modern thinker" and his ability to assimilate a great variety of earlier literary modes and styles: "In a work of art, as in a man, we are best satisfied when we are confidently aware of a wholeness, or integrality, that underlies all the diverse and even conflicting elements."[5]

Auden's literary executor and editor, Edward Mendelson, supported the changes Auden made by printing all the poems in the definitive, posthumous *Collected Poems* (1976) in their revised forms—not only to carry out Auden's wish but also because he believed the new versions to be better "on the whole."[6] In *The English Auden* (1977) and *Selected Poems* (1979) he chose to reprint the earlier versions of most of the poems, partly in response to "the claims of history, and of readers who want the discarded poems."[7] Surely Mendelson is correct, however, in arguing that a poet has the right to apply a moral standard to his earlier poems if, like Auden, he believes it important to expunge them of hateful or false ideas. Mendelson is probably also right in asserting that the history of Auden's reception by his readers reveals gradual acceptance and approval of what initially seemed very "unsettling" changes.[8]

The alterations, excisions, and additions Auden made primarily in the poems he wrote before 1942 reflect his greater certainty about both his beliefs and his craft in the later poetry. Yet the inference some critics have made from Auden's publishing practices—that he was somehow dishonest, insincere, and even frivolous—bears significantly on the critical judgment and opinion of his work. John Haffenden's introduction to the Auden volume in the *Critical Heritage* series, a collection of representative reviews of Auden's individual volumes (and a very useful book in its account of Auden's critical reception), indicates how equivocal the judgment of Auden's poetry has been, especially in the years following his move to America and his return to the Church.[9]

Some critics continued to accuse Auden of frivolity, especially in their reviews of his later volumes, from *Nones* (1951) through his posthumous *Thank*

You, Fog (1974). Although some reviewers who were also his good friends could not write objectively about his poetry, other more detached reviewers allow us to trust the objectivity of their judgments, insofar as detachment is possible in any review. Nevertheless, one cannot reach an objective evaluation by weighing the number of favorable reviews of any volume against the number of unfavorable ones. The general charge against Auden's poetry of lightness is not far removed from Beach's argument that Auden was in some way dishonest, that he wore too many masks, and that his concern with the "surface" of poetry, its forms, language, and tone, outweighed his interest in its content. (Beach's underlying assumption, like Jarrell's, is that poetry should engage with contemporary political circumstances.)

Although not many readers (or professional critics and reviewers, for that matter) thoroughly understood Auden's poetry in the thirties, they assumed that he was entirely sympathetic with communism. After all, he had diagnosed England's ills—its rigid social structure, which put the instruments of production in the hands of a few "managers," the aristocrats and rich commoners; its decadence, which he typically expressed in images of sickness; and its postdepression landscape of abandoned machines and factories—even though he did not, or could not, suggest a cure. His love for the Icelandic sagas—and later, a journey to Iceland with Louis MacNeice—gave Auden a highly expressive metaphor: he used the sagas' starkness and understatement to describe contemporary England. Other sources for his imagery included Old English poetry, Thomas Hardy's poetry, Bertolt Brecht's plays—especially *Threepenny Opera* (1928)—Rainer Maria Rilke's psychologizing of landscape (which Auden imitated in "Paysage Moralisé" [1936]), Sigmund Freud, the psychologist Georg Groddeck's functional view of illness, D. H. Lawrence's ideological books (*Psychoanalysis and the Unconscious* [1921] and *Fantasia of the Unconscious* [1922]), schoolboy games, popular songs, and biology (Auden's scientific bent is unusual among modern poets). Part of Auden's skillfulness in this period was the ease with which he assimilated his reading, what he heard in the cabarets of Berlin, and what he saw both in his native England and in the countries he traveled in (Spain, Iceland, and China). This skillful assimilation, combined with his extraordinary openness to influence, constituted part of the excitement his first readers felt. But above and beyond these characteristics, the apparently iconoclastic, revolutionary tone in many of his poems led readers to cast Auden as a strong spokesman for left-wing views when, in fact, he was never entirely comfortable with them.

Among the most astute of Auden's first critics was Babette Deutsch. In the chapter "Poetry and Politics" in *This Modern Poetry* (1935), Deutsch writes about Auden in the context of his fellow "revolutionaries," C. Day Lewis and Stephen Spender. Deutsch praises their "exactitude of phrase" and their relation to British poetry, which was closer than that of their predecessors, who had admired French literature more than English.[10] Deutsch notes

Auden's delight in the imagery of machines, in contrast to the American Fugitives' disgust for it. Quite rightly, she sees Auden's attack on the bourgeoisie as a form of buffoonery in its fusion of mocker with self-mockery. She suggests that Auden's "obscurity" in his early poetry was not so much his "fault" as it was a consequence of modern education's specialized nature: the common knowledge earlier generations of readers had shared with their poets allowed them all to understand one another better. Finally, Deutsch points out that Samuel Butler's iconoclasm may have been as great an influence on the early Auden as were other, more widely recognized ones.

Among the early works that Auden later repudiated (although he salvaged some poems from it) was *The Orators: An English Study* (1932). When Auden looked back on this early work in 1967, it seemed to him to have been written by an entirely different person; "My name on the title-page seems a pseudonym for someone else, someone talented but near the border of sanity, who might well, in a year or two, become a Nazi."[11]

Auden included very little of *The Orators* in *The Collected Poetry* (1945). Originally, *The Orators* was in three books; the first book contained four prose sections, one of which, "Letter to a Wound," Auden reprinted verbatim. The second and most obscure book, "Journal of an Airman," he dropped entirely. Of the six odes that make up the third book, Auden chose to retain four in *Collected Poetry* (1945): "January 1, 1931," "The Exiles," "Which Side Am I Supposed to Be on," and "Not, Father, further do prolong."[12]

Nevertheless, *The Orators,* in its original form, remains crucial to an understanding of Auden's early poetry. His most extended diagnosis of English society in the thirties, it embodies the sickness and decay beneath the surface of public-school and bourgeois behavior: through his creation of a comic incongruity between the manner and the matter, Auden sustained an ironic contemplation of English society in the process of decay without addressing specific social problems or institutions. In "Address for a Prize-Day," an old public-school boy addresses his school's students on prize day; in "Letter to a Wound," written in the style of a bourgeois billet-doux, the writer speaks not to a beloved but to a secret, festering wound, which critics have taken to be a symbol for the sickness of upper-middle-class life, for homosexuality, or for sin.

David Lehman, in his review of *The English Auden,* places *The Orators* in the context of the modern prose poem, pointing to its easy assimilation of different genres and "subliterary" texts. Turning away from the political implications of *The Orators*—not because he does not acknowledge them but because Auden himself recognized the incipient Nazi in his former, ostensibly left-wing self—Lehman praises the radically different styles present in the works. Just as Eliot mixed voices and accents in *The Waste Land* (1922), Lehman sees Auden's genius here as "an ironic renewal of the rhetorical devices of English prose, stripped from their familiar contexts and playfully re-situated." Lehman points out that the subtitle of *The Orators,* "An English

Study," alludes to the work's parody of the courses in English studies that a public-school student would take and, with a shift of emphasis, to the poem's analysis of England between the two world wars.[13]

Auden's most avowedly left-wing play, *The Dance of Death* (1933), had its first production by the Group Theatre in London on 24 February 1934. Robert Medley, a painter and former classmate of Auden's at the Gresham School, and Rupert Doone, a dancer, had founded the Group Theatre as a way of fusing a theater of mixed forms (dance, mime, and speech) with left-wing beliefs.[14] Medley and Doone suggested to Auden that he write either a *danse macabre* or a ballet on the theme of Orpheus in the underworld for Doone to choreograph and perform in as the leading dancer. Auden, who initially planned to include words in the ballet to create a "choral ballet affair," later chose to submit to Doone and Medley a *danse macabre* as a mixed form that he intended to go beyond the Group Theatre's concept of "total theatre." Its musical and theatrical forms are largely those of popular art (the cabaret and the pantomime)—an appropriate choice for an attempt to communicate directly with the proletariat.

The Dance of Death has as its theme the inherent self-destructiveness of the bourgeoisie. Death, the dancer, represents the death wish of this doomed class, which diverts itself in its last hours with such pursuits as sunbathing, anti-Semitism, drugs, and mysticism. Edward Mendelson sees the play's failure—quite apart from its gross oversimplifications—as a result of Auden's inability to fuse an economic and psychological analysis of the dying middle classes.[15]

John Fuller summarizes clearly *The Dog beneath the Skin* (1935), Auden's best play, written in collaboration with Christopher Isherwood (and anticipating his later cooperative efforts in writing opera librettos and translations of librettos with Chester Kallman).[16] Fuller includes a summary of the text of *The Chase,* an earlier draft of *Dog,* and points out that *Dog* makes up in its denser dramatic texture for what it lacks in political complications. Fuller not only sorts out the interpretive cruxes in other commentaries on the play but also notes such influences on the play as Lawrence's psychological "think books" (as Auden referred to them when he noted that they had dangerously influenced his writing in *The Orators*), *Alice in Wonderland,* Groddeck's and Homer Lane's functional views of illness, and, especially, T. S. Eliot's poetry. Just as Herbert Greenberg suggests that Karl Marx in *The Dance of Death* seems more like Groucho Marx,[17] so Fuller suggests that one of the scenes Isherwood wrote recalls the Marx Brothers' movies in its "violence and offhand illogicality." He finally argues that the apparent vagueness of "the enemy" in *The Dog beneath the Skin* is bound up with "the mysterious inevitability" of the play's actions; Fuller admires its fusion of an engaging lightness of touch with a serious purpose.[18]

The Ascent of F6 (1936), which Faber and Faber published on 24 September 1936, had its first performance at the Mercury Theatre, Notting Hill

Gate, on 26 February 1937. This interval gave Auden and Isherwood time to rewrite in response to criticisms of the play, especially those leveled at it by E. M. Forster and Stephen Spender.[19] Although Spender asserted that the collaboration between Isherwood and Auden was a better work than *The Dog Beneath the Skin,* he still had serious reservations about the new play. He pointed out that the character of their "hero," Michael Ransom, has major flaws: "Ransom is a colossal prig, a fact of which the authors seem insufficiently aware. He behaves in the way in which one projects behaviour when one does not think of any way of living, but simply of ways of behaving in a given situation."[20] Although Forster had a better opinion of *F6* in its first published form, he, like Spender, thought the conception of Ransom's character was contradictory. He also took exception to the treatment of Ransom's Oedipal love: "Mother-love, usually sacrosanct, becomes a very nasty customer in this exciting play."[21] Isherwood wrote Forster to tell him that he and Auden were revising *F6* in part to answer Forster's criticism, especially of its ending, and that they were also changing the representation of Ransom's mother to make her "more like a dictator's public: submitting to him and yet preying on him."[22]

Richard Hoggart's *Auden: An Introductory Essay* was published in 1951, the same year as *Nones,* the first of the six volumes of poetry published after Auden's last long poem, *The Age of Anxiety* (1947). Hoggart's book, as its subtitle suggests, is very helpful in its commentary on poetic techniques and themes in the work. Although Hoggart has some misgivings about Auden, he recognizes what Mendelson later reinforces, that not only did Auden "feel at home in the modern world," but that, as Hoggart puts it, he "is at one of the frontiers of this anxiety-torn world; he is one of those who play out with unusual and revealing clarity, struggles to which, whether we recognize it or not, we are all committed."[23]

Hoggart sees the last of the collaborations between Isherwood and Auden, *On the Frontier* (1938), as unsuccessful in the simplicity with which it treats its oppositions between Ostnia and Westland, the democracy and the totalitarian state. Art here becomes propaganda, perhaps because Auden and Isherwood deliberately set out to write a play that would communicate directly with its audience. Nevertheless, when it was finally produced, in Cambridge on 14 November 1938, it was a success, if a highly qualified one. Among the critical reviewers, C. Day Lewis thought that the characters were paper-thin and that the prose in which Auden and Isherwood cast most of the play was hardly stronger than the occasionally banal lines of poetry.[24]

Edward Mendelson, in *Early Auden* (1981), writes perceptively about two poems crucial to the outlook of Auden's *Look, Stranger!* (1936; the 1937 American edition is entitled *On This Island*): "Paysage Moralisé" and "A Summer Night." Mendelson's main point about "A Summer Night"—that we find the full meaning of an achieved unity only long after the event, not in the fleeting epiphany the moment causes in the participant—is the key to the profound sense of the power of Eros that Auden achieved in the volume—not in the sense of love's immediate gratification but, as Mendelson quite rightly points out, in love as the fusion of instinct and choice.[25]

In 1936, the same year *Look, Stranger!* appeared in England, Bennett Cerf, of Random House, Auden's American publisher, persuaded Auden's English publisher, Faber and Faber, that it should have Auden and Isherwood write a travel book about some place, as yet unspecified, in the Far East. Because the Sino-Japanese War had begun that summer, the two writers decided to go to China; they left on 19 January 1938.[26]

The night before Auden and Isherwood left London to cover the Sino-Japanese War, the Group Theatre gave them a splendid farewell party. Among the guests was E. M. Forster, for whom Auden wrote his dedicatory poem to *Journey to a War* (1939; *Sonnets from China* in *Collected Poems*). Both Auden's biographers, Charles Osborne and Humphrey Carpenter, recount this trip, which was much less a journey to the war front than it was a trip through China itself; both writers shifted the focus of their reporting from the war to other aspects of contemporary culture in Asia. Edward Callan, in *Auden: A Carnival of Intellect* (1983), places this trip in the context of the political situation in China. His book, a concise account of Auden's poetic career, focuses on the themes and the art of the poetry; he demonstrates that *Journey to a War* reveals "a critical point" in Auden's work between his trip to Spain early in 1937 and his publication of *Another Time* in 1940.[27]

Callan also postulates a link between Auden's relationship with Chester Kallman, whom he met in April 1939, and his return to the Anglican church, suggesting that there is an implicit reference to Auden's obsession with Kallman in a passage from his contribution to *Modern Canterbury Pilgrims* (1956): "I was forced to know in person what it is like to feel oneself the prey of demonic powers, in both the Greek and Christian sense, stripped of self-control and self-respect, behaving like a ham actor in a Strindberg play." In the same essay Auden pointed to other influences on his return to the Church: (1) the failure of liberal humanism to bring about peace and prosperity, and (2) the Nazis' rise to power, "not in some remote barbaric land outside the pale, but in one of the most highly educated countries in Europe."[28]

The apolitical stance that Auden's return to the Church appeared to entail led some critics, like Beach, to deplore the changes he made in such major poems as "September 1, 1939" and "In Memory of W. B. Yeats." In this sense, his 1940 volume, *Another Time,* marked Auden's shift in ideology from social and political concerns to existentialist themes. *Another Time* also includes two of the finest elegies in modern British poetry, "In Memory of W. B. Yeats" and "In Memory of Sigmund Freud." These poems celebrate two men whose deaths in 1939 coincided with the outbreak of war in Europe; it was as if these great civilizing figures could not endure the enormities in which the thirties ended.

Auden's first long poem in the forties, "New Year Letter," appeared first in the form of a book, *The Double Man* (1941); it included notes in prose and poetry on the long, epistolary poem, as well as a "Prologue," an "Epilogue," and a sonnet sequence, "The Quest." "New Year Letter" grew in part out of Auden's friendship with Charles Williams, whose *The Descent of the Dove* (1939) offered Auden not only several of his ideas in the poem but also its controlling metaphor of order. Order, here, is the task of both life and art, of Eros and Apollo; furthermore, personal and political orders are related to one another. In his book *Quest for the Necessary* (1968), Herbert Greenberg focuses on what he argues is Auden's major subject, humanity's duality. He reads "New Year Letter" as a poem in which Auden "decides that unified being may be experienced only momentarily, that human existence is a continual 'becoming,' and that by a 'double focus' of faith and doubt the ego in each of us must pursue a solitary quest for self-fulfillment as governed by natural law."[29] Greenberg outlines the content of "New Year Letter" before defining Auden's understanding of the historical circumstances leading to our present failure to reach the "Just City." Only through the acceptance—indeed, the exaltation—of our average, not our exceptional, selves may we undertake the "quest for the necessary" to which Greenberg's title points.

In *Saving Civilization: Yeats, Eliot, and Auden between the Wars* (1984), Lucy McDiarmid explores the divisions each of the three poets sensed between his feeling that he was responsible for becoming involved in political events and the artistic compulsion for detachment. Each one had a different answer to the question of whether a writer could influence his audience through his essays and poetry. The present selection, from the fourth chapter, takes its title, "The Treason of the Clerk" (or intellectual), from Julien Benda's book *The Treason of the Intellectuals* (1928), an attack on politically involved writers. McDiarmid analyzes Auden's "In Memory of W. B. Yeats" (first published in 1939) and "At the Grave of Henry James" (first published in 1941) as crucial instances of Auden's refusal to be political, a stance both Eliot and Auden learned from Yeats. McDiarmid finally observes that Auden committed himself in his elegy for Yeats to the only solution that he, like Yeats himself, could bring about in the face of fascism's threat to democracy: the perfect ordering of a work of art. Although Auden recognized that history influences poetry, he "insists on their autonomy and their coexistence.[30] McDiarmid develops her argument convincingly as she relates Auden's elegies to Yeats's finest late poems, "Long-Legged Fly" and "Lapis Lazuli," and to T. S. Eliot's "Little Gidding." It was precisely this stance of Auden's that led many 1930s intellectuals to question seriously his apparently sudden change in outlook.

During the forties Auden published three long poems in addition to "New Year Letter." "For the Time Being" and "The Sea and the Mirror" appeared in the same volume, entitled *For the Time Being*, in 1944. *The Age of Anxiety*, the only one of his long poems published as a single volume, yet the weakest of them, was published in 1947. The critical consensus is that

"The Sea and the Mirror" is the best of the four long poems. Its subtitle, "A Commentary on Shakespeare's *The Tempest*," is in itself a comic incongruity, since one does not ordinarily think of poetry as a scholarly commentary, or gloss, upon another text. The poem explores the archetypal patterns present in *The Tempest* by fusing Auden's profound readings of Shakespeare (collected in *The Dyer's Hand* [1962]) with his interpretation of Kierkegaard's "categories"—the aesthetic, the ethical, and the religious.

Justin Replogle, whose book *Auden's Poetry* (1969) is among the best appreciations of the later poetry, shows how Kierkegaard's categories have full play in "The Sea and the Mirror." Replogle argues at the same time that we need not be familiar with Kierkegaard to understand the poem's view of humanity. He goes on to assess *The Age of Anxiety* as a less successful work than "The Sea and the Mirror," although one similarly grounded in the Kierkegaardian categories. His view of Auden as a brilliant comic poet helps Replogle make his distinction between Eliot and Auden: they were two poets whose theological views were not radically different but who differed in what their poetry celebrates; Auden's acceptance of secular life formed a sharp contrast to Eliot's longing for transcendence.[31]

Auden describes "For the Time Being" in the subtitle as "A Christmas Oratorio." Like many oratorios, it derives its structure from a biblical narrative, here, the birth of Christ interpreted in Kierkegaardian and modern liberal Protestant theological terms. Like "The Sea and the Mirror," it is partly prose and partly poetry; its resemblance to an oratorio includes the presence of a narrator, whose role resembles that of the Evangelist in a Bach oratorio, a chorus, recitatives, a semichorus, and individual voices or trios, in Auden's poem those of Joseph, Mary, Gabriel, the Shepherds, and the Three Wise Men. There are tutti passages and a chorale. It could have a musical setting, although none has been created for it in its entirety.

The poem's title refers to the time between Christmas and Good Friday, between the Incarnation and the Crucifixion. In the narrator's closing passage, he tells the audience that it has not taken seriously the possibility of commitment to the truth manifest in Christ's birth, partly because human beings fear the possible consequences and difficulty of that commitment, the necessity for sacrifice implicit in Christ's death. The "time being" also refers to the time between birth and death, during which one may choose to accept or refuse the way of faith implicit in the Incarnation.

"For the Time Being" did not receive good reviews on the whole, largely because readers objected to the intellectual density of such passages as "The Meditation of Simeon," which was heavily influenced by Reinhold Niebuhr's interpretation of Kierkegaardian existentialism in *The Nature and Destiny of Man* (1941–43). One of the mixed reviews was by Harry Levin for the *New Republic*. Levin's customary good sense and ability to see a text in its literary-historical context come to the fore in this review as he draws analogies between T. S. Eliot's and Auden's poetic careers. He points to one characteristic of Auden's Christian poetry that has troubled some of its readers and interpreters, its "double negation." For Levin, Auden "is more adept at burying Caesar"—that is, at exposing the failure of a secularized civilization governed on rational principles—"than at praising Christ, more anxious for a Messiah than confident in the Revelation."[32] Finally, Levin expresses his disappointment in what he regards as Auden's failure to see the contemporary political situation in its complexity.

Although Auden's last long poem in the forties gave its name to Leonard Bernstein's ballet music and became part of common parlance, *The Age of Anxiety* has fared least well of the four long poems with the critics. In spite of some favorable reviews by such prominent scholars as Jacques Barzun, M. L. Rosenthal, and Louis Martz, and particularly by Marianne Moore, the burden of many others, as Haffenden notes in his introduction to *W. H. Auden: The Critical Heritage* (1983), was that in spite of some of its technical achievements, *The Age of Anxiety* is without much interest.

Gerald Nelson, in his chapter about the poem in *Changes of Heart* (1969), takes issue with Randall Jarrell's judgment that *"The Age of Anxiety* is the worst thing Auden has written since *The Dance of Death;* it is the equivalent of Wordsworth's 'Ecclesiastical Sonnets'!"[33] Nevertheless, Nelson is far from favorable in his judgment. He reads *The Age of Anxiety* as a quest poem but argues that the characters' quest is false, since the search has its impetus in their drinking; according to Nelson, this quest is only a parody eluding the realities of this world and embracing fantasy. Nelson's most compelling idea is that in this long poem Auden showed enormous interest in the relationship between actor and character, between human being and mask. A character confusing his or her chosen role with actuality has disastrous consequences, ones that a poem like *The Age of Anxiety* effectively dramatizes. Nelson reads the conclusion of the poem, especially Malin's monologue, as very dark in its implications, but only because Nelson does not value insight as highly as he does actions: "What Malin says is important. It is important to recognize Christ, to recognize that 'He speaks / Our creaturely cry.' But it is more important to do something with this recognition."[34] Perhaps sensing the failure of *The Age of Anxiety,* Auden wrote no more long poems, but he did publish three extraordinary sequences: the seven poems of the "Bucolics," the seven poems of "Horae Canonicae" (both of these sets of poems are in *The Shield of Achilles* [1955]), and the twelve poems of "Thanksgiving for a Habitat," in *About the House* (1965). Apart from these sequences, Auden wrote several extended lyric poems between *The Age of Anxiety*'s publication in 1947 and his death in 1973. The best of these poems is "In Praise of Limestone," composed in May 1948 and included in *Nones* (1951).[35]

Among the best commentators on "In Praise of Limestone" and the "Bucolics" is Richard Johnson. In his preface to *Man's Place: An Essay on Auden* (1972), Johnson argues that, although Auden was a philosophical poet whose poems have paraphrasable content, they approach their points indirectly; they do not assert but rather, "present modes of existence that involve the reader in the process of exploration. The patterns of sound, imagery, syntax, rhyme, diction, metaphor, perspective, stanza, and argument are the means by which Auden essays his fundamental subject, man in the world."

Johnson's sensitivity to Auden's poetic achievement allows him to read the "Bucolics" without emphasizing either meaning or method at the expense of the other. For Johnson, "In Praise of Limestone" is a comic poem in its evocation of a pastoral world that admits "frivolity, triviality, unpredictability, and outlandishness," in short, the moderate, fallible beings who have not betrayed this place by leaving it. (Its landscape resembles both the limestone moors of northern England and the Italian countryside Auden came to know when he lived on Ischia.) Johnson finds that in the "Bucolics" Auden viewed human beings as both fallen creatures and evolved creatures. The art of the poem corresponds to this duality; in their simultaneous "definition and celebration" of natural gestures, the poems' poetic methods mirror implicitly the definition of humanity's dual condition.[36]

The "Horae Canonicae" form a meditation on the Crucifixion in which, I have argued, Auden's concern was humanity's relation to history; he expressed the irony inherent in our development of civilization at the cost of unleashing the violence subconsciously present within us.[37] The dramatization in contemporary imagery of the events on the day of the Crucifixion emphasizes the way in which we reenact the fall from innocence to sin and our consequent repentance or guilt every day of our lives. In "Nones" the Crucifixion becomes an attraction that tourists arrive in motor coaches to witness taking place in an Italian town. Ultimately, the "Horae Canonicae" express the limits on our understanding of the Crucifixion and the larger, eternal pattern in which it assumes its full significance.

Stan Smith's "The Sons of Hermes: Last Poems," a chapter from his book *W. H. Auden,* comments on Auden's poems in *About the House* (1965), *City without Walls* (1969), *Epistle to a Godson* (1972), and *Thank You, Fog* (1974).[38] Smith's book, as Terry Eagleton notes in his preface, does not distinguish between the early and the later Auden; Smith prefers to celebrate instead the varied roles and guises Auden assumed, the many hats he wore. Rather than seeing some sort of unity underlying all the poetry, or making a case for either the Marxist or the Anglo-Catholic Auden, Smith praises "the right to play" and "the right to frivolity" that, according to Auden, poets and peasants share.[39] In the later poems Smith finds "the comic perspective of the anthropologist who knows that all cultures are historical artifacts but who can nevertheless admire, respect or forgive the diversity of forms they take."[40] Smith's readings of individual poems are often sociological (placing Auden's attitudes within the social structure) and deconstructive in their definitions of the poems' subtexts and their identification of the ways power relationships are inscribed in the texts.

After his move to America in 1939, Auden turned some of his attention to writing librettos and to literary critical efforts longer than the book reviews and occasional essays he wrote during the thirties. His interest in music in the thirties, especially in the cabaret song, the music theater of Kurt Weill, popular songs, and folk ballads, gave him forms for poetry and drama. When he had worked for the film wing of the U.K. General Post Office, Auden wrote commentaries for two films, *Coal Face* and *Night Mail,* documentaries about the daily lives of miners and the Scottish mail train. Benjamin Britten, who as a very young man had met Auden in 1935, would compose the music for both films. Later, they would collaborate on a work for voice and theater, *Our Hunting Fathers* (1936), first performed at the Norwich and Norfolk Triennial Festival.[41]

Monroe K. Spears's *The Poetry of W. H. Auden* (1962) was the first major study of Auden's work through *Homage to Clio* (1960). Spears's strong interest in prosody, sound, and music lead him, wisely, to emphasize these elements in Auden's poetry, since Auden himself imitated and wrote in an astonishing variety of forms, from the popular song to the opera libretto. I have included Spears's commentary on the libretto Auden wrote for Stravinsky's *The Rake's Progress* (1951).[42] Chester Kallman collaborated with Auden on *The Rake's Progress,* as well as on librettos for Hans Werner Henze's *Elegy for Young Lovers* (1961), Henze's *The Bassarids* (1966), and Nicholas Nabokov's *Love's Labour's Lost* (1973). Auden and Kallman's *Delia: or A Masque of Night* (1953) was never set to music.

Of the five librettos that Auden wrote for composers, *The Rake's Progress* is the one that will be remembered, partly because its composer was a major figure in a way that, in spite of his considerable reputation, Hans Werner Henze is not. In its visual richness, its *tableaux vivantes* taken from Hogarth's paintings, its union of archetypes, and its exploitation of motifs from fairy tales and nursery rhymes, *The Rake's Progress* recreates its eighteenth-century sources, just as Stravinsky's music recalls late baroque composers, especially Mozart. The absolute appropriateness of its words to the music was achieved in part through Auden's understanding of the proper relationship between musical and syllabic values.

The collaboration between Auden and Stravinsky began with the latter's decision to ask Auden if he would write the libretto for *The Rake's Progress.* In a BBC television interview, Stravinsky praised Auden's ear, especially his sense of the way the words in a libretto might receive appropriate stress through the music: "[Auden's] lines were always the right length for singing and his words the right ones to sustain musical emphasis."[43] Stravinsky also wrote affectionately about his friendship with Auden, at the same time commending him as a writer of librettos.[44] Crucial to the interview with Stravinsky is the composer's quotation of Auden's distinction between opera and literature in a grammatical analogy; Stravinsky quotes Auden's statement, "All musical statements are intransitive, in the First Person, singular or plural, and in the Present Indicative," whereas poetry, Stravinsky adds, "does not have these limits."[45]

His inaugural lecture as professor of poetry at Oxford is the major text in Auden's 1962 collection of his reviews and essays, *The Dyer's Hand,* whose title is a phrase from Shakespeare's sonnet 111, in which the speaker thanks the young man for arguing with Fortune's responsibility for Shakespeare's life as a playwright: "Thence comes it that my name receives a brand: / And almost thence my nature is subdued / To what it works in, like the dyer's hand" (lines 5–7). The dye that colors the hand of the dyer became Auden's metaphor for the process of writing poetry, not just in the eponymous essay but also in the other essays, lectures, and reviews collected in *The Dyer's Hand.*

In his criticism, whether theoretical or practical, Auden avoided schematization; he pointed out in his foreword to *The Dyer's Hand* that, because he preferred artists' notebooks to their formal criticism, he chose a similar form for his own essays and reviews. One can define at least two major elements in Auden's criticism: he interpreted Kierkegaard's categories in historical terms (the world of the Homeric epic is aesthetic, the dialogues of Plato ethical, and the Christian world religious). Second, he continued the tradition of T. E. Hulme and T. S. Eliot in his antiromanticism, although *The Enchaféd Flood* (1950), his most profound critical work, is an exposition of romantic literature.

Cleanth Brooks, in the essay "Auden as a Literary Critic" (originally a lecture at the meetings of the English Institute for 1962), comments on those essays he believes to be Auden's best, at the same time that he reveals Auden's own beliefs about poetry underlying them. Brooks correctly sees Auden's zest for classification as the basis for his concern with genre and with theories of comedy and tragedy.[46] In some ways, Auden's criticism, especially in *The Enchaféd Flood,* resembles Northrop Frye's in its identification of archetypes; *The Enchaféd Flood* is subtitled "The Romantic Iconography of the Sea." Composed of lectures originally given at the University of Virginia in March 1949, the volume offers a powerful reading of romanticism through its dominant symbols.[47] Along with the lectures Auden gave as professor of poetry at Oxford, included in *The Dyer's Hand,* the title essay of that volume, and his articles about Shakespeare, *The Enchaféd Flood* represents Auden's literary criticism at its very best.

Brooks, who was among the first to recognize Auden's strengths as a critic, relates Auden's convictions about the criteria for determining the value of poems to T. S. Eliot's belief that poetry should be impersonal ("The progress of an artist is a continual self-sacrifice, a continual extinction of personality") and to his own conviction that poetry should be organic, achieving its unity through its dramatic embodiment of tensions.[48] Brooks also admires Auden's insistence that religion and art should be kept separate, a conviction Auden articulated fully in his inaugural lecture at Oxford; poets express their awe in rites "of worship or homage" that have "no magical or idolatrous intention," nor are they "act[s] of devotion."[49] Like Brooks himself, Auden had "respect for the autonomy of art" and never regarded art "as merely the handmaiden of a religion or of a political party."[50]

In *W. H. Auden* (1981), George T. Wright assesses Auden's later poetry as a whole rather than individual poems. Wright considers Auden's influence on younger American poets, such as Richard Wilbur, Anthony Hecht, John Hollander, and James Merrill, to have been salutary, particularly in the way Auden's experimentations with prosody, including syllabics and stanza forms, gave them a precedent for their own preference for traditional forms in an age dominated by free verse. Furthermore, Wright acknowledges the dualisms present not only in Auden's poetry but also, now that we have a partial biographical record, in his character. One of Wright's most compelling hypotheses is that intellectuals who thought Auden betrayed them by turning away from political subjects did not realize that he had done so out of both his discomfort with being a leader and his growing commitment to the individual and to the personal life.[51]

This sense of betrayal that intellectuals felt when Auden appeared to have turned his back on the left-wing views they believed him to have espoused in the thirties has continued to haunt assessments of Auden's importance and value as a modern poet. Whether they are aware of it or not, some of those critics who believe Auden's 1930s poetry will endure regard Auden's later values as elitist. For example, David Perkins, in his two-volume study *A History of Modern Poetry* (1976, 1987), believes that in the later poems Auden was implying that civilization, even if it is to endure only in remote enclaves, requires well-educated, sophisticated, and witty human beings who do not commit themselves to "views," who devote themselves instead to an effete art in which form and verbal play greatly outweigh content.[52] This charge has been leveled at Auden before, notably by A. Alvarez in *Stewards of Excellence* (1958): "[Auden] has caught one tone of his period, but it is a cocktail party tone, as though most of his work were written off the cuff for the amusement of his friends."[53]

A link between the disagreements among literary critics over the value of Auden's poetry, and Auden's own character, emerges indirectly from the recollections of his two closest friends, Christopher Isherwood and Stephen Spender. In his autobiography *Lions and Shadows* (1947), Isherwood, who had been Auden's classmate at St. Edmund's School in Hindhead, Surrey, recalls his reunion with Auden—whom he calls Weston—seven years after they left school. Isherwood's delight in his and Auden's mimicry of their old schoolmasters anticipates Auden's mimicry in his poetry, his ability to assume an extraordinarily wide range of voices, and his genius for parody—of everything from ballads and cabaret songs in the thirties to Horace's epistolary poems in the sixties. Yet this very capacity has provoked the suspicion of those critics who, like Jarrell and Beach, regard Auden as dishonest.[54]

In the selection from *Lions and Shadows* reprinted in this volume, Isherwood emphasizes the detachment and austerity that Auden believed is central to poetry. Auden's hatred of nature because of its formlessness ("I loathe the sea") and his shift in poetic allegiance from Edward Thomas and Robert Frost to T. S. Eliot reflect his growing adherence to Eliot's antiromantic, impersonal theory of poetry: the poet, in Auden's view, must treat all themes, even love, "with a wry, bitter smile and a pair of rubber surgical gloves."[55] Auden's conviction that poets should be "clinically minded" was inextricably linked to his definition of the poet's role as a diagnostician. (Here again one recognizes the influence of D. H. Lawrence's *Psychoanalysis and the Unconscious* and *Fantasia of the Unconscious;* Lawrence's own sense of himself as a healer is reflected in the titles of some of his critical essays, for example, "Surgery for the Novel—or a Bomb.")[56] The didactic and prophetic voice in such poems as "Consider" ("Consider this and in our time / As the hawk sees it or the helmeted airman"), "Venus Will Now Say a Few Words" ("Since you are going to begin today / Let us consider what it is you do"), or the opening of the fourth part of "1929" ("It is time for the destruction of error") echoes Lawrence's diagnoses of the malaise in English society.[57]

The austere world Auden admired in the Icelandic sagas fused in his early poetry with the boarding-school world he and Isherwood had known to heighten his notion that poets could speak with clinical detachment. His refusal in the thirties to commit himself entirely to left-wing assessments of Great Britain's economic and political structure may indeed have stemmed from the strong element of fantasy and play in his dissections of the life the English bourgeoisie led. This "failure" on Auden's part to be unequivocally clear about his beliefs certainly contributed to liberal intellectuals' disappointment in him, and later, to their feeling of betrayal when he announced his return to the Church. His "easy" assumption of widely differing roles—as if they were analogous to his youthful delight in role-playing, which Isherwood notes in his account of Auden's collection of different hats—probably contributed to the sense of "dishonesty," or "absence of integrity," that some of his critics have deplored.

At the same time one might argue that this very detachment in Auden's voice gives his poetry its peculiar and often powerful effects. In his journal, Stephen Spender formulated the answer he would give to a question he had been asked: whether he really liked Auden. The crucial sentence in his answer must be this one: "I did not think of him as having ordinary feelings and I felt about his early poetry the lack of any 'I' at the centre of it."[58] Auden's advice—even to his friends, Spender notes—resembled a doctor's or a psychoanalyst's in the detached tone of his diagnoses and proposed therapy. Spender points to the "clinical detachment even from the speaker's own hurt" in Auden's early poem "The Letter."[59]

This dispassionate voice, which so easily subverts a reader's expectations, as in his famous "Lullaby"—"Lay your sleeping head, my love /

Human on my faithless arm"—[60]not only is characteristic of Auden in both the early and the later poetry but is also one of his strengths that belies efforts to expose his facile or "insincere" poetic temperament. In fact, few poets have committed themselves so fully to honesty in their art. The changes, revisions, and excisions Auden made in his poetry stemmed from his refusal to say something he no longer believed. His commitment to truth—at least, to as much of the truth as human beings are capable of knowing—underlies all his poetry, no matter what view of humanity, Marxist, Freudian, or Christian, he held at the time.

This commitment appears even in the history of the poems' texts. For example, Auden revised "September 1, 1939," which was first published in 1939, for the *Collected Poetry* (1945) and *Collected Shorter Poems* (1950).[61] (Because Mendelson does not include the poem in *Collected Poems* [1976], it is clearly among those Auden did not wish to preserve.) The last line of the penultimate stanza, "We must love one another or die," troubled Auden; as he later pointed out, the line is "a damned lie" because we must die in any case. In the revised version, he left out the entire stanza.[62] In his essay on Robert Frost, Auden asserted that not only do we want a poem to be beautiful, "a verbal earthly paradise," but we also want it be true, "to provide us with some kind of revelation about what our life is really like and [to] free us from self-enchantment and deception."[63] Certainly in Auden's poetry at its best the didactic strain, the "clinical detachment," and the commitment to poetry as truth and to beauty come together to offer us greater knowledge of ourselves; the degree to which his work helps us recognize and accept our human limitations depends upon our ability to share his fundamentally comic vision, which was based on his ironic contemplation of humanity. Auden was aware of the temptation to be "insincere"; his Prospero, who surely is closely related to Auden himself, asks Ariel just before he leaves his island, in a question that deliberately values life over art, "—Can I learn to suffer / Without saying something ironic or funny / On suffering?"[64]

Auden's commitment to a view of humanity as limited, rather than omnipotent or heroic, seems consistent with the main outlines of liberal Protestant theology. His works have an underlying seriousness, whatever the mimicry or apparent glibness on the surface, that gives them an extraordinary consistency and cogency and makes them worthy of our attention and admiration.

Notes

1. Randall Jarrell, "Changes of Attitude and Rhetoric in Auden's Poetry," *The Southern Review* 7 (1941); Randall Jarrell, "Freud to Paul: The Stages of Auden's Ideology," *Partisan Review* 12 (1945): 440, 437, 441.
   2. Ibid., 450–51.

3. Joseph Warren Beach, *The Making of the Auden Canon* (Minneapolis: University of Minnesota Press, 1957).

4. W. H. Auden, *The Collected Poetry of W. H. Auden* (New York: Random House, 1945); W. H. Auden, *Collected Shorter Poems, 1930–1944* (London: Faber and Faber, 1950).

5. Beach, *Auden Canon*, 245, 253.

6. W. H. Auden, *Collected Poems*, ed. Edward Mendelson (New York: Random House, 1976), 11.

7. W. H. Auden, *The English Auden: Poems, Essays, and Dramatic Writings, 1927–1939*, ed. Edward Mendelson (New York: Random House, 1977); W. H. Auden, *Selected Poems*, new ed., ed. Edward Mendelson (New York: Random House, 1979), ix.

8. *Collected Poems* (1967), 11. Auden, however, in his own foreword to *Collected Shorter Poems, 1927–1957* (New York: Random House, 1966), asserted that he had never, "consciously at any rate," changed his thoughts or feelings, but that he had made many changes in the language of the poems (16).

9. John Haffenden, ed., *W. H. Auden: The Critical Heritage* (London: Routledge and Kegan Paul, 1983).

10. Babette Deutsch, *This Modern Poetry* (New York: Norton, 1935), 241.

11. W. H. Auden, *The Orators: An English Study*, rev. ed. (New York: Random House, 1967), vii; Faber and Faber published the original edition in 1932.

12. Of these four, Auden dropped two, "January 1, 1931" and "Not, Father, further do prolong," from *Collected Shorter Poems* (1966). Mendelson reprinted *The Orators* in *The English Auden*, which also includes the early, unrevised versions of the *Orators* poems Auden did reprint.

13. David Lehman, "In the Cool Element of Prose," review of Auden, *The English Auden*, *Parnassus* 8, no. 2 (1980): 141.

14. Humphrey Carpenter, *W. H. Auden: A Biography* (Boston: Houghton Mifflin, 1981), 138.

15. Edward Mendelson, *Early Auden* (New York: Viking, 1981), 269. This volume is the first of a projected two-volume study of the poet.

16. John Fuller, *A Reader's Guide to W. H. Auden* (New York: Farrar, Straus and Giroux, 1970), 79–95.

17. Herbert J. Greenberg, *Quest for the Necessary: W. H. Auden and the Dilemma of Divided Consciousness* (Cambridge, Mass.: Harvard University Press, 1968),

18. Fuller, *Reader's Guide*, 85, 90.

19. Charles Osborne, *W. H. Auden: The Life of a Poet* (New York: Harcourt Brace Jovanovich, 1979), 139.

20. Stephen Spender, "Fable and Reportage," *Left Review* 2 (November 1936): 779–82, reprinted in part in Haffenden, *Auden: Critical Heritage*, 195.

21. E. M. Forster, review of *The Ascent of F6*, *The Listener*, suppl. 31, 14 October 1936, vii, reprinted in Haffenden, *Auden: Critical Heritage*, 191.

22. Brian Finney, *Christopher Isherwood: A Critical Biography* (New York: Oxford University Press, 1979), 163.

23. Auden, *Selected Poems* (1979), ix; Richard Hoggart, *Auden: An Introductory Essay* (New Haven, Conn.: Yale University Press, 1951), 219.

24. C. Day Lewis, unsigned review of *On the Frontier*, *The Listener* 20, 24 November 1938, 1145 (reprinted in Haffenden, *The Critical Heritage*, 280–81).

25. Mendelson, *Early Auden*, 154–56, 164–68.

26. Carpenter, *Auden*, 204, 223, 233.

27. Edward Callan, *Auden: A Carnival of Intellect* (New York: Oxford University Press, 1983), 135.

28. W. H. Auden, untitled essay, in *Modern Canterbury Pilgrims*, ed. James A. Pike (New York: Morehouse-Gorham, 1956), 41, 60, 61, 41.

29. Greenberg, *Quest for the Necessary,* especially chap. 1, "Introduction: At the Core," 1–13; 99.

30. Lucy McDiarmid, *Saving Civilization: Yeats, Eliot, and Auden between the Wars* (New York: Cambridge University Press, 1984), 121.

31. Justin Replogle, *Auden's Poetry* (Seattle: University of Washington Press, 1969).

32. Harry Levin, "Through the Looking Glass," a review of *For the Time Being, New Republic* 111, 18 September 1944, 347–48, reprinted in Haffenden, *Auden: Critical Heritage,* 333.

33. Gerald Nelson, *Changes of Heart: A Study of the Poetry of W. H. Auden* (Berkeley and Los Angeles: University of California Press, 1969), 77–107; Randall Jarrell, "Verse Chronicle," *The Nation,* 18 October 1947, 424–25.

34. Nelson, *Changes of Heart,* 106.

35. Mendelson's composition date; Mendelson notes in *Collected Poems* (1976), "Where provided, these [dates of composition] represent the dates on which the poems first achieved approximately their present form" (14).

36. Richard Johnson, *Man's Place: An Essay on Auden* (Ithaca, N.Y.: Cornell University Press, 1973), xi, 63, 163–64.

37. George W. Bahlke, *The Later Auden: From "New Year Letter" to* About the House (New Brunswick, N.J.: Rutgers University Press, 1970), 161.

38. Stan Smith, *W. H. Auden,* in the series *Rereading Literature,* gen. ed. Terry Eagleton (Oxford: Basil Blackwood, 1985), chap. 9.

39. W. H. Auden, "The Dyer's Hand: Poetry and the Poetic Process," *Anchor Review,* no. 2 (Garden City, N.Y.: Doubleday, 1957), 300–301. An altered version of this passage appears in "The Dyer's Hand," in W. H. Auden, *The Dyer's Hand and Other Essays* (New York: Random House, 1962), 88–89.

40. Smith, *Auden,* 199.

41. Carpenter, *Auden,* 177–78, 188–89.

42. Monroe K. Spears, *The Poetry of W. H. Auden: The Disenchanted Island* (New York: Oxford University Press, 1963), ch. 4.

43. Igor Stravinsky, *Themes and Conclusions* (Berkeley and Los Angeles: University of California Press, 1982), 286–90.

44. Igor Stravinsky and Robert Craft, *Themes and Episodes* (New York: Knopf, 1967), 97.

45. Ibid., 289–90.

46. Cleanth Brooks, "Auden as a Literary Critic," in *A Shaping Joy: Studies in the Writer's Craft* (New York: Harcourt Brace Jovanovich, 1971), 126–42.

47. W. H. Auden, *The Enchafèd Flood, or, The Romantic Iconography of the Sea* (New York: Random House, 1950).

48. T. S. Eliot, "Tradition and the Individual Talent," in *Selected Essays* (New York: Harcourt Brace and World, 1964), 7.

49. Auden, *Dyer's Hand,* 57.

50. Brooks, "Auden as Critic," 142.

51. George T. Wright, *W. H. Auden,* rev. ed. (Boston: G. K. Hall, 1981); Twayne published the original edition in 1969.

52. David Perkins, *A History of Modern Poetry,* 2 vols. (Cambridge, Mass.: Harvard University Press, 1976, 1987).

53. A. Alvarez, *Stewards of Excellence: Studies in Modern English and American Poets* (New York: Charles Scribner's Sons, 1958), 105.

54. Christopher Isherwood, *Lions and Shadows: An Education in the Twenties* (Norfolk, Conn.: New Directions, 1947), 182–84.

55. Ibid., 191.

56. D. H. Lawrence, *Phoenix, The Posthumous Papers of D. H. Lawrence,* ed. Edward D. McDonald (London: Heinemann, 1936), 517–20.

57. *Collected Poems* (1976), 61, 49, 53.

58. Stephen Spender, *Journals 1939–1983,* ed. John Goldsmith (New York: Random House, 1986), entry for 11 April 1979, 355.

59. *Collected Poems* (1976), 39; Mendelson dates its composition as December 1927.

60. Ibid., 131.

61. "September 1, 1939" was first published in the *New Republic,* 18 October 1939; it was reprinted in *Another Time* (1940) before appearing in its revised form in the later collections.

62. Carpenter, 330.

63. Auden, *Dyer's Hand,* 338.

64. "Prospero to Ariel," in *The Sea and the Mirror* in *Collected Poems* (1976), 316.

ESSAYS

◆

[From "Freud to Paul: The Stages of Auden's Ideology"]

RANDALL JARRELL

There are three stages of the works (and the ideas which are their sources or elaborated by-products) that we call Auden. In the beginning there is the Old Auden, the *Ur*-Auden. What should I call this stage? *Freud and Grettir? The Law of the Members?* Here everything of importance happens inside the Realm of Causal or Magical Necessity. Here—in *Poems,* in *Paid on Both Sides,* and in most of *The Orators*—is the world of the unconscious, the primitive, the childish, the animal, the natural: it is Genesis. The basic structural picture (in Wittgenstein's sense) underlying these poems is that of the long struggle of genetic development, of the hard, blind journey of the creature or its kind. Existence is an essentially dialectical evolution, presented with particular directness in Freudian or saga terms—*i.e.,* in terms succeeding or preceding those of the higher religions. The primary subject of the poems is the discontinuities of growth, the unrecognized or opposed Necessity that determines men and Man. The "change of heart" is meaningless except as a preliminary to change—is, generally, an evasion by which we avoid changing. But even the real choices, the continued-in changes, possess a deterministic pathos. Our fundamental activity is a guilty revolt against a guilty Authority, a revolt predetermined to immediate or eventual failure, a revolt by the neurotic and diseased (to the Auden of Stage I medicine is a branch of psychiatry, and all illness is functional) against a neurotic and diseased culture.

. . . .

In *Look, Stranger,* and *The Dog Beneath the Skin* Auden changes over into a second, essentially transitional stage which continues until *New Year Letter*—itself a transition from the Moral Auden to the New Auden. It is easy to find titles or mottoes for this second stage: *The Moralist from the Machine; The Questing Beast; Reason as Agape, or, The Saviour with the Vote.* Here everything important happens in the Realm of Logical Necessity. Here we are free to choose—are implored or forced to choose, are told again and again that our choices are meaningful, that the right choice is predestined to success. A change of heart is a change of vote—what is meaningless about

Reprinted from *Partisan Review,* 12 (Fall 1945) by permission of Mrs. M. S. Jarrell.

that? Existence has become a *problem* that Auden reasons about, advises us about, exhorts us to make the right choice about; it is categorized, rather than presented, in secular, liberal, humanitarian, sentimental, metaphorically-scientific terms. The typical poems are problem poems. The political moralist raids a generalized, popularized Science for the raw materials and imagery of a morality which he constructs to satisfy the demands of the self and of the age, but which he implies is Scientific: a favorable mutation becomes for him "a morally good act," and even Destiny presents itself (as it does to his father-in-law) in political terms, to be voted for or spoken against. Animals, misguided former voters bogged down in the partial but final solutions brought them by their wasted votes, are patronizingly condemned by the political adviser because they are not free, like us, to go on voting (and being advised). Auden's ethics appear in an abstract, vituous and interminable Volume II, all the particulars of which are derived from a Volume I that consists of a single sentence: *We must do something about Hitler.* We are all guilty, the will itself is evil (the judgment is a bitter pill with a sugar-and-morphine center); but we can, practically speaking, escape our guilt by recognizing it, by *willing* a sort of Popular Front of the Universe. The quoted *Freedom is the recognition of necessity . . .* changes, through the growingly optimistic determinism of Hegel and Engels, into Auden's consolatory fable: *To recognize necessity is to have escaped it.* Thus the fundamental structural picture underneath the poems is that of the *fairy tale quest* (and the assimilated Quest of the Grail, temptations of the Buddha or the Messiah, etc.): so much so that genetic development, the underlying structural picture of the first stage, is itself expressed in terms of the quest. Success is no longer struggled for interminably and found at last a failure, but is won, in an instant, by choosing correctly—*i.e.,* voting. Good will *is* Grace: in this ideally democratic fable the third son—a humble and unexceptional hero distinguished from his able and eager brothers by his amorphous generalization, his foetalization—tramps goodheartedly, selflessly, will-lessly over the conditions of the universe, choosing, choosing, up to a final choice: a choice rewarded by an external, causally unrelated, paradoxical "success." Actually his normal state is its own reward, his real reward. "Success" is merely the morphological stamp of approval necessary to impress the undiscerning hearers of the parable; it is truly success only insofar as it resembles the state it rewards. Thus the third son, in his most developed and Audenish, his *truest* form, sits happily at home, already successful, and reads indifferently the love-letters of his more primitive forbear, trudging unnecessarily over the tundra or gasping on the peak.

There is only one real name for Auden's latest period: *Paul;* but it is hard to resist *Grace Abounding; The Teleological Suspension of Ethics; Waiting for the Spark from Heaven to Fall.* Here everything that is important happens in the Realm of Grace. The fundamental structural picture underlying the poems is that of *waiting humbly for Grace;* man's ultimate accomplishement is *sitting still*. We are damned not merely for what we do, but for doing anything at all—and properly damned, for what *we* do is necessarily evil: *Do not, till ye be done for* is our only possible slogan. In Stage II action and the will are evil, in Stage III everything (except the Wholly Other, God) is evil; Auden, like a backward Cato, leaves no speech without its *Carthage has fallen*—for he, like Niebuhr, accepts the Fall not merely as a causal myth but as the observed essence of all experience. But the speeches no longer support any Universal Popular Front; who are we to help out God's world? (Better wait it out instead.) The earlier *We must do something about Hitler* has become *We must realize that we ARE Hitler. . . .* The change of heart and its accompanying changes of behavior are now important only as a sign that we have *been* changed, elected—just as they were in Calvin; but the iron confidence of the theocrat (recreated for our age, in an unprecedented feat of the histrionic imagination, by Karl Barth) has scaled away, exposing its shaky armature of guilt and hope. The determinism of Stage I has returned, but transfigured by that Christian optimism which, in its avid acceptance of the worst evils of our world as necessarily inseparable from our fleshly existence, is more frightening than the most pessimistic of secular views. This already determined text of existence is neither presented, as in Stage I; nor categorized, as in Stage II; but *commented on*. Auden's work now consists of commentaries or glosses of every kind—dramatic, philosophical, critical. He becomes fond of writing criticisms or reviews which, under a vague show of criticizing a work some magazine has hopefully handed him, are secondary commentaries or glosses on those primary commentaries or glosses which are his creative works (so that readers of his reviews are continually exclaiming, "*Now* I see!"); these primary and secondary commentaries are indistinguishable in dialectic and imagery—purple patches, heartfelt confessions, and magical feats of dialectical ingenuity reach their highest concentration in reviews of minor theologians.

In this stage Auden has not forsaken ethics in the least—how could so confirmed a moralist? But his morals are now, like the law in Luther or Niebuhr, merely a crutch to beat people into submission with, to force home to us the realization that there is none good but God, that no works can either save us or make us worth saving. The Old Auden he has been forced to forget entirely—just as, in Freud's myth, we *have* to wipe from our conscious memory all the experiences of our earliest childhood. . . . But the Secular Auden of Stage II is the New Auden's favorite target of attack. Herod—hitherto represented by everybody as an aboriginal ogre, Freud's Father of the Primal Horde—is presented in *For the Time Being* as the Humane, Secular, Liberal Auden of Stage II. This explains the fervid rudeness of the attack: Auden is attempting to get rid of a sloughed-off self by hacking it up and dropping the pieces into a bathtub full of lye. . . .

II

But under all the changing surface forms of Auden's development—often almost grotesquely at variance with one another—there is a constellation of a few persistent organizing forces, the examination of which is a key to the understanding of the changes themselves; particularly if we realize that in development the opposite of an attitude is often more immediately allied to it than any intermediate position—and that Auden's rationalizations of his changes, however irrational they may seem, should rarely be considered of any *causal* importance.

A complex of ideas, emotions and unconscious attitudes about anxiety, guilt and isolation—fused or not yet separated in a sort of sexual-authoritarian matrix—is the permanent causal core of Auden's ideology; it is structural and basic in his nature—compared to it most other things are skin or hair, the mere bloom of rouge. In Auden's work the elements of *anxiety, guilt, isolation, sexuality* and *authority* make up a true Gestalt, a connected and meaningful whole.

. . . .

In Stage I Auden has rebelled, though guiltily, against a guilty Authority; he represents the new, potential Good rejecting the old and hardened Evil of an Authority which had itself come into power by revolting against, killing, and eating an earlier Authority (according to the Greek myths and according to Freud's myth in *Totem and Taboo*). In Stage II he tries to *reform* the Father, the State, Authority: everybody concerned has become much less guilty, and Auden's method of operation is now to persuade Authority into a recognition of its essential goodheartedness, into a reconciliation with himself and with the Reason which is over all things, gods and men alike. His relation to Authority is notably ambivalent—naturally so, since the relation is primarily that of Reform. A certain childishness (not too rare in young English intellectuals, who are sheltered and cherished in comparison with our own wild boys) becomes apparent in his attitudes—I remember a reviewer's talking of the "typical boyish charm" of the Auden poem of this period. Auden is managing to stay on surprisingly good terms with Authority by assuming the rôle of *enfant terrible* of the reformers—a very goodhearted and very childish one, the *enfant terrible* of the old father's long soft summer dreams. He becomes fond of saying that his favorite writers, those he would like most to *be,* are Lear, Carroll, and the author of *Peter Rabbit*—who themselves (as Auden wistfully realizes) reformed or rejected society in their ways, though not in any ways that kept them out of the nicest nurseries. . . .

In Stage II Auden nourishes a residual, partially perverse affection for any maladjustment to authority, for any complex or neurosis his development may have left lying around in him: after all, Authority itself, in the process of reform, has to get adjusted to poor ill-adjusted me. He feels an uneasy but thorough dislike for that "goddess of bossy underlings, Normality," and all the nursery schools and feeding-formulas that follow in her train; he betrays an astonishing repugnance to such concomitants of Progress as antisepsis and central heating, prays *Preserve me from the Shape of Things to Be,* and invents as *his* educational slogan: "Let each child have that's in our care / As much neurosis as the child can bear." All this corresponds to the petulance with which Alice, an eminently reasonable child, greeted any divergence of Wonderland from one's own household's routine—which *is* Reason.

In Stage III Auden repudiates with fear and repulsion any attempt to revolt against Authority, to reform Authority, to question Authority, or to remain separate from Authority in any way. Such an attempt is an insane depravity that is the root of all sin. He knows that (as Kierkegaard puts it in his wonderful, if unintentional, eight-word summary of Calvinism) *the only thing which interests God is obedience.* This is lucky: it is all He gets. But Auden is no Calvin—no logician, either—and tactfully overlooks any direct hand of the Creator in the creature's guilt. The only responsibility that Auden, as a representative neurotic theologian, does not thankfully push over on to God is the responsibility for his own guilty depravity; *that* he is responsible for, he confesses—with the abject, appealing leer of Peter Lorre in *M*—but everything else in the universe God is responsible for. This satisfies at one stroke Auden's anxiety—he is assured that he can and should do nothing himself; his need for guilt and his need to be reconciled to that guilt; and his need of an inexorable and unconditioned Authority.

When we have constructed God as the Wholly Other than ourselves, the wholly evil; when we have decreed that the image of God has been "wholly blotted out" in man by the Fall, we naturally find the problem of mediation between the Wholly Other and what it is wholly other than, a logically insoluble problem. We *require*—that is, we have made ourselves require—a self-contradictory, paradoxical, absurd mediator. Authority is now considered to be absolutely unconditioned, at once the Everything and the Not-Everything: shall *we* attempt to depose or limit God by demanding that he accord with our morality, our reason, our anything? The demands of Authority are equally unconditioned: but our own troubling actual existence wholly disappears in our believing, vicarious identification with Authority. Fortunate circumstances! since existence is wholly evil: "In every good work the just man sins." In every act we

> do
> Evil as each creature does
> In every definite decision
> To improve; for even in
> The germ-cell's primary division
> Innocence is lost and Sin,
> Already given as a fact,
> Once more issues as an act.

If Luther had only known about that germ-cell's primary division! The advances of Science almost have enabled Auden to beat Luther and Calvin at their own game. But then they were handicapped by taking it so much more *seriously*. The later Auden is rarely serious: he is either solemn or ingeniously frivolous, like some massive and labyrinthine town-clock from which a corked Topsy and a gilt Eva somersault to mark the hours of Time, but from which Uncle Tom himself, rattling the keys and surrounded by the flames of Judgment, emerges to herald the advent of Eternity.

The Buddha said that he taught nothing but suffering and the escape from suffering; Auden today could say that he teaches nothing but guilt, *which is* the escape from guilt. To be able to spend his time feeling guilty over the primary fission of the germ-cell instead of over that primary fission of the atom which produced in a few minutes half a million casualties—what a God-sent mercy this ability is to Auden, what a final expression of the depths and necessities of his being! What escape from responsibility or from guilt can equal this responsibility, this guilt? And, after all, is not the death of these poor guilty creatures (damned as they were by their lack of any connection with God through that one Mediator, Christ) only one more relatively unimportant effect of the germ-cell's division, that primary actualization of the *fact* of the first Fall—the Fall which has transformed every succeeding action of man into a guilty horror? How unimportant these inevitably trivial secular issues must seem to us to whom God has brought it home that there is only *one* issue: the obedience of the guilty soul to God, the soul's salvation by the grace of God.

Over and over Auden attacks every "good" act, every attempt to "improve." He reiterates that "it is not enough to bear witness [*i.e.,* to be a martyr] for even protest is wrong." He writes, with that overweening humility which is the badge of all his saints, the humility of Luther, Calvin, Kierkegaard and Barth: "Convict our pride of its offense / In all things, even penitence." So far as his penitence, so far as all (theological) things are concerned, it is hard to put up more than a token resistance to his contention. When we look at the world around us and within us, and then think of a statement like Niebuhr's, that only rebellion against God "is sin in the strictest sense of the word," how bitter it is not to be allowed to include that theology itself within the category of *sin, in the strictest sense of the word.* But I am applying ethical concepts to a realm in which, as the most casual witness must have observed, all ethics is suspended.

. . . .

In Stage III Auden is completely alone, but the knowledge of his isolation is not a burden but a blessing: he knows that we have always been alone, will always be alone, except in our paradoxical, absurd union with the Wholly Other, God; and he knows that he is fortunate not to be blinded by illusions of any impossible union with the creatures rather than with their Creator. Our isolation is the complete aloneness of the man who stands for every minute of his life, in fear and trembling and abject dread, before his God. One could describe this isolation with authoritative immediacy by paraphrasing the many pages of Kierkegaard and Kafka from which Auden derives both the spirit and the letter of his treatment. Few of the ideas of Auden's last stage have the slightest novelty to a reader acquainted with Luther, Calvin and Barth; even the expression of the ideas has no novelty to the reader familiar with Kierkegaard and Kafka. But this is a God-send for everybody concerned, since the theological ideas which Auden does not adopt but invents are all too often on the level of those brown paper parcels, brought secretly to the War Department in times of national emergency, which turn out to be full of plans to destroy enemy submarines by tracking them down with seals.

. . . .

The stages of Auden's development can even be diagrammed. In Stage I Anxiety and Guilt are fused in an isolated sexual core, consciously repelling or cowering under (and unconsciously attracting or yearning up to) the Authority that hangs in menacing ambivalence just overhead. In Stage II an active Anxiety dominates this core; it has pushed Sexuality to the side as far as it can, and attempts rather unsuccessfully to mitigate its confessed Guilt and Isolation by *reforming* the Authority it pulls down to it in Auden's traditional Jacob-and-the angel wrestling match. But in Stage III Anxiety, Guilt and Isolation are themselves the *relations* of Authority to the core; they *are* Grace (its mirror-image, as Auden puts it), the means by which Authority is manipulating the core into salvation. (Sexuality, mutated into Agape, is itself floating somewhere up near God.) The reader may complain about my last diagram: "But what is left to be the core?" That is the point I was making: there is nothing left. The one thing the Christian must realize is that he is "less than any of God's creatures," that he is swallowed up in Authority, the wholly determining Authority of God.

This was early plain to Auden: about New Year, 1940, he disapprovingly judged that the Calvinist tradition makes man "the passive instrument of daemonic powers"; but by the anniversary of this date, in the *Nation* of January 4, 1941, he is giving the theologian Niebuhr (who in Cromwell's time would undoubtedly have been named Death-on-Pride Niebuhr) a little neo-Calvinist lecture *à la* Kierkegaard: he is "not sure" that Niebuhr "is sufficiently *ashamed* [*my* italics]," mourns over Niebuhr's "orthodoxy," and ends by threateningly demanding that Niehbuhr decide once and for all "whether he believes that the contemplative life is the highest and most exhausting of vocations, or not." Just so, in late 1939, months and months before, he had complained that the doctrines of the theologian MacMurray are distorted by his "determination to believe in the existence of God," and had suggested that those doctrines would lose little—and, obviously, gain a lot—if expressed as Auden expressed them: "Man is aware that his actions do not express his real nature. God is a term for what he imagines that nature to be. Thus man is always making God in his own image." (In a little over a year he is sure that God is the Wholly Other.) Those years were fun for Auden, but death for the theologians. . . .

III

After observing in Auden this permanent anxiety, guilt and isolation, adhered to with unchanging firmness in every stage of his development, justified for different reasons in every stage, we cannot fail to see that these "reasons" are reinforcing rationalizations of the related attitudes which, not even rationally considered—much less understood—have been for Auden a core impervious to any change.

They form a core that Auden has scarcely attempted to change. He is fond of the statement *Freedom is the recognition of necessity,* but he has never recognized what it means in his own case: that if he understands certain of his own attitudes as *causally* instead of logically necessary—insofar as they are attitudes produced by and special to his own training and culture—he can free himself from them. But this Auden, like most people, is particularly unwilling to understand. He is willing to devote all his energies and talents to finding the most novel, ingenious or absurd rationalizations of the cluster of irrational attitudes he has inherited from a former self; the cluster, the self, he does not question, but instead projects upon the universe as part of the essential structure of that universe. If the attitudes are contradictory or logically absurd there, he saves them by taking Kierkegaard's position that everything really important is above logical necessity, is necessarily absurd. In the end he submits to the universe without a question; but it turns out that the universe is his own shadow on the wall beside his bed.

Let me make this plain with a quotation. On the first page of the *New York Times Book Review* of November 12, 1944, there appeared a review of the new edition of *Grimm's Tales*—a heartfelt and moral review which concluded with this sentence: "So let everyone read these stories till they know them backward and tell them to their children with embellishments—they are not sacred texts—and then, in a few years, the Society for the Scientific Diet, the Association of Positivist Parents, the League for the Promotion of Worthwhile Leisure, the Coöperative Camp for Prudent Progressives and all other bores and scoundrels can go jump in the lake."

Such a sentence shows that its writer has saved his own soul, but has lost the whole world—has forgotten even the nature of that world: for this was written not in 1913, but within the months that held the mass-executions in the German camps, the fire-raids, Warsaw and Dresden and Manila; within the months that were preparing the bombs for Hiroshima and Nagasaki; within the last twelve months of the Second World War.

The logical absurdity of the advice does not matter, though it could hardly be more apparent: people *have* been telling the tales to their children for many hundreds of years now (does Auden suppose that the S.S. men at Lublin and Birkenau had not been told the tales by their parents?); the secular world Auden detests has been produced by the *Märchen* he idealizes and misunderstands, along with a thousand other causes—so it could not be changed "in a few years" by one of the causes that have made it what it is. But the moral absurdity of the advice—I should say its moral imbecility—does matter. In the year 1944 these prudent, progressive, scientific, coöperative "bores and scoundrels" were the enemies with whom Auden found it necessary to struggle. Were *these* your enemies, reader? They were not mine.

Such mistaken extravagance in Auden is the blindness of salvation, a hysterical blindness to his actual enemies (by no means such safe enemies as the Prudent Progressives) and to the actual world. But it is hard for us to learn *anything*. When the people of the world of the future—if there are people in that world—say to us—if some of us are there: "What did you do in all those wars?" those of us left can give the old, the only answer: "I lived through them." But some of us will answer, "I was saved."

[From *The Making of the Auden Canon*]

Joseph Warren Beach

Occasionally I have been asked by friends acquainted with the nature of this study [the changes Auden made in the texts of his poems while preparing the *Collected Poetry* (1945) and *Collected Shorter Poems* (1950)] how my findings here affect my estimate of Auden's poetic work. And I might be expected to make at least a brief statement on this point.

A close examination of his work in general, and of his dealings with it in making up the canon of 1945–50, has confirmed my original high estimate of his imaginative powers as applied in this or that poem or series of poems taken individually. Auden impresses me still as the most gifted of the poets who have been so often bracketed with him as constituting a school of radical writers. And among contemporary poets in the English language he stands very high for the daring originality and brilliancy of his imaginative and linguistic effects.

And when it comes to subject matter and thought, he has the added distinction of being perhaps the most representative of poets in his time writing in the English language. He has seen a good deal of the world and witnessed history in the making. He has been very much aware of the main contemporary currents of thought in political theory, science and psychology, the fine arts and literature, philosophy and religion. He has been a prodigious reader, and remarkable for the ease and suggestiveness with which he has made use of his reading for the nourishment of his creative faculties. He has written notable poems on Voltaire and Pascal, on Freud and Yeats and Brueghel. He knows as much of Darwinism as can be learned from Samuel Butler, Bernard Shaw, and Gerald Heard; as much of socialism as can be learned from the Communist Manifesto; as much of psychology as can be learned from Groddeck, John Layard, and Jung's *Integration of the Personality*. In "New Year Letter" his allusions to poets and philosophers are in terms of confident familiarity; and he can be epigrammatic on the subject of Blake, Catullus, and Rilke, of Rimbaud, Baudelaire, and Kipling; on Descartes, Berkeley, Aristotle, Rousseau, and Hegel. He has discovered St. Augustine, Kierkegaard, and Reinhold Niebuhr. In physical science one takes for granted that he has read Eddington and Jeans, and, still better, his list of

Reprinted from *The Making of the Auden Canon* (Minneapolis: University of Minnesota Press, 1957) by permission of the University of Minnesota Press.

Modern Sources in the notes includes Hyman Levy's *Modern Science* and serious metaphysical treatises by Collingwood and Whitehead. No poet of our time has covered more ground, or ground more favorable to the growth of speculations suited to the felt needs of the time. He is to poetry what Aldous Huxley is to prose. But he is not to be mistaken for a Julian Huxley, a William James, a Santayana, or an Einstein. Like Tennyson he has endeavored to make himself acquainted with the philosophical thinking of his time, and he has been much more confident and dogmatic than the great Victorian in drawing conclusions.

All of this has a distinct bearing on the philosophic passion which may give added force and ponderability to the imaginative creations of a poet. Many great poets have had considerable learning beyond the limits of belles-lettres—witness Dante, Chaucer, Donne, Milton, Goethe, Coleridge, Shelley, St. John Perse. It is a marked weakness of most poetry since Tennyson that it has been so out of touch with the serious thought of our time. And in spite of the invincibly literary strain in Auden that leads him so often to "fall for" uncritical thinking in the realm of theory, it is a great distinction in him that he stands out among modern poets by his earnest effort to be an educated modern thinker.

But in any attempt to place his work as a whole in a scale of poetic "greatness," one is faced with the very difficult problem posed by the role of spiritual prophet assumed by him or thrust upon him by his enthusiastic followers and interpreters. And here we are obliged to take note of certain features of his mentality and poetic character that do not go any too well with his function as a prophet. In the long run, in writing with these pretensions, it is not possible to make a sharp separation between the imaginative and the intellectual faculties. The way a poet thinks is bound to have some effect on the images that he conceives and on the form and texture of the work in which these images are assembled and combined.

When I speak of the poetic character, I have in mind the character assumed by a poet in presenting his thoughts to his audience; and in this particular case I have in mind the way the poet conceives of himself as a performer. A prophet, if he is self-conscious enough to conceive of himself at all as performer, thinks solely of the powers at his command for communicating his spiritual message. He is simply a carrier of the truth that is in him. But it is recognized by Auden's most sympathetic admirers that he conceives of himself as one bound to dazzle and amuse. His poetic function, in our sophisticated age, requires him to wear masks and assume roles; and these vary greatly from poem to poem and from stage to stage of his career.

No one has shown greater virtuosity in assimilating this and that style from his predecessors. Dazzling certainly and hauntingly impressive were several of the choruses in *Paid on Both Sides* inspired by Anglo-Saxon models; dazzling and amusing in the manner of Edward Lear many passages in *The Age of Anxiety* with, this time, their *parody* use of Anglo-Saxon meters, epithets, and alliteration. And parody is much employed to relieve the solemnity of his religious poems, "The Sea and the Mirror" and "For the Time Being." One could not ask for anything more feelingly "incantatory" than his use of the Italian sestina in "Paysage Moralisé," with its teasingly provocative recurrent line-end symbols. No poet ever packed more associative feeling and thought into the images of valleys, mountains, islands, cities, water, and into that mere abstraction, sorrow.

Auden's use of imagery from the boys' game of secret agents and conspirators gives a pleasing air of mystery to many of his revolutionary poems and poems featuring heroic pilgrimages "beyond the frontier." His style in his teen-age period is brightened by many a device from Eliot and Robinson, and in later poems he has produced effects suggestive of Eliot and Hopkins. In "A Communist to Others" he makes good use of Burns's tail-rhyme stanza for satirical effects in the spirit of Burns. In his "light verse" period he wrote amusing cabaret songs, and in his propagandist plays with Isherwood, saucy lyrics that would pass for "proletarian."

Whatever modes he took over from earlier writers were most perfectly assimilated to his own purposes in the more discursively reflective poetry of 1937–40, in which prose tonalities tend to dominate; and it is in such poems as "Journey to Iceland," "At the Grave of Henry James," "In Memory of Sigmund Freud," "Spain 1937," and "September 1, 1939" that he is most perfectly himself and least the performer. These poems are not devoid of irony and sophisticated refinements of thought; but there is little suggestion of the satirical mask and the assumed theatrical role. They are earnest, direct, and manly in their rendering of the poet's sentiments. It is true that in his meditation "At the Grave of Henry James" he makes great play with James's mannerisms, his frequent use of French words, his curiously figurative language, and his elaborate periphrastic periods and locutions. But this is done in the kindliest spirit of a devoted disciple mimicking the style of a revered master. It is more by way of compliment than of lampoon, and it serves to reduce the emotional heat of a poem that is in essence a confession of sins both esthetic and spiritual.

In all periods of his writing, it is made interesting and provocative by the use of familiar idioms and items from familiar experience, and by the air of mystification which makes it all so intriguing and exciting. It is when you come to figuring out the precise intention in terms of prose discourse that you run into real trouble. For here it is that you have to reckon with the chameleon quality of the poet's mind. At first the effect of this quality might seem most bewildering, because most occult and disguised, when the poems of a given period are taken by themselves. One is more aware of the changing colors, and can make more allowance for the fact of change, in a general view, as one follows the development and sequence of doctrinal ideas through distinct periods with their distinguishable ideologies and philosophical positions. But here too the mask and the role are operative in creating ambiguity.

For a time this very ambiguity may serve as a solvent for the contradictions or incongruities among the several overlapping positions, as new points of view begin to invade the old. But gradually, if we insist on knowing where the poet stands at a given moment, we grow more and more uneasy.

It is true that, by discreet revisions and eliminations in the poems of the thirties, and by throwing the poems of all periods together in a heap without regard to their temporal sequence, the author does his best to iron out the contradictions and incongruities. And here perhaps the ordinary reader, who does his reading perforce in one of the later collections, will do well to settle down cozily in his deck chair, give up trying to take his bearings, and submit to the sleepy charm, as distinct outlines are blurred in the general haziness that envelopes the landscape. But for anyone with access to the earlier volumes, the uneasiness becomes still more acute as he compares the original texts with those of 1945 and 1950, where so many relatively unambiguous poems are translated into the terms of Auden's later thinking, only to find themselves rather shockingly out of place. And at this point we are obliged to conclude that the poet, with the best of intentions, is virtually misrepresenting the thought which actually informed the earlier writing. . . .

We are here concerned with what is sometimes called the integrity of a work of art. I am thinking of this use of the word by Matthiessen in his admirable pioneering critique of Eliot. The integrity of a work of art derives, in the last analysis, from the integrity or integrality of the artistic conception. And this in turn involves the integrity of the poet's mental process, since it is impossible to separate entirely the forms taken by the poet's imagination from the way he thinks.

In using the term integrity, or better integrality (a more cumbersome but rather more precise word in this context), I am not making it a synonym for honesty or even sincerity, in the ordinary sense of that word. I am not suggesting that, in writing, or in rewriting his poems, Auden was motived by an intent to deceive his readers or even himself. Through all his writings there runs, I feel, a core of moral earnestness, a wish to be right with himself and with whatever principle of ethical significance there may be in the world. That a man should change his opinions, or shift his position in regard to great issues, with more light and more mature understanding, is a highly honorable proceeding and reflects credit on the human intelligence and our capacity for learning and improving ourselves. And that a man should have the candor to publish to the world such changes of opinion and position is again highly honorable and to be admired. In our time there are innumerable writers and artists and men in every calling who have followed a course parallel to Auden's.

And how, one may say, can we question the right of an author to be his own judge as to the intent of a piece of writing, or to make it over so as to give it a new direction? What I have suggested is that such a making over of a work of literary art is not to be accomplished by cutting out a few offensive passages, or by merely hanging the work in a different gallery in different company; and that it is vain to suppose that now it means something essentially different from what it did. Again, it is surely any writer's privilege to drop by the way poems which seem to him to be inartistic or to carry meanings that seem to him unworthy. But when he retains other poems of the same period and inspiration which carry much the same meanings, but so mingled with other quite different meanings as to invest the whole with a disquieting air of ambiguity, the question of integrity, or simple consistency, is acutely raised.

Consistency is perhaps the less misleading term, suggesting as it does an analogy with other works of art in which the material consistency of the medium is of prime importance. Such media are the potter's clay and the cook's cake-mix. Consistency may go with a considerable number of diverse ingredients; and the most seductive flavors in culinary confections are secured by the combination of many substances as seemingly incompatible as oil and vinegar, or sugar and spice. And here we are reminded of the emphasis recently laid on paradox and tension as strengthening features of poetry, and of Robert Penn Warren's view that, if one is to avoid shallowness and sentimental flatness, the final positives of a poem must be "earned" in their struggle with the negatives that are so prominent in our ordinary thinking and experience. Paradox and tension are certainly prominent features of Auden's poetry, but this analogy would be misleading if applied to the special feature I have in mind. There can be no question about the strengthening effect for poetry of tensions set up between things which actually coexist in all our experience, such as light and dark, bitter and sweet, or the realistic and the idealistic view of human nature. What I have in mind in the poetry of Auden is opposites which cannot well coexist logically or practically, like incompatible meanings of the same word in the same context, or conflicting lines of conduct in a given situation recommended in the same breath.

We must agree that in Auden's most ambiguous work the combination of ingredients is almost invariably piquant and intriguing. And the critical problem is simply whether the effect of the single poem, or still more, the effect of his poetry as a whole, has that final consistency or integrity which in the end satisfies us and gives us the feeling that, as Wordsworth would say, we have been tendered "feeding pleasures." . . .

In considering Auden as a poet representative of his time, what I have called his chameleon quality might be counted to him for a merit. For our time, like any other, like Donne's or Tennyson's, has been notable for the variety and complexity of its intellectual crosscurrents and conflicting emotional attitudes; we have hardly begun yet to sort out the ideas and attitudes which, in simplifying historical perspective, may come to be thought of as dominant. And it may be considered an advantage to find between the covers of one book a maximum reflection of the characteristic movements of the time. But that is a consideration more important for the student of *Kul-*

turgeschichte than for the votary of the arts. Or at any rate what we prize in literary art is not confusion but richness in the representation.

In a work of art, as in a man, we are best satisfied when we are confidently aware of a wholeness, or integrality, that underlies all the diverse and even conflicting elements. And we are most satisfied when there is a consistent thread running through the whole course of a man's life or the whole body of an artist's work.

In the case of Auden, it is our doubt on this point that makes us hesitant to class him with writers in whom we have this sense of wholeness or integrity. We do not take in his work the confident satisfaction that we do in the work of a Voltaire, a Swift, a Molière, a Wordsworth, a Keats, or a Browning. Or to take examples from the poets of our own time, we do not feel in his work the integrity that we feel in poets of lesser gifts—in Spender, or Marianne Moore, or in Robinson Jeffers; or in poets of comparable or greater gifts—Wallace Stevens, or Dylan Thomas, or Frost, or Eliot. Through a man's work we are reaching out to the man. And if it is true that the style is the man, we feel with these that we are making contact with at least as much of the man as shows in his work, and that we know sufficiently with whom we are dealing. With Auden we are not sure of this.

We know that he is a very gifted actor and mimic; and he has beguiled many an hour with his impersonations. But we cannot give ourselves up to him without certain reservations. Isherwood noted how as a young man his character changed with his hat. And we are never sure from moment to moment which of his many hats he will next be wearing.

It is, in the last analysis, a question of identity, and other things being equal, our fullest admiration goes to the poet who on this point never leaves us in doubt.

[From *This Modern Poetry*]

BABETTE DEUTSCH

Not dogged courage, but a bold note of challenge is heard in poetry today, sounding most thrillingly from across the water. The bitterness of the War poets, Sassoon, Graves, Wilfred Owen, is foreign to these young Englishmen, though they are well aware of living under the shadow of war. They have come to grips only vicariously with the evils of poverty, the agony of industrial slavery, the horrors of class warfare, that such writers as Arturo Giovannitti, Michael Gold, Carl Sandburg, recorded with some vigor and much earnestness twenty years ago. . . . Among the less cheerful of them, sardonic laughter has found a new object—their own inadequacy. The plea for strength is seldom uttered. These young men are acutely conscious of the age in which they are maturing: not the horns and motors at their back, but the airplane engine humming overhead, the drill grinding at their feet to make a cave for refuge from the gas-bombs of the next war, are what occupy them. And always, beyond the horizon, lies new country, defying the old order whose collapse they would hasten. Sometimes one seems to hear under their shouts of enthusiasm a murmured paraphrase of one of Kipling's old imperialist songs:

> If th' Union were what th' Union seems:
> Not the Soviet Union of our dreams,
> But only Stalin, brass, and paint,
> 'Ow quick we'd chuck 'er,—but she ain't!

But though they have been stimulated and supported in their faith by the Russian experiment, they appear to be realistic enough to insist that if they are to build the new Jerusalem in England's green and pleasant land, the task must be done by British workmen, if not with English bricks and English mortar.

They are revolutionaries both technically and politically, a fact which makes them almost unique in literary history. For while the poet is often in advance of his time and in opposition to the governing power, those concerned for the niceties of their art are apt to ignore the social question, as the more earnest propagandists are apt to let esthetic considerations go by the board. C. Day Lewis, however, with his colleagues, W. H. Auden and Stephen Spender, have gone to school to Eliot, to Wilfred Owen, and more particularly to Hopkins. They have learned as much from Hopkins's theory as from his inimitable practice, returning to the simplicities of the nursery rhyme, to the easy lilt of the ballad, rather than exploiting "sprung rhythm" with the fastidiousness of its Victorian godfather. They accept the conversational tone and to some extent the free associations of Eliot, though their transitions from the style of one period to that of another are perhaps not as swift as his, if possibly more various. They do not frequently follow Elizabethan practice, and, not having had to revolt from free verse, they do not often employ the tight stanza of Gautier. They are not averse to internal rhyme, which, unlike end-rhyme, fails to accentuate the metre, but they incline more to the assonances employed by Wilfred Owen. Since they do not share his fondness for Keats, they avoid the lush quality which is sometimes at variance with what Owen has to say. They feel his passionate desire to uproot the forces of evil which make our world what it is, but not having known the actual horrors of the front, and so less appalled by the anguish war entails than belligerent in their advocacy of a new social order, their poetry inclines, unlike his, to drama and didacticism.

In one important respect they differ from all of these "ancestors," as they like to call those men on whose spiritual powers they are able to draw. Their imagery refers largely to the machine age, and their symbolism, derived from this urban and industrialized society, as well as from the study of geology, biology, and the findings of Freud and [Kurt] Koffka, is almost allegorical in its definiteness. The vocabulary of industrial warfare: the spy, the bully (or thug), the abandoned works, the ruined farm, and the social parasite seen as a menace to the healthy organism, the effects of a dominating money power seen as manifestations of disease—these recur in their work with hammering persistency. And alike in their concrete details and in their frequent puns they are more anti-poetic than their predecessors. Two quotations from Lewis will illustrate both their exactitude of phrase and the spirit which animates their poetry. He dismisses one division of the enemy—the comfortable, unimaginative bourgeois—thus: "Counters of spoons and content with cushions / They pray for peace, they hand down disaster." And thus simply he states what he and his companions demand: "Men shall be glad of company, love shall be more than a guest / And the bond no more of paper." Contrast this with Alfred Prufrock's despairing symbolism—"I have measured out my life with coffee spoons;"—and with his creator's stricken prayer in *Ash Wednesday:*

> Terminate torment
> Of love unsatisfied
> The greater torment
> Of love satisfied . . .

> Grace to the Mother
> For the Garden
> Where all love ends.

The difference in method and attitude is at once apparent.

Technically, their debt is to the poets of their own country, rather than, as their predecessors' was, to the poets of France. Indeed, as was noted above, they travel back some six centuries to take lessons from Langland, and find in his homely Anglo-Saxon verse a suitable form for their address to the plow-man's modern counterpart. Not that the English laborer would understand the idiom of Lewis or Auden, but the vigorous rhythm and marked allitera-tion of *Piers Plowman* appeals to these poets for its summoning qualities. Like Hopkins, they are in too great haste to get the thing said to wait upon grammatical usage; like him, they constantly play upon words, revel in puns and knottier ambiguities. This clipped manner of speech, with its elisions and compressions, may signify, as in Hopkins's case, passionate conviction, or, as in the case of Eliot, an assumption that one is addressing intimates only. Indeed, nothing is stranger—until one has analyzed it—than the contrast between the tone of these poets and their ultimate intention. They proclaim the dear love of comrades, they announce the imminent birth of a new world of real brotherhood, in phrases charged with paradox, in music often harsh with mockery. Auden, the most obscure, in some respects the most stimulating, nicely illustrates this divergence and its meaning.

His poems are scarcely intelligible until one has read them in their entirety. Not only is nearly every poem an inseparable entity, but, further-more, most of the pieces are supported by the body of his work. The whole here is greater than its parts. One becomes accustomed to the abrupt syntax: "In his day-thinking and in his night-thinking / Is wareness and is fear of other, / Alone in flesh, himself no friend." One comes to understand that when he speaks of "a memory of fish" he is referring not to the pond or the dinner-table, but to a remote period in evolutionary history. One learns to think quickly, although what happens in the mind of the attentive reader is perhaps not thought, driving the staples of logic for a bridge across the gaps, but intuition flinging hasty planks or flying over at the tail of a balloon. But one must beware of being waylaid by references too new to assimilate in passing. Here is none of the delight in machinery which allowed MacKnight Black to talk about turbines and dynamos as though they were bursting buds, none of the disgust for it that made the Fugitives long for the peace of the plantation. Here, moreover, is not that intense realization of war which fills the verse of Sassoon and Wilfred Owen with appalling pain. Auden takes both machinery and war for granted in a fashion impossible to his seniors. He expresses neither praise nor dispraise. It is all part of the landscape, or as Hopkins might say, the "inscape" of the modern world to which he belongs, the world which he sees crashing toward destruction and rebirth. Foreseeing the destruction, he speaks of "Equipment rusting in unweeded lanes." Accepting the struggle as inevitable, he commands: "Cover in time with beams those in retreat / That, spotted, they turn though the reverse were great." In the course of a poem sung to a jazzed tune which gives it an effectiveness it would otherwise lack, a poem filled with peacetime imagery, he observes:

> In my spine there was a base;
> And I knew the general's face:
> But they've severed all the wires,
> And I can't tell what the general desires.

The acceptance of the machine, and more especially of machine warfare, which allows him not merely to introduce it casually and frequently, but actually to convert it into metaphor, is one of the distinguishing marks of Auden's verse. But more significant than this are the unexpected gaps and reversals which make it difficult to know where to have him next.

It is plain enough that he is satirizing capitalist society. The Announcer in his *Dance of Death* describes a good deal more of Auden than is contained in that sharp little comedy with his opening speech: "We present to you this evening a picture of the decline of a class, of how its members dream of a new life, but secretly desire the old, for there is death inside them. We show you that death as a dancer." From behind the curtain the Chorus responds: " 'Our Death.' " This is but an echo of the passage in one of his poems where the poet cries out that love

> Needs more than the admiring excitement of union,
> More than the abrupt self-confident farewell,
> The heel on the finishing blade of grass,
> The self-confidence of the falling root,
> Needs death, death of the grain, our death,
> Death of the old gang . . .

Here is the reason for the sudden air-pockets that Auden's poems seem to strike in their bold flight. How shall a man, in himself or as representative of his class, consent to death? Here is the explanation of the severed wires, the ignorance of the general's wishes in the lines quoted above. How in this crisis shall the general—the will—be understood? How, knowing the need for the extinction of the old gang, and naturally reluctant to go down, shall a keenly conscious member of it avoid satirizing not merely society, but the enemy within?

If one is to understand Auden's poetry one must recognize that he is attacking the Old Gang, the declining class, and therewith attacking everything in himself which clings to that sick part of society. The attack—since he is a gay as well as an angry young man—takes the form of buffoonery.

And the obscurity of his verse comes from sources over and above the expressive novelty of his technique, the abrupt syntax, the urban and mechanical imagery, the puns. It is due in part to the fact that he turns without warning from mocking the social order he would defeat to mock himself and mock his friends who, because of their breeding and background, are interfering with that defeat.

There are passages in Auden's work that the blind could read, as when he considers the older generation:

> These ordered light
> But had no right,
> And handed on
> War and a son
>
> Wishing no harm.
> But to be warm
> These went to sleep
> On the burning heap.

Or again, when he addresses his contemporaries or those elders in whom the blood still runs:

> Shut up talking, charming in the best suits to be had in town,
> Lecturing on navigation while the ship is going down.
>
> Drop those priggish ways for ever, stop behaving like a stone:
> Throw the bath-chairs right away, and learn to leave ourselves alone.
>
> If we really want to live, we'd better start at once to try;
> If we don't, it doesn't matter, but we'd better start to die.

This poem is richer for one who hears under it the ironic echo:

> For I dipt into the future, far as human eye could see,
> Saw the Vision of the world, and all the wonder that would be;
>
> Saw the heavens fill with commerce, argosies of magic sails,
> Pilots of the purple twilight, dropping down with costly bales;
>
> Heard the heavens fill with shouting, and there rain'd a ghastly dew
> From the nations' airy navies grappling in the central blue;
>
> Far along the world-wide whisper of the south-wind rushing warm,
> With the standards of the peoples plunging through the thunder-storm;

Till the war-drum throbb'd no longer, and the battle-flags were furl'd
In the Parliament of man, the Federation of the world.

Similarly, when, in the *Journal of an Airman,* Auden writes: "His collar was spotless; he talked very well, / He spoke of our homes and duty and we fell," those who remember the verses in which the poets of antiquity praised the patriots who died for their country will savor the satire more keenly. Which brings up another point in regard to Auden's obscurity in particular and the obscurity of contemporary poetry in general.

It is an ironic commentary on popular education that one of its results has been to make it impossible for the poet to communicate except to a narrowly limited circle. Where every one has a minimum of information, every one pretends to be educated, but only the fewest attain more than a shallow learning. The necessity for specialization, with the advance of science and technology, is also somewhat to blame for this situation. The result is that the poet, knowing more of the past than his fellows, more sensitive than they to the present to which that past is tributary, and speaking out of that richer awareness, can be intelligible to the merest handful of people. Moreover, even within this civilized circle, there are bound to be smaller circles: what is comprehensible to people, however cultivated, living in a given quarter of London, will not be equally comprehensible to people, however alert, who live in a very different quarter of New York, or Charleston, or Chicago, and vice versa. When Auden speaks of air-dromes, of music-halls, of the unemployed, one can translate the British scene into American terms. But when he assumes—as he generally does—familiarity with the life that goes on in English country-houses, familiarity with the College Quad and the Cathedral Close, even the traveled American, instructed by generations of British novelists, supplemented by Henry James, T. S. Eliot, and the creator of Jeeves, will have but superficial or second-hand knowledge of the substance of that life, the object of Auden's attack. Add to this that the poet, appreciating the multiple barriers to communication, decides to abandon all pretense of talking to outsiders, however intelligent, and addresses the small group of his intimates. The difficulty would seem to be insurmountable.

It is not. Hopkins, whom these young men have good reason to imitate, made, in a letter to Bridges, an observation which they might underscore. Speaking of the obscurity his friend found in his own verse, he wrote: "Granted that it needs study and is obscure, . . . you might, without the effort that to make it all out would seem to have required, have nevertheless read it so that lines and stanzas should be left in the memory and superficial impressions deepened, and have liked some without exhausting all." Elsewhere he said that a poem should have one of two kinds of clearness: "either the meaning to be felt without effort as fast as one reads or else, if dark at first reading, when once made out, *to explode*." Auden is, in more senses than one, explosive. The best of his verse, like that of many of the predecessors against whom he is taking arms, offers superficial impressions which are deepened with re-reading. Because he depends less on connotative effects than do those poets who went to school to the symbolists, these impressions are themselves somewhat foreign. But surrender to the alien element, not unlike that of the child who flings himself into the sea without water-wings, offers the most rapid and exhilarating mode of learning. Thus Charles Madge instructs his audience:

> This poem will be you if you will. So let it.
> I do not want you to stand still to get it.
> You will have it if you go high-speed; it slides in
> Between velocities; you will not need to begin
> But to have begun and to be going; to have started . . .

Another possible analogy is that of children learning to read and write. They can understand words and phrases that they do not themselves employ, use in conversation words that they cannot read, and grasp the meaning of words on the printed page that they are unable to write. Similarly, the amateur of contemporary verse may understand in a poem more meanings than he can formulate or restate, even with some necessary loss, in his own words, and he must exercise some ingenuity to enjoy what he sees.

The key to Auden's position may be found in a sentence from the opening section of *The Orators:* "What do you think of England, this country of ours where nobody is well?" and in his thirtieth poem, in which he prays for power (not sweetness) and light. In this poem he addresses God as one who forgives all but "will his negative inversion"; forgives all, that is, save the will toward death. Among Auden's spiritual forebears not the least important is the one most ignored—Samuel Butler. Like that mid-Victorian modern, he would put the sick in jail and the criminal in hospital: though for Auden it is not the individual, but a social class that is diseased. Like Butler, he would throw off the dead hand of the past, but keep faith with his real ancestors, those whose strength and sanity he can still praise and seek to emulate. Like Butler, the young poet recognizes the force of the unconscious, the seat of racial memory, the keeper of the secrets of desire and fear. Above all, he is with the historian of *Erewhon* in his faith that man is an unifinished creature who has learned how to give himself a swifter foot, a louder voice, and longer hand by virtue of the machine, but who seems to be the victim of his own ingenuity, and who must become cleverer than fish or bird if, with all his accomplishments, he is not to go the way of the giant saurian. . . .

[From "In the Cool Element of Prose" (Review of *The Orators: An English Study*, rev. ed.)]

DAVID LEHMAN

In the English-speaking world, the prose poem never quite graduated to the status of a genre—until recently, perhaps—largely because it didn't really have to. The opportunity to write prose poetry, by whatever name it might be called, had almost always existed for the writer in English; whereas in France the prose poem occurred as a more or less complete rupture with the past, there is a profound sense in which, for example, Ashbery's *Three Poems* extends the impulse behind an earlier work, the *Centuries of Meditation* by Thomas Traherne. The inflexible metrical rules and strict conventions of French verse made inevitable Baudelaire's conclusion that the medium of prose alone presented an authentic alternative to a condition of slightly seedy classicism; imposing far fewer constraints than its French counterpart, English blank verse seemed flexible enough to allow the prose of the world to mingle within its domain. Rebellions would still be needed, but when they came their leaders would wave a different gallic banner, that of *vers libre* rather than *poèmes en prose;* verse would demand its emancipation, but not from the strictures of lining. More to the point, there existed in the English literary heritage no shortage of works that enthusiasts could claim for the province of prose poetry. Thus Shelley speaks of "the astonishing poetry of Moses, Job, David, Solomon, and Isaiah," while Coleridge refers to "the writings of Plato, and Bishop Taylor, and the *Theoria Sacra* of Burnet," which "furnish undeniable proofs that poetry of the highest kind may exist without metre, and even without the contra-distinguishing objects of a poem." In "a little anthology of the poem-in-prose" published in the New Directions annual of 1953, the American poet Charles Henri Ford includes passages from Shakespeare and Thoreau as well as a Donne sermon; one wonders only that so zealous an editor didn't see fit to print a "Now" of Leigh Hunt or one of the prose songs of Ossian which so profoundly affected young Werther.

It is no accident that, among English harbingers of the modern prose poem, we find hoaxes like that perpetrated by Macpherson, cosmological

Reprinted from *Parnassus: Poetry in Review* 8, no. 2 (1980) by permission of *Parnassus*.

reveries like Poe's *Eureka,* memorable fancies like those of Blake, and other enterprises of undeniable eccentricity. By its anti-traditional tradition, the form would seem to authorize and encourage activities symptomatic of what I am tempted to call the original syndrome—that is, the latecomer's thirst for the new. A pronounced and deliberate quality of otherness characterizes such landmarks of French prose poetry as *Spleen de Paris, Une Saison en enfer, Les Chants de Maldoror, Le Cornet à dés,* and the *"Plume"* poems of Henry Michaux, to name but a few; strange bedfellows, they militate against the possibility of any precise definition of the prose poem as a genre. To be sure, there is something in the French critical temper that gravitates toward codification, and Professor Suzanne Bernard in her massive study of the subject can confidently list conditions that must be met for a work to enter the ranks of certified prose poems.[1] It is hard to know whether serious poets on either side of the ocean take that sort of thing to heart, but if they do it is at their peril; to conform to rules, even (or especially) sensible ones, can only result in a loss of liberty.

A voluntary surrender of the poet's prerogative accounts, at least in part, for why prose poems written self-consciously "in the French manner" (but also, alas, in the English language) have always struck me as less satisfactory than works which may have analogue or precedent but which fiercely declare their independence from any recognizable "line." I am thinking of Stein's *Tender Buttons,* Ashbery's *Three Poems,* and individual prose poems by Elizabeth Bishop ("12 O'Clock News"), John Hollander ("On the Calendar"), Frank O'Hara ("Meditations in an Emergency"), Edwin Denby ("Aaron"), James Schuyler ("Footnote"), and some others. Many American practitioners of the prose poem seem determined even to avoid calling their productions by that name. Though its very title recalled the Rimbaud of *Une Saison en enfer,* William Carlos Williams denied that *Kora in Hell* had anything in common with "the typically French prose poem," whose "pace was not my own." Why this resistance, this mistrust? To avoid sounding like a cheap domestic model of the expensive foreign brand, for one thing; for another, to guard jealously the writer's autonomy. Above all else, the use of prose as a medium for poetry comes as a liberation—or, rather, as a constitutional right. It guarantees the freedom to make use of the languages of "dust and twigs and flies," of annual reports and gossip columns, railway timetables and textbooks; it enables the writer to create his own context without reference to generic conventions. Paradoxically, the prose poem affords a home for writings that would not be at home in any genre whatsoever. It is designed to allow for *sui generis* works, works which are—to use the expression Duke Ellington reserved for superlative praise—"beyond category."

The Orators: An English Study is such a one; by making it available once again (along with other early writings that the poet would later disown), *The English Auden* presents an admirable opportunity to reassess what is arguably the most controversial book of prose poetry the century has produced. It is a work which must, I think, be restored to the canon, though not without properly considering the vicissitudes of its publishing history; the problems it raises recall the sparks that flew over the awarding of the Bollingen Prize to Pound. What guided Auden's hand, after his famous step westward on the eve of World War II, was the instinctive need to be consistent, to achieve an identity between written words and mental convictions, to regard sincerity and intellectual honesty as prominent among the criteria by which he sternly judged his literary productions, past and present; the "dishonest, or bad-mannered, or boring" poem was to be issued a dishonorable discharge. Thus judged and found wanting was *The Orators,* which Spender calls "Auden's most English book," "the most uninhibited, high-spirited, and self-revealing work of the young Auden." Upon its first appearance, in 1932, it was received with great enthusiasm; it was, critics felt, as innovative in its texture and as disturbing in its vision as *The Waste Land* had been a decade earlier. Moreover it spoke to the young men of its time with a voice to which they could respond with terrific excitement.

Still is not difficult to understand the hostility which *The Orators* was later to arouse, sometimes from its former champions. For the 1945 edition of his *Collected Poetry,* Auden consented to retain only the "Letter to a Wound"; when in 1967 he finally permitted the book to be reissued (as a document of historical importance, a kind of blast from the past), it was with considerable embarrassment. "My name on the title-page," Auden ruefully wrote, "seems a pseudonym for someone else, someone talented but near the border of sanity, who might well, in a year or two, become a Nazi." No doubt it was the "Journal of an Airman" that made its author most uncomfortable, with its paranoid outbursts, its yearnings for a "leader," its wishes for the subordination of womankind, its impatience with things flabby and bourgeois, an impatience that hindsight may find dangerously close to the totalitarian urges so prevalent in the European Thirties. If the "Journal" is approached for its ethical and political implications, the reader will certainly find it alarming, even ominous; one wonders how it could come about that a man of avowedly leftist inclinations, whose instinctive liberalism survived the period, could have written as he did, unaware of the trap he had fallen into. Perhaps, Monroe K. Spears has suggested, there is a "double irony" at work in *The Orators,* with the effect that the mocker is himself the most mocked of all; perhaps it is the very nature of a "double irony" that it leaves everyone confused, for the right or wrong reason.

Auden could scarcely have failed to consider the purely literary defense that could be mounted on behalf of the book. For a young writer with experimental tendencies, whose interest in modern poetry inclines toward the verbally innovative and as such is exuberantly amoral, the dazzling and audacious surface of this manual of styles deflects attention from the bothersome obscurity of its content. Indeed, it may even be forcibly argued that it is precisely this obscurity that makes the book so manifestly attractive at a first or second reading. How emancipating it must have felt to compose a "Statement" or "Argument" whose structure is known but whose terms remain unknown quantities; how invigorating a test of the reader's agility. These were poems, after all, not campaign speeches or public addresses; where their logic led was somehow beside the point. If this manner of reasoning might have nourished the young Auden, however, it represented the antithesis of the position he adopted in the Forties. Then, armed with the conviction—perhaps intellectual dread would be a more accurate term—that all of the civilized world somehow contributed to the Nazi terror, passively or actively, by tolerating it or acquiescing before it, and that all must share in the enormity of guilt, Auden wanted to revise the record belatedly, to dismiss *The Orators* as "a case of the fair notion fatally injured"—the good literary idea marred by what Spender called "schoolboyish ruthlessness"; the shrewd diagnosis delivered by the infected doctor; the prophecy, even, that would hasten the very doom it forecasts.

About the brilliance of *The Orators* there can be no doubt. As *The Waste Land* moves from parody to echo, from biblical lamentation to truncated anecdote, changing tones and diction at will, blending the accents of high Elizabethan drama with Cockney barroom slang, so does *The Orators* seem a collage—not, in this case, of lifted lines and remembered fragments, but of a whole nation's speaking and writing habits. "He do the police in different voices": the phrase from *Our Mutual Friend* that was Eliot's original title for *The Waste Land* is at least as applicable here, if not more so. Where Eliot lifts phrases and lines, Auden mouths distinctive modes of utterance: the commencement speech, the diary notation, the love letter (as it might appear in an epistolary novel), the forms of expository prose, the accents of Anglican responses. In so doing Auden demonstrated the merit of conceiving a prose poem as an ironic renewal of the rhetorical devices of English prose, stripped from their familiar contexts and playfully re-situated. As "an English Study," then, *The Orators* parodies the courses on "English studies" that a British public school student could be assumed to have taken.

But the subtitle has an equally important second sense; the work is intended to be a "study" of England as it behaved *entre deux guèrres,* still cringing from the shocks of the first World War as the second inexorably approached. The "Address for a Prize Day" introduces Auden's version of Eliot's overwhelming question: "What do you think about England, this country of ours where nobody is well?" With the ventriloquist's trick of putting these words in the mouth of a cheerfully brutal headmaster, Auden achieves the "double irony" I have mentioned: if the problem of England's *malaise* and *maladie* is defined on the playing fields of Eton, the terms of the problem derive from *The Divine Comedy,* it being Auden's humorous fancy to present Dante in pedestrian dress and thrust him into the gymnasium that stands by metonymy for the whole of England. The headmaster shares with Baudelaire—another of Dante's disciples—the sense of life as a hospital whose patients incessantly change their beds, if not their sheets. Much has been made of the influence exerted on Auden at this time by Homer Lane, whose "progressive" pedagogy stressed the view that all of man's physical ailments spring from mental or emotional disturbances—that, indeed, both crime and sin are symptoms of psychosomatic ailments. And so, just as each of Spenser's seven deadly sins is identified by a specific disease in *The Faerie Queene,* Auden's excessive lovers of self are deaf to all external sound; the excessive lovers of their neighbors are heavy smokers; the defective lovers tend to be "anemic, muscularly undeveloped, and rather mean"; the perverted lovers, prone to influenza from the start, end as "incurable cases"; Hell is not "other people" but our own failures of love. Whatever Auden's own reservations, this piece resonates with his characteristic touch. How like Auden to use the conceit of a "Divine Commission" filing a report on England; how like him to adhere broadly to Dante's design and then to divide and categorize, with the rigor and precision of a biologist, a people, its manias, and its sources of discontent.

As a rhetorical strategy, the inventory is of particular appeal to the poet-in-prose, and Auden's "Argument" and "Statement" illustrate two directions that the form can take. As a parody of Anglican prayers and of liturgical language in general, the middle section of "Argument" beseeches "private" detectives and "public" houses to lend their aid to the defective lovers. The movement from the general to the surprisingly specific is one humorous by-product of a characteristically modern attempt to be all-inclusive:

> For the devoted; for the unfaithful; for
> those in whom the sexual crisis is delayed; for
> the two against one, and for the Seven against
> Thebes,
> O Goat with the Compasses, hear us.

> For the virgin afraid of thunder; for the
> wife obeyed by her husband; for the spinster
> in love with Africa,
> O Bear with the Ragged Staff, hear us.

Notice the witty use of false parallelism ("for the two against one, and for the Seven against Thebes"), as though it were the special power of the inventory as a literary device to effect a leveling of reality, a kind of identity between apparently unlike phenomena.

"Statement" is a series of lists, a procession of persons defined first by their talents and then by the manner in which they achieve either destruction or salvation. For example:

> One slips on crags, is buried by guides.
> One gets cramp in the bay, sinks like a stone
> near crowded tea-shops. One is destroyed in his

bath, the geyser exploding. One is arrested
for indecent exposure.

One is saved from drowning by a submerged
stake. One healed by drinking from a holy well.
One is honoured by a countess with a gift of
grapes. One is hailed as the master by monthly
reviews. One is known in his club as "the Skipper."

The list permits the poet to shift gears incessantly, to move from magic or
myth to history and empirical reality, to render the sense of relativity inherent in such a concept as "success," which may be accidental and military
("One wins a battle through a change in the weather") or materialistic, the
reward for technical ingenuity ("One makes a fortune out of a locking device
for lifts"). The constant repetition of the word "one," like an incantatory
note, provokes the poet to draw back from his work and comment on it, in a
passage which recalls the distinctive rhythms and "insistence" of Gertrude
Stein:

An old one is beginning to be two new ones.
Two new ones are beginning to be two old ones.
Two old ones are beginning to be one new one.
A new one is beginning to be an old one. Something
that has been done, that something is being
done again by someone. Nothing is being done
but something being done again by someone.

"Letter to a Wound," which concludes the first part of *The Orators,* is a
poignantly ironic description of the salutary effects of disease. "You" throughout refers to the wound, with which the writer lives in a state of intimacy,
like a spouse. During the initial stages of the illness, the sufferer reports, "I
had outbursts, wept even, at what seemed to me then your insane jealousy,
your bad manners, your passion for sporting things." As time goes by,
however, the disease becomes an asset, a way of differentiating oneself from
one's fellows, a new aperture through which to view the world. "I pitied
everybody. Little do you know, I said to myself, looking at my neighbor on
the bus, what has happened to the little man in the black hat sitting next to
you." Finally, the relationship matures; man and wound become inseparable,
and the writer feels impelled to express his gratitude. "Thanks to you, I have
come to see a profound significance in relations I never dreamt of considering
before, an old lady's affection for a small boy, the Waterhouses and their
retriever, the curious bond between Offal and Snig, the partners in the
hardware shop up front."
    This is more than a wry romanticizing of a significantly undefined
illness, more than just an account of the way we cling to our neuroses,

regarding our limitations as virtues, our ailments as necessary to our way of being. For in contrast to other parts of *The Orators,* the tone here is mild and subdued rather than brash, and the reader is left with a feeling of bemused pity. It is true that the element of satire is ever present—"You are so quiet these days that I get quite nervous, remove the dressing. No I am safe, you are still there"—but the piece ironically points to larger truths: that the contemplation of beauty owes much to disease and disaster, reminders of our mortality; that the bearer of the wound gets to shoot the charmed bow; that the damaged groin of the fisher king may yet father forth. The letter writer is guilty of the excessive love of self that culminates in perversity if not perversion, yet the wry note Auden strikes makes us regard the letter as a parabolic description of the modern artist, at odds with himself, yet deriving inspiration from this division and from the incessant dialogue, like ongoing peace negotiations, between the stalemated factions. This perception of the psychic cost exacted by one's art is developed with greater ingenuity and finesse in the high comedy of "Caliban to the Audience," Auden's most remarkable prose poem, which comes in the guise of a commentary on *The Tempest* (in *The Sea and the Mirror,* 1944).

Here it is "imprisoned Ariel" that appears to take the wound's place in the writer's heart and mind. Grateful for his freedom, Ariel faithfully provides solutions to any novelist's problems: "who should be killed in the hunting accident, which couple to send into the cast-iron shelter, what scent will arouse a Norwegian engineer, how to get the young hero from the country lawyer's office to the Princess' reception, when to mislay the letter, where the cabinet minister should be reminded of his mother, why the dishonest valet must be a martyr to indigestion but immune from the common cold." But Ariel the ever-obedient servant refuses to oblige in one particular: he will not collect his fee and promptly disappear when discharged. There comes the inevitable crisis, the "sour silences" and "curdled moods," when with the subsiding of the creative "fever" the artist has neither the will to command Ariel nor the ability to get rid of his haunting presence. Now, therefore, the shaving mirror held up to the artist's nature no longer reflects a liberator's face but "a gibbering fist-clenched creature," the Caliban in everyman, upon whose intractable clay even Ariel's magic is powerless. Ariel's master has become Caliban's servant; the artist as Prospero must mediate between these rival impulses, as the ego mediates between superego and id, but this is far from a simple task. Again we are reminded that, as hosts, we are helplessly dependent on the wounded and wounding organisms that have taken up lodgings within us in response to our unthinking invitations. In accents that recall those of "Letter to a Wound," Caliban soberly asesses his (their?) prospects:

> From now on we shall have, as we both know only too well, no company but each other's, and if I have had, as I consider, a good deal to put up with from

you, I must own that, after all, I am not just the person I would have chosen for a life companion myself; so the only chance, which in any case is slim enough, of my getting a tolerably new master and you a tolerably new man, lies in our both learning, if possible and as soon as possible, to forgive and forget the past, and to keep our respective hopes for the future within moderate, very moderate, limits.

If in its exposition of the dilemma, as in its metaphorical invention, this pastiche of Jamesian grandiloquence surpasses the most moving portion of *The Orators,* that is scarcely to denigrate the latter. Rather it underscores the conviction that "Caliban to the Audience" stands together with "In Praise of Limestone" as twin magnificences of Auden's American period.

By far the longest section of *The Orators,* the "Journal of an Airman" is both the most politically objectionable and the most technically audacious; in addition to prose and verse, the journal includes a chromosome design, geometrical figures put forth as psychological tests, spurious definitions, "G.H.Q. Commands," and "The Airman's Alphabet" which renders "Ace" as "Pride of parents / and photographed person / and laughter in leather," and "Bomb" as "Curse from cloud / and coming to crook / and saddest to steeple." One has the feeling here of an almost organic structure that could accommodate all manner of impulse, all possible styles of communication.

The English Auden permits us to take preliminary steps towards answering certain inevitable questions: Which of Auden's "periods" is the most impressive? Will his influence on future poets abate or gain in intensity, with beneficial or deleterious results? Was Auden right, or misguided, to censor such works as *The Orators?* From the wealth of material now available, will it be possible to arrive at a selection that would constitute the "essential" Auden? In any such reckoning, the early, "English" writings will, in my estimation, fare very well indeed. For James Merrill, John Hollander, and Richard Howard, each of whom has been moved to write memorable verse in tribute to this master, Auden's technical know-how, his brilliant wit and lively wordplay, and his fine mediation between the public and private realms are exemplary. Upon a review of *The English Auden,* one finds these virtues and more: one can also see the scaffolding on which the consciously avant-garde writer can hang his banner. The very methods the early Auden employed in composition—at a certain point he made poems out of an anthology of lines Isherwood chose from other, discarded poems of his—prefigure the tricks up the sleeve of the New York School.

In an overview of Auden's career, *The Orators* assumes a special significance. While its history dramatizes the crucial change of heart the poet underwent, there is a surprising continuity between the concerns articulated here and those of the later work; if the theme of male bonding and tribal initiation is found to be somewhat sinister, still the critique of English society is as penetrating as the gaze Auden would later cast "Across East

River in the night." To the extent that writers are hedonistic in their approach to the literary past, *The Orators* will survive as an eccentric masterpiece, a risk worth emulating. It assures Auden an eminent place within the tradition of the new; among other things it demonstrates with a singular vitality the attractions of prose as a medium for poetic experimentation.

Note

1. *Le Poème en prose de Baudelaire jusqu'à nos jours* (Librairie Nizet, 1959).

[From *A Reader's Guide to W. H. Auden* (*The Dog beneath the Skin*)]

John Fuller

Auden's *The Dog Beneath the Skin* (written in collaboration with Christopher Isherwood, but still largely his own) struck a happy balance between suggestive symbolism and myth, and direct caricature and propaganda; between doggerel, knockabout and pastiche, and some of Auden's finest lyrical and analytic poetry. It is easily the most successful and original of the three plays written with Isherwood.[1] Curiously, it was not entirely well received at the time,[2] but it is the kind of work that improves with keeping: what may originally have seemed raw and youthful has now attained a fine period flavour.

The origins of the play are of some interest. Auden and Isherwood had already collaborated on an unpublished play called *The Enemies of a Bishop*,[3] which presented the victory of the Bishop over his enemies as a paradigm of Homer Lane's victory over false healers. Bloomfield reports Isherwood as saying that this play was based on Lampel's *Revolt in a Reformatory*, which he and Auden had seen together in Berlin, and Isherwood himself writes that they "revised the best parts of it and used them again, five years later, in *The Dog Beneath the Skin*." Actually, Auden's earlier draft of *Dog*, called *The Chase* (a typescript of which exists in Exeter College Library, Oxford), is also largely about a revolt in a reformatory. Since it was this draft which Auden showed to Isherwood early in 1935, and upon which they collaborated, it becomes dificult to imagine what in *Dog* might have been cannibalized from *Enemies of a Bishop*. One suspects that there has been a confusion here between the two earlier plays.

The extent of the collaboration is also now uncertain. Isherwood has said: "I always thought of myself as a librettist to some extent with a composer, his verse being the music; and I would say 'Now we have to have a big speech here,' you know, and he would write it' (*London Magazine*, June 1961, p. 51); but he holds that most of the play is by Auden. Bloomfield reports Auden as crediting Isherwood with "Act I, scene ii, with the exception of the song, about half of Act II, scene i, and the Destructive Desmond episode."[4] Since *The Chase* survives, it may be of interest to give a resumé of

Reprinted by permission of Thames & Hudson Ltd.

its action for purposes of comparison with *Dog*. The typescript presumably dates from after May 1934, when the Vicar's Sermon—which has not been typed out in the typescript and is merely referred to as "the sermon from *Life and Letters*"—appeared in that magazine under the title of "Sermon by an Armament Manufacturer."

The Chase

ACT I

CHORUS: Cf. *Dog*, p. 11. Mr Fordham is automating his mine, and a strike results.

SCENE I: Introduces the Vicar, and three newspapermen whom he tells of the missing heir. The newspapermen describe the principal of the Reformatory, Augustus Bicknell (the name is made up of Auden's father's second name and his mother's maiden name). The texture is similar to that of *Dog*, including in this scene pantomime doggerel, parody of Kipling and a song-and-dance.

SCENE II: The Reformatory. George and Jimmy are new arrivals. The Vicar distributes moral largesse, but the boys are ready to revolt ("2nd Boy: We demand der free air. Der zunlicht. 4th Boy: Good ole Fritz"). Introduces Bicknell and Sergeant Bunyan, who plays the O'Grady game. Bicknell is sanctimonious. George and Jimmy escape.

SCENE III: "Curtains open at the top of the Cyclorama, disclosing the Witnesses, old men identical in nightshirts and night caps" (cf. *Dog*, p. 15).

SCENE IV: The Vicarage. The Vicar's cook tells him he must have a cold supper because she is helping with the strike meeting. The Vicar indulges in a fantasy about the First World War, and stumbles on George and Jimmy who are hiding in the garden. Encouraged to help them by the Witnesses, the Vicar distracts Sergeant Bunyan's attention while they dress up in the toolshed as a dog and a woman. There is then an interlude in which the Prompter apologizes for the delay, and the Conductor consults him about names he can't read of those to appear in the heir-finding ceremony.

SCENE V: Cf. *Dog*, p. 17. The Vicarage Garden. The Vicar introduces "Miss James" (Jimmy) to Bicknell as his secretary-chauffeur. Alan Norman is chosen to find the missing heir, and is given the dog (George). The second newspaperman is drunk. Mildred Luce delivers her diatribe (cf. *Dog*, p. 31). Alan departs.

ACT II

CHORUS: Cf. *Dog*, p. 117, the Act III chorus beginning "A man and a dog are entering a city."

SCENE I: Cf. *Dog*, p. 120, Act III, sc. i. The Ninevah Hotel. Miss Vipond tells the hotel to let the dog stay. Alan goes to her room.

CHORUS:	"Fordham has answered with a lock out."
SCENE IIA:	A picnic in a deserted mine. No news of Alan. Bicknell woos "Miss James." General Hotham and Hayboy (a research chemist) talk about the presumption of the lower classes. The Vicar answers them with the speech "You too are patients" (printed in *New Verse*, Feb. 1935).
SCENE IIB:	Iris waits for news, sings "Seen when night was silent" (cf. *Dog*, p. 65). The Witnesses appear as explorers.
SCENE IIC:	Bicknell protests love to "Miss James." Sergeant Bunyan says that there is trouble at the Reformatory: the boys are off to the strike meeting.
SCENE III:	Cf. *Dog*, p. 138, Act III, sc. iv. The epithalamium at the Ninevah Hotel. The dog discovers a letter from Francis Crewe, the missing heir, to Miss Vipond saying that he's been shot during street fighting at the Power House. The Witnesses appear at a toll-gate ("The way be careful to remember is never lost / But to our tolls for upkeep you must pay the cost").
CHORUS:	The strike continues. Jimmy is with the strikers.
SCENE IV:	A concert at the Reformatory. "Miss James" gives out prizes (and asks the winners if they are ready with keys, bombs, barbed wire, etc.). He is taken away by the police.

ACT III

CHORUS:	Cf. *Dog*, p. 155.
SCENE I:	The dog (in front of a drop representing slum street) asks the audience who he is. "Undergraduate: You're a s-s-symbol of M-M-M-Marx and Lenin? . . . Dreadfully clever little girl: You're the dog. George: Bravo."
SCENE II:	The Police Station. Alan is brought in. The Police are called out to a demonstration at the Power House. A policeman brings Alan workman's clothes. Dialogue between Alan's feet (cf. *Dog*, p. 112). George tells Alan about Francis's letter.
SCENE III:	Outside the Infirmary. Alan says good-bye to George.
SCENE IV:	The operating theatre. Operation on Francis Crewe (cf. *Dog*, p. 104), who dies ("Francis: Be true, be true / To Pressan. She / Will teach you what to be"). The police charge the crowd offstage.
CHORUS:	Cf. *Dog*, p. 111.
SCENE V:	The Vicar says Jimmy has been shot while trying to escape, and expresses impartiality (cf. the Curate's speech in *Dog*, p. 175). The General wants reinforcements to attack traitors in the Reformatory, and asks the Vicar to preach a sermon to the audience "to call 'em round." The Vicar refuses and is arrested. The sermon (the General's "special record") is played from a gramophone, while recruits pour on to the stage. The Reformatory is stormed; a machine-gun covers the audience, shooting down Alan as he runs through the auditorium. He dies in front of Iris. The Reformatory is fired, and Mildred Luce exults.

CHORUS: "If we end to-day with the apparent triumph of reaction or folly: there is an alternative ending / And the choice is your own" (cf. *Dog,* p. 179).

The Chase is evidently, with its involved interrelation of plots, a politically more ambitious play than *Dog,* but it has a far less interesting dramatic texture and range, even though it similarly bulges with theatrical devices. This is probably due to a sharp division of interest between the reformatory revolt and the search for the missing heir. Moreover, the relation of both these themes to the industrial unrest in the background is sketchy in the extreme, though it is intended to provide the point behind the violent and pessimistic climax to the play. The answer lay in telescoping the plots: thus, in *Dog,* George, Jimmy and Bicknell disappear, and Francis Crewe himself becomes the dog who accompanies Alan Norman. Although this telescoping means that the action of *Dog* is compelled to become much more episodic than that of *The Chase,* it also provokes the central message of the play in its new form: that only by an act of imaginative sympathy and self-abnegation (becoming the dog) can the hero come to understand his predicament and escape from it. Francis is the real Leader of the play. The new title (provided by Rupert Doone) emphasizes the centrality of this developed idea.

The dedicatory quatrain may be found in the BM Notebook, fol. 85, a page much influenced by Blake.[5] It invokes the revolutionary as a healer or a poet, who, in his anatomy of a corrupt society, comes to understand the powerful role played by the bourgeoisie ("the genteel dragon"), just as Francis Crewe comes to see through the villagers of Pressan Ambo.

The opening chorus is in Auden's characteristic panoramic-descriptive mode, with imagery developed to a musical simplicity and accuracy that was to become more and more common in his middle period. Its initial idyllic appeal to a genuine love for England provides a perfect dramatic contrast to the agricultural desolation and chaotic proliferation of exurbia which is described in the second part. This is the landscape of decadent capitalism grinding slowly to a halt, the outward manifestation of an inner anxiety which is presented in the semi-choruses as the insomnia of the young men from among whom is about to be chosen a hero to undertake the Quest for the missing heir.

The Witnesses who play such a large role in *The Chase* as representatives of Necessity are reduced here (p. 15) to one embodiment only: they appear as the chorus leaders who conclude the chorus by singing eight of the ten stanzas of Part III of the long poem called "The Witnesses," published in *The Listener* in July 1933. This poem elaborates and explains the function of the Witnesses "to curse and bless." It describes the despair of a hero who discovers that he is "not the truly strong man": his exploits, therefore, though heroic, have been in vain, for the Witnesses are displeased. Like the Watchers (see CSP, p. 52), they represent for Auden a mysterious duality which is a governing principle of human life (see also *The Orators,* p. 34, with its overtones of Lawrence's cosmology as expounded in Chapter 13 of *Fantasia of the Unconscious*). Although in their full role in *The Chase* they attain a playful Cocteauesque humour (there is much play with telephones and motor-bicycles), they plainly allow Auden to pursue his developing interest in the numinous. As Necessity and Time ("the clock"), therefore, they create for the guilty Quest hero (the restless neurotic or radical bourgeois) an atmosphere of indefinable menace which Auden evokes with allusions to the plagues of Egypt, Birnam Wood coming to Dunsinane and the Scissor Man from *Struwwelpeter.*

The action begins in "a musical comedy or pantomine village garden" (stage direction from *The Chase*), with the stereotyped characters introducing themselves in verses reminiscent both of Gilbert and Sullivan and of the doggerel of Lyceum pantomimes in the thirties.[6] When Alan Norman is chosen to find Sir Francis Crewe, the chorus invoke Love (p. 26: "Enter with him," called "I shall be Enchanted" in CP, and "Legend" in CSP) to accompany him on his quest. Love is seen as the archetypal bewitched fairy-tale figure who accompanies the hero, helping him with his tasks, and then demands to be sacrificed in order that he may return to his real shape (cf. *The Frog Prince*). In this sense, therefore, the "love" of the chorus is (*a*) the quality that the successful hero needs in order to pacify the Witnesses; and (*b*) the dog, Francis, the real hero who assists Alan, and who is seen sniffing about, being kicked and patted, throughout the chorus. On page 28, incidentally, it is still being called George (see my synopsis of *The Chase,* above). Mildred Luce's speech embodies the kind of vengeance that Auden was writing about in *Paid on Both Sides:* her vain appeal to her watch shows that the Witnesses ("we are the clock") are not responsive to such vindictiveness.

Alan's journey has all the inconsequential logic of a dream. Indeed, some of the scenes suggest the direct influence of Lewis Carroll: compare the King of Ostnia with the King of Hearts (p. 46) or the Poet with Humpty Dumpty (pp. 94ff). Alan's naïvety and obstinacy are exactly suited to the kind of revue-sketch world he moves through. The didactic point of these scenes is clear enough, so that Auden is able to concentrate his more complex elaboration of their relation to his theme into the choruses which punctuate them. The scene is the Europe of the inter-war period, typified by Ostnia, a corrupt East European monarchy, and Westland, a fascist dictatorship, countries which were to reappear in the later Auden and Isherwood plays.

The scene on the boat where Alan meets the two Journalists was written by Isherwood (except for the Cowardesque song "They're in the racket, too"). With its neat and very conventional characterization, its well-observed dialogue which isn't afraid to take ironic short cuts across the pages of middle-brow fiction, and its continual undercurrent of light farce, this scene sets the general tone of the play. The description of Ostnia, for instance (p. 38), creates an expectancy of something not far removed from the Fredonia of the Marx Brothers film *Duck Soup.* Indeed, the whole scene in the Palace at

Ostnia (p. 46), with its parody of the Mass, and the King's fussy, apologetic execution of the workers, has a violence and offhand illogicality reminiscent of the Marx Brothers. And yet in the introductory chorus (p. 43) Auden holds up Ostnia and Westland as serious types of contemporary capitalist communities, whose follies are similar to England's, and whose poverty, expanding "like an air-bubble under a microscope slide," will soon affect England's "treasure and . . . gentlemanly behaviour." The old man "of the sobriquet of Tiger senilely vain" is Clemenceau, whom, in a review in *Scrutiny* (March 1933, p. 413), Auden had called a senile homicidal maniac, and the "naughty life-forcer in the Norfolk jacket" is Bernard Shaw.

The King has directed Alan to Ostnia's Red Light district, and the chorus on page 54 describes his journey through the city ("where loyalties are not those of the family") to find it. The description here of cruel poverty and deprivation has a force and pity which sets the scene at the brothels (p. 57) at an ironical distance. Those who visit the brothels are "rebels who have freed nothing in the whole universe from the tyranny of the mothers, except a tiny sensitive area": the Chorus's accusation is suggestively and characteristically phrased, and bears enough weight to allow the predicament of Sorbo Lamb, former heir-finder turned dope-addict, to be presented on the same cartoon level as the brothel proprietors' songs.

The following scene in the Westland lunatic asylum (about half of which was written by Isherwood) is an evident satire on German nationalism. Stephen Spender criticized the scene (*New Writing*, Autumn 1938), saying that it was not frightening because the Nazis were not really lunatics: perhaps the point is rather that the lunatics of *Dog* are not frightening because they are not as mad as we now know the Nazis to have been. The scene is high-spirited, not bitter, and its prophecy of doom seems too genially dismissive. The First Mad Lady's Song is adapted from an uncollected sonnet in *New Verse*, October 1933.

On their way out of Westland, Alan and the Journalists encounter the financier Grabstein, a figure probably based roughly on Sir Alfred Mond, industrialist, politician and one of the architects of ICI (compare "President of the XYZ"). Auden had reviewed Hector Bolitho's biography of Mond in *Scrutiny*, December 1933. Compare Grabstein's "I've founded hospitals and rest homes" (p. 88) with Bolitho, p. 219, where a similar point is made about Mond; and compare Grabstein's "I've studied all the Italian Masters" with Auden's point in his review that Mond was no artist and that his taste for Italian painting was not relevant.

The chorus on page 91 (called "The Cultural Presupposition" in CP) is one of Auden's most famous poems, famous rightly for the way it moves triumphantly from its point about man's self-consciousness and knowledge of death to its point about the dependence of a flourishing highbrow culture upon a slaving and oppressed proletariat. It does this not by any facile neatness or didacticism, but by a simple rhetorical appeal to biblical authority. Auden may have been influenced, as in other choruses in *Dog,* by Eliot's choruses in *The Rock* (1934). More particularly, the echoes of the Beatitudes here may have come via Owen's poem "Insensibility," which Auden included in *The Poet's Tongue,* published in the same year as *Dog.*

In his search for Sir Francis Crewe, Alan had been told by Grabstein to try Paradise Park.[7] The brutes that Alan meets here are all self-deceivers. The Poet, Grabstein's son, is a Poundian egotist: he is "the only real person in the whole world" and insists on speaking in several languages, quoting Aeschylus and Villon (a line already used by Pound in *Mauberley*). When Alan doesn't understand, the Poet is forced to speak English, and quotes Dryden. *"Cinders"* (p. 95) is the title of an early Auden poem (in *Oxford Poetry 1926*). The two lovers are similarly self-absorbed: their song is a loose variation on Lear's *The Owl and the Pussycat,* and manages to include an allusion to *Sweeney Agonistes* ("Two as one and one as two," p. 96). Neither they nor the invalids know anything about Sir Francis Crewe. The self-consciousness defined by the previous chorus, and demonstrated in Paradise Park, assumes the extreme form of absorption in disease, the Lane theory finally coming into the open in the chorus on page 102.

If disease has a psychological origin, as Lane's theory holds, it follows that conventional surgery is a waste of time. The belief "in the physical causation of all phenomena," exposed by the parody of the Creed in the next scene, underlines the futility of the Surgeon's quasi-religious procedures (Isherwood compared an operation to a religious ceremony in *Lions and Shadows,* p. 294: perhaps this idea was his). It is hard to see how the bullet in Chimp Eagle's bowel could have a psychosomatic origin, especially as he got it during strike action at the docks (p. 100). However, in his Wagnerian duet with Alan (pp. 108–9), he knows that Francis is in England, and that he (Chimp) has forgotten his "choice and lot" (it is Francis disguised as the dog disguised as the nurse, curiously enough, who hastens his death by giving him an injection of hydrochloric acid). Chimp thought that he could succeed by simple political action.

The night interlude which follows (pp. 111ff), though it contains two of the most striking choric passages in the play, is merely marking time on Alan's journey back to England. The dialogue between his two feet is taken from *The Chase,* now given a quasi-political point by the addition of Cockney dialect. It also attempts to maintain interest in the mystery of Francis's whereabouts, but the melodramatic confidence about the roller-skates has a limitingly Mortmere air. In the following chorus (p. 117) the hawk's eye moves in from "Villas on vegetation like saxifrage on stone" down through the suburban "sorrow" clinically catalogued, into the heart of the city as Alan and the dog make their way to the Ninevah Hotel, symbol of capitalist excess. In the vestibule he meets the two Journalists, and the Second Journalist is given the opportunity to sing his rhyming-slang song "Alice is gone" (to the tune of "Jesu, the very thought of thee" according to *The Chase*). The restaurant scene burlesques the sexual tyranny and (Isherwood's scene, this) the militant philistinism of the rich: Destructive Desmond's appeal to the cabaret audience as he is about to slash the Rembrandt is borrowed from the presentation of Christ to the Jews, and the cry of "Barabbas! Barabbas!" Alan's involvement with this world is represented by his affair with the film star, Lou Vipond. To the accompaniment of an ironic epithalamium sung by the hotel staff, he makes love to her as a shop-window dummy ("*When the dummy is to speak,* ALAN *runs behind it and speaks in falsetto*"), a device which represents the isolated self-regard of conventional romance. Sex is thus (as the speech by the dog's skin, p. 144, makes clear) merely an "idea in the head."

The skin represents the instinctive life, and it draws the contrast between itself and the clock in the hall, which represents fate. Francis's assumption of the skin (which is revealed to the audience in this scene) is therefore essentially an attempt to break out of duality. However, he later (p. 172) elaborates the social reasons for it, and when he helps Alan to escape from the Ninevah Hotel in the skin, and Alan is kicked by the Manager, says, "Ha ha! Now you know how it feels!"

The chorus on p. 155 re-emphasizes the inevitable conditioning and fate of the divided individual. Auden draws on Georg Groddeck's *Exploring the Unconscious* (1933) for some of the detail. Compare "his first voluptuous rectal sins" with "The earliest sins . . . are connected with the rectal tract" (Groddeck, p. 89), and "the greater part of the will devoted / To warding off pain from the water-logged areas" with "certain lower parts of the adult body always contain an excess of fluid. . . . A great part, a very great part of our unconscious mental energy is used up merely in warding off pain from these water-logged places" (Groddeck, pp. 51–52). The last notion is a particularly dotty one, since Groddeck proposed that the water-logging was due to the effect of gravity. The chorus is really attacking the escapism and optimism of the man who imagines that "five hundred a year and a room of one's own" are a sufficient "change of heart." In its allusion to the final sonnet in *Poems* (1930), "Sir, no man's enemy," this probably shows a fresh awareness in Auden of the difficulties in which the individual is involved: he may easily be able to beware of others, whose illnesses he can correctly ascribe to their various spiritual failings, but will he be able to beware of himself, whose own heart whispers: "I am the nicest person in this room"? Two years later, in a broadcast, Auden was still tackling solipsism in much the same terms (*The Listener,* 22 December 1937, p. 137). The solution in this chorus looks rather perfunctory: in a pastiche of the "Give. Sympathize. Control" passage from *The Waste Land,* Auden resorts to an abbreviated didacticism.

Alan and Francis return to find Pressan Ambo in a fit of jingoism. The Vicar, who with General Hotham has founded a rather Mosleyite Boys' Brigade, delivers a sermon on the origins of sin, or more particularly on the revolt of Satan against God, which he compares to the growth of international Communism. His conviction that God is on his side in this new battle develops into self-righteousness, and the self-righteousness into hysteria. This splendid prose piece acts as the climax of the play, evoking as it does the ironical fourth Ode in *The Orators,* where the psycho-political struggle is suddenly seen from the side of reaction. Auden reprinted the sermon in CP, and the view has arisen (probably due to Beach) that this means that Auden now approves of the witch-hunting Vicar. On the contrary, a prefatory note in CP makes it plain that the subject of Auden's satirical attack is still the same as it was when the piece appeared as "Sermon by an Armament Manufacturer" in *Life and Letters,* or as the General's gramophone record in *The Chase:* that is, the type of the Super-Ego convinced that it is the Voice of God. Of course, out of context it was bound to appear rather more of an in-group satire than otherwise, but criticism of Auden for "changing sides" here is simply mistaken.

Francis reveals himself and denounces the village. He has observed them "from underneath," recording his observations in a diary,[8] and did not like what he saw. With a handful of recruits from the village he leaves to join "the army of the other side," passing out through the auditorium while the Journalists photograph the villagers, who have all turned into animals. Stephen Spender criticized *Dog* (*New Writing,* Autumn 1938) on the grounds that it presented "a picture of a society defeated by an enemy whom the writers have not put into the picture because they do not know what he looks like although they thoroughly support him." It is plain, however, just as it is plain in a work like Upward's *Journey to the Border,* that the hero joins the Communist Party. The vagueness (as in Upward) is part of the mysterious inevitability of it all, an inevitability supported by the final line of the "Epilogue," the Marxist "To each his need: from each his power," and by the whole drift of this deliberately grand and rhetorical chorus in which love is urged to wake from its dream and prove its vigours.[9] The play's extraordinarily lively and eclectic means to this serious end has deceived many into thinking less of it than they might. It deserves frequent revival.

Notes

1. Originally published 1935; paperback edition published 1968 (London: Faber and Faber). The other two published plays on which Auden and Isherwood collaborated are *The Ascent of F6* and *On the Frontier.*

2. The range of critical attention may be gathered from Kenneth Allott in *New Verse,* Feb./March 1936, and Ian Parsons in the *Spectator,* 28 June 1935.

3. See Isherwood in *New Verse,* Nov. 1937, and B. C. Bloomfield, *W. H. Auden: A Bibliography* (Charlottesville, University of Virginia Press, 1964), p. xvii.

4. For a full account of the evolution of the published version, and of the authors' altercation with Faber and Faber, see Bloomfield, pp. 13–14.

5. Manuscript Notebook (Add. MS 52430). See Bloomfield, Item J3. A full description may be found in John Whitehouse, "Auden: An Early Poetical Notebook, *London Magazine* 5 (May 1965) pp. 85–93.

6. See A. E. Wilson, *Christmas Pantomime* (1934), pp. 247ff. Auden has said that pantomime is "the most important single influence" on *Dog* (Breon Mitchell, *Oxford German Studies* 1 [1967], p. 169). Dick Whittington was a popular pantomime subject at the time (Wilson, p. 165).

7. Cf. Hegel, *Philosophy of History* (trans. J. Sibree, 1900), p. 414: "Paradise is a park, where only brutes, not men, can remain."

8. The idea of the diary may have come from J. Field's *A Life of One's Own*, which Auden reviewed and praised in *The Listener*, 28 Nov. 1934, p. viii.

9. One line of this chorus is based on a phrase of Winston Churchill's in *The World Crisis* (1923), his history of the First World War, describing Germany's March offensive: "It was an hour of intolerable majesty and crisis." See Auden's review in *Scrutiny*, March 1933, p. 413.

[From *Auden: an Introductory Essay* (*The Ascent of F6* and *On the Frontier*)]

Richard Hoggart

"The Ascent of F6," chiefly because it has a stronger central thread, is more worth study than either "The Dog beneath the Skin" or "On the Frontier." One of the scenes—that between Ransom and the Abbot—has a force not approached in either of the other plays. There is the usual alternation of prose and verse, this time with some attempt at heightening the tension by moving into verse at moments of crisis—as when Ransom and his mother address one another in blank verse (actually, unimpressive), or when Ransom, on F6, railing at the blizzard, echoes Lear confronting the storm; there are some incantatory passages and some striking dramatic gestures ("I have found a spider in the opulent boardroom. / I have dreamed of a threadbare barnstorming actor, / And he was a national symbol"); and there are some parodies of popular and cabaret songs, mainly by Gunn, though the best—"At last the secret is out"—is from the chorus.

In general, "The Ascent of F6" is not as careless as the other two plays. Its construction is tighter: after some simplified assaults on such things as the unscrupulous Press, the technique of sensation, imperialism and threadbare public-speaking, have been cleared out of the way, it concentrates on one main theme—the climbing of the mountain and its significance for Michael Ransom.

Ransom is a scholar and ascetic, sensitive and yet a man of action, whose greatest enthusiasm is mountain climbing. He is finally persuaded by his mother, after his statesman brother James and others have failed to move him, to lead an assault on F6. The Ostnians are also preparing a party with the same object, since the natives of the region, which both countries want, believe that the first white man to conquer F6 will rule them for a thousand years. By the time F6 is finally climbed three of Ransom's friends—Lamp, Shawcross and Gunn—have lost their lives. Just before the first death and in the very middle of the climb, Ransom has his interview with the Abbot, in which his dilemma is discussed at length but still not fully faced.

The dilemma arises from the realisation, by a man of exceptional gifts, that corruption seems inevitably to follow from the use of power, that the

Reprinted by permission of Chatto & Windus/Hogarth Press.

will is usually impure, but that to react therefrom into isolation may be itself another form of sin. By virtue of his qualities Ransom is potentially a man of power, and knows this; he is, in fact, obsessed with the problem of power, suspicious of himself, and yet unable to analyse his own motives satisfactorily. He has become profoundly mistrustful of his own driving force; he sees the mark of the serpent on all men's actions and on their relations one with another, and his mountain climbing, like his scholar's withdrawal, is in part an escape to a "purer" battle with impersonal forces. We meet him first sitting alone on the summit of the Pillar Rock above Wastdale, telling the beads of his obsession in a rhetorical prose soliloquy, which begins by commenting on the selfish springs behind Dante's creative activity and widens to comment on the endlessness of self-deceit and self-justification, and on the impossibility of communication except with "the unqualified and dangerous dead," to whom alone Ransom will pay homage.

Ransom can detect the infection in the will of others; he recognises his brother's lust for power; he understands his friends (who are also his subalterns, since he is a natural leader)—he envies Lamp's simple singleness of purpose, but knows he could never possess it himself; he sees the value of a weak but comparatively uncomplicated youth like Gunn (a surface-sketch for Emble in "The Age of Anxiety"); he is able to give good if unacceptable advice to the permanent head-prefect Shawcross, who hides his refusal to face the weaknesses of his own character in homage to his ego-ideal Ransom. When Ransom finally removes his shadow and obliges Shawcross to face himself, alone, Shawcross realises that even his admiration for Ransom was "only another kind of conceit." He cannot meet the challenge of his new nakedness, and kills himself.

Ransom sees all this and sees some way into himself—but not far enough. He talks of "those to whom a mountain is a mother," but fails to apply the moral to himself; until the final dénouement at the top of the mountain he is trying to understand his personal daemon, wondering whether the better course would be to turn back, but still, in all essentials blindly, going on. The Abbot presents him with a clear choice, but one which he cannot seriously consider, partly because he is not yet ready for those particular alternatives, partly because he already sees the insufficiency of the Abbot's choice. The Abbot's crystal shows Ransom the special form of his own temptation, in the pleading faces of the lost and lonely who want a healing god and ask Ransom to assume power over them: "Restore us. Restore us to our uniqueness and our human condition." Ransom is haunted by the vision; he has no lack of pity; but he knows that pity can betray, and so produce worse results than it sets out to cure. (Auden has talked of this same point recently: "The vice of pity, that corrupt parody of love and compassion which is so insidious and deadly for sensitive natures.")[1]

The Abbot's call is direct: "The Daemon is real. Only his ministry and his visitation are unique for every nature" (and, it is implied, are more complicated for those more complicated). The existence of the daemon proves that life is evil and, since the daemon works through the will, the will is always evil. One may try to evade the daemon or to ignore it—like Shawcross, who tried to lose his personality in another's; or one may wrestle with it as Ransom is doing in trying to conquer F6. All these ways, says the Abbot, are wrong: by opposing our will to the daemon we bind ourselves more tightly to it. Even the sense of pity is the daemon's ally; if Ransom thinks to climb F6 and then descend to help the world, he will fail, for: "As long as the world endures, there must be order, there must be government; but woe to the governors, for, by the very operation of their duty, however excellent, they themselves are destroyed . . . government requires the exercise of the human will; and the human will is from the Daemon."

So, in language reminiscent of Eliot's "Ash Wednesday," the Abbot urges the cleansing of the will by the way of complete renunciation. But he finally admits that he is himself a man of power, and that even here, in this place of withdrawal, he is haunted by memories of the sensuous world. Ransom is muddled, but sees the inadequacy of a spiritual isolation which is also a form of spiritual pride and a refusal to be committed.

He only sees those motives more clearly at the very end. To each of his party the mountain has represented a different thing; they all came for the wrong reasons. But the others had come partly out of allegiance to Ransom; they die in part the victims of his pride and cowardice. His driving force may have been less obvious than his brother's, but is no more admirable. At the top of the mountain, in a scene silly with expressionist fancies, the symbolism is made manifest in the figure of the daemon which has drawn Ransom to the climb. The daemon is real, but is self-created, his own daemon; it is finally revealed as Mrs. Ransom, ready to receive Michael on her bosom. She has always given her overt love to James, although her love for Michael was the greater. She wanted Michael to learn strength thereby, since "the truly strong man is he who stands most alone." But Michael was not sufficiently strong; in climbing the mountain, he expressed his desire to displace his brother and possess his mother's love for himself. So he lies destroyed, as the Hidden Chorus sings over him a fine rhetorical dirge on the weakness of man. The implications of this chorus, like those of the discussion with the Abbot, are a good deal wider than any suggested by the very crude Freudian symbolism of the final scene. A mother-fixation may properly be shown as part of the problem, but to make it the culmination of the whole climb and the climax of the play is to ignore the more complex problems already posed for the sake of a theatrically startling close.

Throughout the action two highly stylised citizens of a mechanical society, Mr. and Mrs. A., deliver choral commentaries on their own dreary lives. They derive a vicarious thrill from the newspaper accounts of Ransom's exploits; he is the dying god, not preaching at them, but doing dangerous things for them; and so they feel dashing too—and go to Hove for the week-end.

They are relatives, much more shallowly conceived, of Quant, in "The Age of Anxiety." But their monotonous reels of rhyming couplets bore. And though the movement of the verse is meant to underline the monotony of their lives, one doubts whether those lives are by any means as dreary as Auden conceives them. Auden is so particularly—and personally—interested in the exceptional man that he too quickly classifies the unexceptional. He cannot see them as in themselves very interesting; they interest more as objects of pity and concern than as personalities whose richness is hidden under the humdrum. "Our moments of exaltation have not been extraordinary, but they have been real," say Mr. and Mrs. A.; but one suspects that, though Auden believes this, he does not really feel it naturally. It seems as though he has to remind himself at intervals that the lives of the ordinary obscure family, and of "the little men and their mothers, not plain but / Dreadfully ugly," can be anything other than deadly dull, a "closed life the stupid never leave." In Ransom, who has so much in common with Auden, the attitude breaks out in the exasperation of: "Under I cannot tell how many of these green slate roofs, / The stupid peasants are making their stupid children." Much earlier in Auden there was: "Those shall be taught who want to understand / Most of the rest shall love upon the land." And: "All of the women and most of the men / Shall work with their hands and not think again."

No doubt many people are dreary, perhaps more than most of us realise. But Auden too soon forgets that, though the most obvious characteristic of many people is their unlimited patience in "putting up with things" as they come, most have moments of remarkable intuitive grasp, and the spiritual problems of the most ordinary are as pressing as those of the better-endowed. He seems too quickly willing to consign them—much as he consciously fights the tendency in his later work—to collective living in a state of childlike innocence, leaving the exceptional few to fight the battle of belief and grace.

But this is to be too harsh towards Auden. It over-emphasizes an impression one nevertheless gains from some parts of his work—that though he has a profound concern for ordinary people, he lacks certain insights into the nature of their lives; and that this lack is connected with his special regard for the Michael Ransoms, the exceptional men.

"On the Frontier"

The "melodrama" "On the Frontier" is, in contrast with "The Dog beneath the Skin," a very tidy piece—and has much less sparkle. There are seven scenes in three acts, and five interspersed choruses, spoken by groups of workers, prisoners, dancers, soldiers and newspaper readers. The scenes are set either in Valerian's study or in the Ostnia-Westland room. Ostnia is the decaying democracy, and Westland the leader-stoated total state of "The Dog beneath the Skin." Most of the characters are the usual types in silhouette, and there is much social comment, sometimes vivid, sometimes banal.

We are presented with an animated cartoon on the quarrels of national states, the machinations of international capitalists, the deceptions of the Press, the psychology of fascism and the inner decay of the democracies. The Westland and international-capitalist armament manufacturer Valerian, for example, delivers set speeches as a bogeyman keeping the workers quiet with dope and welfare. What he says may be largely true, but sounds like a dramatised ABCA talk staged by a subversive subaltern. No matter what Auden's aim may be in these plays, he would have done better either to have omitted such things as Valerian's long soliloquy on the common man, cared-for and unfree, or to have realised them in terms of incident. Valerian's Leader is another puppet constructed from psychological jottings—the lonely little man with a tyrant's urge for power, inwardly gnawed by anxiety; calmed by music, because underneath, like everyone else, he wants love, but soon thrown into hysterical rage again.

Against these two are set, firstly, one bourgeois family from each country, the Thorvalds and the Vrodnys, expressionistically occupying opposite halves of the stage in the same scenes. Into each half the respective national broadcasting systems pour a barrage of hate when war breaks out; into each come the increasing miseries of war—and reach their climax when a starved Westland spinster, whose adoration of the Leader has been an outlet for her thwarted love, is smitten with a suitably Groddeckian disease. Eric Thorvald and Anna Vrodny, whose love has leapt frontiers, die on either side of the stage, asserting that their real enemies are not those they have been called upon to fight. Eric, who has been a pacifist, but finally fought, utters the main moral of the play—that the times demand active commitment:

> Yet we must kill and suffer and know why.
> All errors are not equal. The hatred of our enemies
> Is the destructive self-love of the dying,
> Our hatred is the price of the world's freedom.

Behind the ordinary families are the representative choral groups, most of them extraordinarily dull. The newspaper readers speak in prose, and the soldiers sing a fine cynical ballad, but the rest make oversimple statements in rhyming couplets flatter even than their sense warrants:

> Oil that bearing, watch that dynamo;
> When it's time to strike, brother, I'll let you know.

> Stoke up the fires in furnace number three;
> The day is coming, brother, when we shall all be free!

It is this kind of ingenuous leftism which distinguishes "On the Frontier" even from "The Dog beneath the Skin." It was written in 1938, specifically for a left-wing audience, and was by some rated the best of the three plays when first produced. This is probably because it is as bold as a poster, startling in its contrasts, obvious in its propaganda and unambiguous in its assaults. It remains one of Auden's most ephemeral efforts at popular writing. From it one remembers only some of the verse exchanges between Eric and Anna which, with their irregular rhythms and patterns of weak rhymes, strike a quieter, graver, as well as a deeper note than any other passages in the play.

Notes

1. "A Note on Graham Greene," printed in *The Wind and the Rain*, Summer 1949, from an NBC broadcast by Auden.

[From *Early Auden* (*Look, Stranger!*)]

EDWARD MENDELSON

. . . The waters take a different but equally active form in a poem Auden wrote the following month, May 1933—the sestina beginning "Hearing of harvests rotting in the valleys" (*EA,* 136; *SP,* 29) (later titled "Paysage Moralisé"). Now, instead of dreaming of a chaotic storm or a passive lake, he asks if flowing waters might make fertile his barren landscape. For the first time he hopes neither to be somewhere else, nor changed to some transfigured condition, nor held to the safety of a small group, nor joined with the masses. Instead, epitomizing in the simple emotional term "sorrow" all the unhappiness that gives rise to vain hopes of escape, he asks if that glacial unhappiness could "melt." If this could happen, he would no longer be caught in his wish for an impossible change, but would be free to work responsibly, would be free to rebuild the broken fragments of his world.

Within the exigencies of the sestina form Auden achieves a masterful symbolic play of psychology and history. The poem offers a summary account of civilization in terms of action and desire. We live in sorrowful cities, trapped by an inhospitable landscape. Looking back to a time we imagine to have been less sorrowful than ours, "We honour founders of these starving cities." But our nostalgia for the past has no basis in historical fact; it is the projection of our present unhappiness. Our image of the heroic past is false: the will and energy we admire in the city's founders is only the inverted "image of our sorrow." They lacked as we do the decisive happiness we project onto them, and it was their own futile hope of a cure "That brought them desperate to the brink of valleys." As we dream now of a past without sorrow, they dreamt then of a happy future, "of evening walks through learned cities." That their dream was futile is proved by our unhappiness now. Their new cities brought no peace, only a different dream of some distant place never infected by sorrow: "Each in his little bed conceived of islands / Where every day was dancing in the valleys . . . / Where love was innocent, being far from cities." These are the Islands of Milk and Honey, an Enlightenment dream shattered daily when "dawn came back and they were still in cities." No fantasy could distract them for long, since "hunger was a more immediate sorrow."

Now romantic visionaries came, promising unity and peace on utopian islands. Yet of those who went forth in quest, "So many, fearful, took with them their sorrow," and got no farther than other "unhappy cities." Other travellers, "doubtful," "careless," "wretched," came no closer to Utopia. And so the centuries of search and dream leave us with the same sorrow in which these cities began.

The sestina's envoi states our circumstance bluntly: "It is the sorrow." No more need be said. The nurturing sea lies frozen—"shall it melt? Ah, water / Would gush, flush, green these mountains and these valleys / And we rebuild our cities, not dream of islands." Only in the last line do "these cities" become "our cities." The melting flood, if it comes, will release our private dream into public responsibility. What the watershed divided, now will gather in the valleys.

Auden in this poem is fully conscious of the difficulties he has set for himself. The ancient founders and explorers, the thinkers of the Enlightenment and the dreamers of the Romantic age, all hoped to escape or to diminish human sorrow, but Auden's hope is different. Knowing that sorrow is everywhere and can never lessen, he hopes instead that it may *melt*— change its form, become available for use, make a vineyard of the curse. No reason or logic offers any promise that this might happen. But in imagining the results of this miraculous event Auden infuses his poem with the accentual energies of Gerard Manley Hopkins' religious poetry: "Water / Would gush, flush, green these mountains and these valleys." Hopkins used such language as a sign of faith's conquest of rational limits. Auden, less confident, can use it, for the moment, only in the conditional mood, to express a possibility. Yet after years of entrapment in a language of irony and contradiction, sorrow and self-defeat, he speaks in a language of hope.

. . . .

"A Summer Night" brings love very much down to earth, down to "this point in time and space," and so far from thoughtless heaven that for the first time in Auden's career he associates love with conscious choice rather than simple instinct. The worlds of Eros and responsibility coincide as never before: "this point" is both a place of love and "chosen as my working place." For the first time, Auden is neither astonished nor wary at a love that lasts longer than an hour or a night, and knows he will wake to "speak with one / Who has not gone away." This poem, in fact, marks the first time in his work that he manages to speak with a lover at all. Earlier there had been either touching or talking, but never both.

This is the full text with stanzas numbered for the benefit of the discussion that follows. Half-concealed in the third stanza may be found the ring that symbolizes the married love Auden praised in *The Book of Talbot:*

1   Out on the lawn I lie in bed,
        Vega conspicuous overhead
          In the windless nights of June;

Forests of green have done complete
The day's activity; my feet
   Point to the rising moon.

2   Lucky, this point in time and space
Is chosen as my working place;
   Where the sexy airs of summer,
The bathing hours and the bare arms,
The leisured drives through a land of farms,
   Are good to the newcomer.

3   Equal with colleagues in a ring
I sit on each calm evening,
   Enchanted as the flowers
The opening light draws out of hiding
From leaves with all its dove-like pleading
   Its logic and its powers.

4   That later we, though parted then
May still recall these evenings when
   Fear gave his watch no look;
The lion griefs loped from the shade
And on our knees their muzzles laid,
   And Death put down his book.

5   Moreover, eyes in which I learn
That I am glad to look, return
   My glances every day;
And when the birds and rising sun
Waken me, I shall speak with one
   Who has not gone away.

6   Now North and South and East and West
Those I love lie down to rest;
   The moon looks on them all:
The healers and the brilliant talkers,
The eccentrics and the silent walkers,
   The dumpy and the tall.

7   She climbs the European sky;
Churches and power stations lie
   Alike among earth's fixtures:
Into the galleries she peers,
And blankly as an orphan stares
   Upon the marvellous pictures.

8   To gravity attentive, she
      Can notice nothing here; though we
          Whom hunger cannot move,
      From gardens where we feel secure
      Look up, and with a sigh endure
          The tyrannies of love:

9   And, gentle, do not care to know,
      Where Poland draws her Eastern bow,
          What violence is done;
      Nor ask what doubtful act allows
      Our freedom in this English house,
          Our picnics in the sun.

10   The creepered wall stands up to hide
      The gathering multitudes outside
          Whose glances hunger worsens;
      Concealing from their wretchedness
      Our metaphysical distress,
          Our kindness to ten persons.

11   And now no path on which we move
      But shows already traces of
          Intentions not our own,
      Thoroughly able to achieve
      What our excitement could conceive,
          But our hands left alone.

12   For what by nature and by training
      We loved, has little strength remaining:
          Though we would gladly give
      The Oxford colleges, Big Ben,
      And all the birds in Wicken Fen,
          It has no wish to live.

13   Soon through the dykes of our content
      The crumpling flood will force a rent,
          And, taller than a tree,
      Hold sudden death before our eyes
      Whose river-dreams long hid the size
          And vigours of the sea.

14   But when the waters make retreat
      And through the black mud first the wheat
          In shy green stalks appears;

When stranded monsters gasping lie,
And sounds of riveting terrify
   Their whorled unsubtle ears:

15   May this for which we dread to lose
Our privacy, need no excuse
   But to that strength belong;
As through a child's rash happy cries
The drowned voices of his parents rise
   In unlamenting song.

16   After discharges of alarm,
All unpredicted may it calm
   The pulse of nervous nations;
Forgive the murderer in his glass,
Tough in its patience to surpass
   The tigress her swift motions.[1]

The goal of this poem, from its large structure down to its details of
metre and rhyme, is reconciliation. It hopes to join the private and public
realms; the present, past, and future; and the opposing powers of instinct and
choice. For all its improvisatory air its structure is directed single-mindedly
toward its reconciling cadence. The poem begins with a present moment of
unity, moves through a time when that unity is broken, and ends with its
recovery in another form. This pattern occurs in the poem as a whole and also
in both its halves. In the first eight stanzas the pattern informs the private
realm of friendship and love; in the second eight, the public realm of society
and revolution. In the final stanzas the two patterns and the two realms join.

Even in the opening lines opposites are reconciled. The very first line
places the poet both "out" and "in" at once; the second stanza sets the scene as
one that is both "chosen" and unwilled ("lucky"), a place of work and sexy
leisure. He discovers it and is discovered by it: in Stanza 5 he learns he is glad
to look in eyes that return his glances, while in Stanza 3 he is metaphorically
discovered, drawn out of hiding, by an opening dove-like light. (These latter
metaphors, with their distant echoes of the Annunciation, suggest religious
resonances Auden was not yet prepared to acknowledge more directly.) The
poem, like its opening line, moves both out and in. In Stanza 6 the first line
rushes outward to the four cardinal points of the compass, "North and South
and East and West"; the next line arrests this outward motion by stating a
relation with "Those I love"; and now the arrested motion turns to evening
repose as all "lie down to rest." The moon that sees them all cannot compre-
hend the love that joins them—its perspective is too distant to tell a church
from a power-station or sense the love that informs our gardens.

This love is the unity of the poem's present. Although it must break, it
will survive in memory. This pattern of breaking and recovery, the poem's

central mode of reconciliation, would be quite conventional were it not for one extraordinary detail. We shall recall our lost moment of unity not simply out of nostalgia, but because our recollection of it will fulfill the real purpose it has in occurring now. We experience it in order that we may recall it later. Our unity is not at all like a modernist image or epiphany, valuable for its immediate intensity, but an event whose full meaning exists only in time's extension. This idea is present in Stanzas 3 and 4, although partly obscured by Auden's practice of ending stanzas with a period where grammar would demand a lighter stop. In Stanza 3 he sits "Equal with colleagues in a ring." This sentence, despite the period at the end of the stanza, continues in the subordinate clause that opens Stanza 4. He and his colleagues sit in their ring *"That"* later, though parted, they may recall its enchantments. Auden's prose account mentions four persons, a number whose visual counterpart is normally a square or cross (as in the cardinal points of Stanza 6). But the poem makes an imaginative transformation, and sets the four colleagues in a ring, because the ring is an emblem of the poem's sense of ultimately unbroken time. Miranda's love song in *The Sea and the Mirror* will make the same statement of cause and effect: "So, to remember our changing garden, we / Are linked as children in a circle dancing" (*CP,* 325; *SP,* 148). The ring is our seal of faithfulness even in change. The 1940 poem "In Sickness and in Health," its title borrowed from the marriage service, identifies it as a wedding ring: "this round O of faithfulness we swear" (*CP,* 249; *SP,* 114). And in fact Auden was faithful to his image of the faithful ring, recalling it in these poems years after he wrote "A Summer Night."[2]

When Prospero ends *The Tempest* by gathering the wise and the royal together—"Please you, draw near"—Antonio is still silent, having neither asked nor accepted forgiveness. When Auden forms his charmed and loving circle he too acknowledges an unloved and unloving world outside. We need not look to the future to face separation. It exists now, dividing those protected within our ring from those we never invited.

From the moment Auden found his poetic voice he was alert to the outsider who was barred from community, but at first he scarcely regarded the exclusion as unjust. When he himself was the outsider, he tried to claim that he had chosen or accepted his position. As he grew older all this changed: he learned that the pain of exclusion was real, and that some of its victims were innocent and unwilling. "A Summer Night" includes an allegory of this change. In the poem's first half, with its mood of calm celebration, the excluded Other is one who can feel no pain at all: the orphaned moon staring blankly at love's marvels. But by the second half, it is not only the moon who is left out of our sunny picnics. There are "multitudes" gathering, whose hungers cannot be satisfied by our love feast.

To do justice to these wretched multitudes—even to become aware of them—the poem must shift from the private affective realm to the public economic one. At its midpoint, in the final line of Stanza 8, the poem subjects its vision of love, for the first time, to the irony of a different perspective. In our enclosed gardens we endure with a sigh love's "tyrannies"—a word that acknowledges the existence of more painful tyrannies elsewhere. The first line of the poem's second half admits we "do not care to know" about those tyrannies, or about political violence, or about the "doubtful act" of inequality that allows us our prosperity and peace. In these transitional lines Auden poses the moral paradox that would become familiar in the writings of George Orwell: the paradox of one's love for the English calm and recognition of its manifest virtues, while at the same time one knows it to be sustained by hidden injustice in colonies and mines.

At the moment the poem reaches this divided sense, a border rises abruptly into view. The garden no longer rests at the center of a compass rose from which love extends without limit. Now the "creepered wall *stands up* to hide" the few "Whom hunger cannot move" from the many "Whose glances hunger worsens." Where the poem's first half managed to be *out* and *in* at once, the second divides our "freedom *in* this English house" from the "gathering multitudes *outside.*" A vision of love, like Nower's curative dream in *Paid on Both Sides,* can dissolve personal division, but social division remains.

Yet those divisions too will be broken—by revolution within and without. While the wretched threaten its walls, our world inside has lost its "wish to live." Their external revolution will fulfill our fantasies of destruction, those apocalyptic projections which "our excitement could conceive, / But our hands left alone." Since we cannot resolve thought and action, the crumpling flood will resolve it for us. It will realize our dream of dissolution, and sweep away all that we valued. Auden had hoped for that flood a few weeks earlier in "Paysage Moralisé"; now he foresees its imminent arrival, and his hope is balanced by regret.

Where "Paysage Moralisé" hoped to rebuild its cities after the flood, "A Summer Night" hears the actual "sounds of riveting." These contemporary sound effects, with their faint Socialist Realist overtones, accompany a more ancient image of the waters receding from Ararat. Auden's politics in this poem are more visionary than practical. He imagines a garden of Eden in the first half (Stanza 4) and a New Jerusalem in the second. In Stanza 14 the new city and the new wheat spring up while Leviathan lies gasping on the strand. The new order is ruled not by workers' committees but by love. The public revival of the city in Stanza 14 corresponds to the private recollection of love in Stanza 4, and the poem concludes by praying that these two recoveries might become one. The love we feel now may "belong" to the rebuilding strength of the future. The drowned parental voices of the private life will rise through the happy childish cries of the new order as death is overcome by charity. Personal love, transfigured into public concord, will have power to calm nations and grant even the murderer forgiveness and peace. With the tough patience of a persistent love whose emblem is the equals' ring, the new Love will surpass the "swift motions" of violent enmity.[3] Yet at the depths of the poem's harmonies, in the slightly awkward and tentative character of its hymns to the future, is a sad presentiment that its political hopes are unlikely to prove true.

"A Summer Night" is curiously reticent about the source of its exaltation. Auden's earlier poems did not scruple to invoke the name of Love or provide intimate reports of Love's actions and desires. This poem uses the word *love* only once, in the relatively weak sense of wide friendship (Stanza 6), a sense in which Auden had not used the word before. Where the word *love* is virtually demanded by the poem's argument, in the two concluding stanzas, Auden refuses to use it. Stanza 15 speaks of "this" which should need no excuse in the revolutionary future and for which we dread to lose our privacy; but the poem nowhere says what "'this" is. Nor, in Stanza 16, does the pronoun "it"—that which calms and forgives and is tough in "its" patience—refer to any antecedent more specific than the word "this" in the stanza preceding. There is no mystery about the unnamed antecedent of these two words: it is Love. And as the syntax makes clear, it is not "Our privacy" we dread to lose, but the Love the privacy made possible.[4]

Auden evidently had reasons of his own for suppressing Love's name in his one poem that seemed most to require it. He had effectively profaned that name by using it to refer to various loves that were less than fully human— either the simple impulsive Eros which the "it" of this poem has patience to surpass, or the interest itself in an impossibly distant heaven. To use the same name for the power he would later call agape would amount to a desecration. In his prose writings, however, this state of affairs was exactly reversed. There he used the word *love* only once, in referring to the absence of love as the motivation for theft. In this light his review of *The Book of Talbot* may perhaps be forgiven its quality of gush.

Love's transformation brought with it a transformation of other forms of desire, and for a moment even dispelled the nostalgic wish that burdened Auden's earlier poems. Before this, Auden kept trying vainly to convince himself of the error of nostalgia. When he wrote nostalgically he made use of a characteristic pattern of three elements in sequence: a lost undivided Eden, a barrier, and an inescapably divided Present. In "A Summer Night" he makes no effort to dismantle this durable pattern of thought, but instead pushes it forward in time, so that the coherent moment of unity is no longer in the past but in the present. Now the divisive barrier does not block us from a desired imaginary past, but instead will rise up in the future, as the later moment of the parting of friends. Unable to exorcise his nostalgic wish, Auden accepted its structure, and learned to render it harmless.

In Auden's work during the next five or six years this historical pattern developed into two different and contradictory versions, which in some instances occupied the same poem. On the one hand, he retained the modernist nostalgia for a coherent arcadian past, but added to this a corresponding revolutionary projection of a utopian future. On the other, he made explicit the historical idea implied in his Old English recollections, the idea that history is essentially continuous and that Eden and Utopia are fantasies that evade the tasks of the present. This newly explicit sense of continuity would also find expression in the form and texture of his poems, whose eager acceptance of received metres paid homage to the unbroken patterns that persist in human time, while his increasingly accessible vocabulary and diction reversed the evolutionary movement toward isolation in his earliest work. His new sense of time brought with it a new sense of the feasibility of education. The past could teach the present. Education was no longer to be postponed in hopes of a revolutionary future; it was urgent now.

Important as these new attitudes were, they manifested a deeper and more crucial change. Until this time Auden had understood repetition—in nature, history, and poetry—as the romantics and modernists understood it, as a mortifying compulsion, a doom to which everyone was condemned and which heroes struggled to escape. Throughout Auden's earliest poems "ghosts must do again / What gives them pain" (*EA*, 55; *SP*, 17). All this changed in "A Summer Night." Repetition now became the ground of memory, the medium of love, and for the first time Auden praised events that occurred a second time.

. . . .

There is far more in "Look, stranger" (*EA*, 157; *SP*, 43) than its warm slow language of description. It also illustrates a theory of perception and its ethical consequences. In the first stanza "The swaying sound of the sea" can "wander like a river" through the ear's "channels." Here perception is imitative: the mind acts as a microcosm of what it observes. The sound of the large body of water moves in the ear like a small body of water, and both sounds move aimlessly. In the third stanza, visual images move in a similar way. The "full view / Indeed may enter / And move in memory," just as "these clouds" appear to "pass the harbour mirror," moving from reality in air to reflection in water, where they "saunter" all summer.

No urgency intrudes on this holiday island, where sound and image move in memory but have no other effect. The visiting "stranger"—as in "The Watershed" apparently a double for the poet himself—should simply enjoy his passivity, "Stand stable here / And silent be," and "pause" where the cliff forever opposes the foam. Here all motion is part of an unchanging natural balance, and no deliberate human acts require action in response.

It is different elsewhere: "Far off like floating seeds the ships / Diverge on urgent voluntary errands . . ." Everything else in the poem is a matter of passive sensory impressions of unconscious natural objects; here Auden adds a deliberate interpretive understanding of conscious artifice and actions. These two varieties of perception oppose each other even in these two lines. To the perceiving eye the ships seem purposeless, part of nature. The truth is different and less poetic. The phrase *urgent voluntary errands* abjures all sensory metaphors. The sympathy with nature sought and mourned by the romantics, the wisdom of the senses, is not enough. The senses discover facts but evade meanings. Implicit in the poem are challenges to its author to find his own urgent errand, to leave his poetic isolation behind him, and to learn that he and his audience can be more active than the unmoving stranger the poem addresses.

In the film *Beside the Seaside* the island was no more than the Isle of Wight and its pleasures. In Auden's lyric it took on a more immediate and personal significance. A few months later he used it in the title he chose for his second book of poems, as a reference both to England and to the isolation of the poems themselves from any purpose outside their own existence. When he compiled this second book in the spring of 1936, he began with the working title *Thirty-One Poems,* than changed it to *Poems 1936.* Faber & Faber used this latter title in the proofs, but the directors of the firm decided it sounded too much like the title of a full collected edition and asked Auden for something more specific. Writing from Iceland, he suggested either *It's a Way,* from the book's final line, or *The Island* (or, he added, "On the analogy of *Burnt Norton* I might call it *Piddle-in-the-hole*").[5] But the mails were slow, and by the time Auden's reply reached England, the printing schedule had obliged Faber's directors to come up with a title of their own. They chose *Look, Stranger!,* complete with exclamation mark. With his redemptive fantasies behind him, Auden was in no mood to buttonhole passing strangers with a title like this one. "It sounds," he wrote to his American publisher, "like the work of a vegetarian lady novelist. Will you please call the American edition *On this island.*"[6]

Notes

1. *EA,* 136; *SP,* 29. All the early versions of the poem—a typescript, the text in *The Listener,* 7 March 1934, and that in *Look, Stranger!*—are verbally identical, except that the book version misprints "voice" for "voices" in Stanza 15. I have followed the punctuation of the book version, with minor emendations in end-line pointing. The *Listener* text is titled "Summer Night"; other 1930s texts are untitled.

2. He alludes to this aspect of his vision of agape in a passage near the start of Part III of *New Year Letter* (1940) in which he describes a vision of pure Being: "O but it happens every day / To someone. . . . / But perfect Being has ordained / It must be lost to be regained."

3. "The tigress her swift motions" adapts Wilfred Owen's vision of warriors in "Strange Meeting": "They will be swift with the swiftness of the tigress."

4. Revising the poem for the 1945 *Collected Poetry* Auden apparently recognized how elusive he had been, and altered "this for which we dread to lose / Our privacy" to "these delights we dread to lose, / This privacy"; and in the final stanza changed "it" to "them" (i.e., the delights). Although the new "delights" allude to the "opening light" in Stanza 3, the change drastically alters the force of the poem. Around 1942–43, when he made these revisions, Auden's protestantism was too calvinistically severe to grant much authority to mystical visions of love.

5. Postcard to T. S. Eliot, n.d. (postmarked in England 7 July 1936 but evidently sent there earlier from Iceland to be forwarded) ([In the possession of Valerie Eliot]).

6. Letter to Bennett Cerf, n.d. (October 1936) ([In the] Columbia University [Library]).

[From *Auden: A Carnival of Intellect* (*Sonnets from China*)]

Edward Callan

. . . Between [Auden and Isherwood's] setting out for China on January 19, 1938, and their emigration to America exactly one year later, January 19, 1939, they made decisions that altered the courses of their lives, and, in Auden's case, changed his view of the poet's role in society. His earlier travel-book, *Letters from Iceland,* had directly invoked the spirit of Byron in the cantos of *Letter to Lord Byron.* But however Byronic their setting out from London as war correspondents, their book on China is remarkably un-Byronic; and in the course of Auden's verse contribution, the sonnet sequence "In Time of War," there emerges the new notion of a hero with everyday virtues, like the characters in E. M. Forster's novels—or as Auden's "Verse Commentary" puts it: "the Invisible College of the Humble, / Who through the ages have accomplished everything essential" (*Journey to a War* [*JW*], 298). The artists whose spirit the sonnet sequence invokes are the quiet-voiced Forster and Rilke, not the posturing Byron.

2

Journey to a War has four parts. The first, "London to Hong-Kong," is a series of poems by Auden on the outward journey via the Mediterranean, Suez, and the Red Sea. (It includes "The Voyage," "The Sphinx," and "The Ship," written on the journey, and "Macao" and "Hong-Kong" added later.) The second part, "Travel-Diary," is Isherwood's prose account of their experiences in China—derived from their separate diaries—which comprises most of the book. The third part, "Picture Commentary," has forty-five photographs, mostly by Auden, and two stills from the Chinese film *Fight to the Last.* The fourth part is Auden's main verse contribution: "In Time of War: A Sonnet Sequence with a Verse Commentary." Of the twenty-seven sonnets in this sequence, twenty are retained, slightly revised and rearranged, as "Sonnets from China" in *Collected Poems.*

Both in form and theme the sonnets in this sequence signal a change in Auden's outlook. Technically they follow Rilke, a poet who endured war but had no wish to glorify it, and who greatly respected individual human worth and creativity. Many of these sonnets are not directly about the war in China. They are wartime reflections on the human condition and on the role of the artist in time of war. In the revised and rearranged form "Sonnets from China," the first three sonnets constitute a prologue on the evolution of human consciousness. They imply, as much of Auden's later poetry frequently does, that only plants and animals are innocent or good by nature, and that man may use his freedom for either good or evil as he chooses. The next seven, a retrospect of human history markedly anti-Romantic and far from Marxist in outlook, combine the evocation of a series of historical epochs with portraits of personified types who supplied successive ages with models of heroic personality: the Agriculturalist, the Soldier, the Prophet, the Poet, and so on. The Poet depicted in Sonnet VII, for example, is the Rousseauean Romantic, god-like in his self-esteem. . . . He is also the self-righteous satirist. . . .

The tenth sonnet, closing the first half of the sequence, is an interesting sonnet on the Enlightenment (for which Auden sometimes uses the German *Aufklärung*). Its theme is that the Enlightenment, by banishing the mythical, the mysterious, and the illogical, prepared the way for their reappearance in the unconcious. . . .

Auden made Sonnet X the culmination of the retrospective survey of his own Western intellectual heritage—a placement that gives weight to its questioning of wholly rational values (expressed elsewhere in his view that Hitler's rise in a center of humane learning cast doubt on the proposition that liberalism was self-supporting). Since this sonnet was composed in 1936, prior to his visits to Spain and China, it confirms that the stages of his return to Anglicanism enumerated in *Modern Canterbury Pilgrims* are stated in exact sequence: first, the puzzle of the election of Hitler in an advanced liberal society; second, Auden's recognition of religious persecution in Barcelona; third, his meetings with Charles Williams and his reading of Kierkegaard.

The second half of the sequence "Sonnets from China" moves on to the immediate situation in China by way of a transitional sonnet affirming the value of song: "Certainly praise: let the song mount again and again"; but insisting that even song must take account of human doubleness—of the capacity for evil as well as good. . . . There follows a group of sonnets dealing directly with scenes from the war, with individual sonnets devoted to the dead, the wounded, air-raids, diplomats exchanging views, and so on. There are fewer of these vignettes in the revised sequence than in the original, but all share the detached viewpoint of an observer from outside the struggle. They are, in a sense, photographic, and a number are directly related to photographs in Auden's "Picture Commentary." One of them in particular, a Petrarchan sonnet on a dead soldier, has an interesting history.

Auden had finished writing it on April 20, 1938, the day he and Isherwood returned to Hankow after a visit to the front near Soochow during March, and a subsequent visit to the ancient capital, Sian. On the following day they attended a party with a number of Hankow intellectuals including the poet Mou Mou-tien who presented them with some verses written in their honor. Not to be outdone Auden replied with the sonnet he had written the day before. There was also a journalist present, Ma Tong-na (anglicized to Macdonald), who interviewed them for the newspaper *Ta Kung Pao*. His interview, printed on April 22, included a Chinese rendering of Auden's sonnet together with a manuscript facsimile. The second line, "Abandoned by his general and his lice," was too brutal for the Chinese translators; or, as Isherwood puts it, "maybe, even, a dangerous thought (for generals never abandon their troops under any circumstances)." The Chinese translators emended the line to read: "The rich and poor are combining to fight" (*JW,* 161). This modification marks, perhaps, the first of many expressions of embarrassment at Auden's new determination to view events not with the single-mindedness of a propagandist but in the double focus of the struggle between good and evil.

The revised arrangement of "Sonnets from China" gives the sequence a tighter structure and a much more pointed conclusion. The anti-Romantic theme, for example, becomes more pronounced. The three final sonnets, which now include the sonnet to E. M. Forster used as a dedication to *Journey to a War,* justify the work of artists and also of ordinary people who live simple, creative lives even in the face of apparent defeat by an all-powerful tyranny: "When all our apparatus of report / Confirms the triumph of our enemies" (*CP* [1976], 156). As a representative of artists who cultivated the inner life rather than public attitudes, Sonnet XIX calls on Rilke, "Who for ten years of drought and silence waited, / Until in Muzot all his being spoke." Sonnet XX develops this theme of voluntary personal commitment to justify the sacrifice of the nameless soldiers killed in China, and to set them above narcissistic tyrants "Who want to persist in stone forever." Sonnet XXI moves to the particular case of E. M. Forster, an artist who, in contrast to the god-like poet of Sonnet VII, neither domineers nor lectures us on what to do, but quietly sets before us parables in which we may see ourselves.

> As we dash down the slope of hate with gladness,
> You trip us up like an unnoticed stone,
> And, just when we are closeted with madness,
> You interrupt us like the telephone.
>
> (*CP,* 157)

This sonnet on E. M. Forster not only justifies the artist as observer, but insists that art and the inner-life have a place in our affairs. It is the first of an extraordinary series of poems, mostly elegiac, on art and artists that Auden wrote within a year of his journey to China.

The sequence "Sonnets from China" shows that Auden had reached a critical point in his intellectual development between early 1937, when he went to Spain, and late 1939, when he assembled the collection *Another Time*. Several of the poems in *Another Time* are on existentialist themes and show that within a year after his arrival in America his beliefs had unquestionably changed. By the end of the thirties he had become, philosophically, not a Communist, but a would-be Christian—at first existentialist, or Kierke-gaardian, in outlook. "Sonnets from China" and its successor, "The Quest: A Sonnet Sequence," show that at the time of their writing Auden had adopted an anti-Utopian vision that accepts doubt and ambiguities in place of doctri-naire certainties.

In essays and reviews of the same period Auden frequently returns to the themes that the Renaissance is at an end and that the liberalism it nurtured is not self-supporting. Reviewing Reinhold Niebuhr's *The Nature and Destiny of Man* in June 1941, he said: "For the past hundred years Occidental liberalism has lain snug in the belief that the relation of its arts and sciences, its ethical and political values, to the Christian faith was simply historical. It has taken Hitler to show us that liberalism is not self-supporting."[1] And some ten years later while discussing Romanticism in *The Enchafèd Flood* he said: "We live in a new age in which the artist neither can have a unique heroic importance nor believes in the Art-God enough to desire it, an age, for instance, when the necessity of dogma is once more recognized, not as the contradiction of reason and feeling but as their ground and foundation" (*EF*, 153). In retrospect, "Sonnets from China" may be seen as an overture to Auden's major American themes. . . .

Note

1. "The Means of Grace," *New Republic* 104 (June 1941): 756–57.

[From *Quest for the Necessary* ("New Year Letter")]

HERBERT GREENBERG

An extended analysis of the modern situation in relation to the war, "New Year Letter" . . . represents a last attempt to do without belief in God, to continue to find sufficient cause for awe and obligation in Eros; and in some respects it shows the strain of this effort. In the United States, the poem appeared in a volume called *The Double Man,* and since the point of this study is that, in a sense, the double man is the theme of *all* Auden's work, Richard Hoggart's suggestion that this is the more suitable title is difficult to resist.[1] The poem decides that unified being may be experienced only momentarily, that human existence is a continual "becoming," and that by a "double focus" of faith and doubt the ego in each of us must pursue a solitary quest for self-fulfillment as governed by natural law. But these things will be clear if we take the poem on its own terms, and towards this end, and towards an understanding of poetic method, its actual title is indispensable. "Letter," suggesting an unceremonious meditation, prepares us for the air of "reverent frivolity" encountered, the freedom of reference and allusion, and the discursive bent, as "Letter to Lord Byron" had acknowledged, common to letters: "I want a form that's large enough to swim in, / And talk on any subject that I choose." "New Year," on the other hand, reveals the orientation organizing Auden's material. Instancing our customary celebration of the New Year, Kenneth Burke has said that "the human mind is prone to feel beginnings and endings *as such.*"[2] The poem testifies to this, arguing that "the machine has now destroyed / The local customs we enjoyed," that with the war a "whole system . . . Shudders her future into stone," that Marx is now "one with those / Who brought an epoch to a close." It asserts of those fighting in Europe:

> . . . each one knows
> A day is drawing to a close.
> . . . .
>
> That all the special tasks begun
> By the Renaissance have been done.

We live, Auden believes, at the end of the Protestant era or, as he has it here, the Renaissance, and the poem is his analysis of the factors bringing this era to disaster and of the situation we confront in readying ourselves to set out anew.

The poem, in other words, is about death and the necessity for rebirth, the rebirth, in "Epithalamion's" words, "Asked of old humanity," and this theme is reflected in diction and imagery when it observes that art is not "A midwife to society," or when it pictures the devil as a celebrant of the womb, or explains that some dreamed the Russian revolution had realized "potential Man, / A higher species brought to birth / Upon a sixth part of the earth," but that, though the "rays of Logos" take effect, "dwarf mutations are thrown out / From Eros' weaving centrosome." Bringing an epoch to a violent close, the war is the death incurred for having failed our task; it is a parody birth issuing, like Miss Gee's cancer, to protest a reality frustrated. Europe lay trembling in apprehension. "As on the verge of happening / There crouched the presence of The Thing":

> All formulas were tried to still
> The scratching on the window-sill,
> All bolts of custom made secure
> Against the pressure on the door,
> But up the staircase of events
> Carrying his special instruments,
> To every bedside all the same
> The dreadful figure swiftly came.

The pressure so steadfastly resisted by formulas and the tightened bolts of social rigidity is actually projected, of course, by a stifled unconscious, and it is to superintend the release of this force that the surgeon figure, Time, arrives. "We would rather be ruined than changed," thinks Malin in *The Age of Anxiety*. It is a consistent point with Auden. If we cling to the past and refuse to change, with the coming of time the unconscious makes our changes for us.

Though the direction of the poem is towards a fresh beginning, a new Re-naissance, no such rebirth actually occurs:

> Our news is seldom good: the heart,
> As ZOLA said, must always start
> The day by swallowing its toad
> Of failure and disgust.

Despite this repellent inversion of the birth image, the poem concludes with a prayer, a request for guidance. As has been said in parallel circumstances of *The Waste Land,* it moves toward a point outside itself, this being Auden's decisive acceptance of Christianity. In shaping this end, the poem does contemplate rebirth as an experience of regenerative contact with the unconscious; in religious terms again reminiscent of Eliot, it affirms the possibility of a moment out of time when we touch upon eternity, "Unconscious of Becoming," and from which we depart "Obedient, reborn, re-aware." The obligation to transform our lives is reenforced, though we still face the problem of how to do so.

As a means to organizing analysis, the poem's three sections each concentrate on a period of time reaching its close at the New Year; the first part focuses on the climate and aftermath of the war year, 1939, the second ("Tonight a scrambling decade ends") upon issues raised by the thirties, the third on broad developments since the start of the Renaissance. In addition, each of the sections is unified by what Kenneth Burke would call a "representative anecdote," a projection of man in a particular stance revealing the section's chief preoccupation. Though brought to the surface by imagery, these imaginative constructs are not really sources of organization, evoking a symbolic response, but emblems of an organizing view in force independently and active throughout. Like the imagery of birth objectifying the thematic implications of New Year, their function is mainly to bring to the attention an intellectual orientation and make possible the play of wit as inquiry proceeds. Part I, then, may be entitled "Man Under Judgment," Part II "Man and his Devil," Part III "Man as Seeker of the Way."

The first section measures the disorder of contemporary circumstances—hatreds crystallized into "visible hostilities"—against the ideal order possible in art and reaches the conclusion that we stand indicted and have much to atone for. It is not that art can teach us to be good, for "Art in intention is mimesis / But, realised, the resemblance ceases"—art presents "Already lived experience" and shapes its materials into an order of its own, different from "Life-order," which is the task of living men. But the order of art still constitutes a judgment upon us, as a paradigm of the possible. As poet, Auden admits that he has sinned against his craft. And evoking the theme of man under judgment, he imagines himself tried for his misdeeds by a "summary tribunal" of dead masters, the presiding judge, it is interesting to note, being Dante and an associate magistrate, Blake. As "ancestors," these represent a poetic conscience, and Auden confesses that he has been careless and hasty in his work, he has adopted the "preacher's loose immodest tone." But a greater offence is murder, that of a civilization plunged into the havoc of war. Here judgment requires some detective work:

> The situation of our time
> Surrounds us like a baffling crime.
> There lies the body half-undressed,
> We all had reason to detest,
> And all are suspects and involved

> Until the mystery is solved
> And under lock and key the cause
> That makes a nonsense of our laws.

The "Whodunit" analogy is cleverly elaborated, and the conclusion is that "guilt is everywhere."

"Man at the Crossroads" might be a subordinate title for Part II, which formulates his role as "Seeker of the Way" with an image of an indecipherable signpost on a barren heath, roads branching ahead in all directions and the ruins of the old order behind. But since Auden's chief interest is in the errors bringing us to an impasse, tendencies of mind, this section belongs to the devil, the tempter who split man's consciousness and encourages error. More than a lively personification, the devil is Auden's means of portraying the results of the Fall. This section is really an analysis of the privileges and perils of self-consciousness, and a last effort to account for evil as a deficiency of knowledge. It concedes that our knowledge must always be defective and perhaps in this takes an important step towards the Christian view that evil is inherent in man, but it also offers the hopeful observation that the devil's true function is to "Point us the way to find truth out," that in his flashy legerdemain lies the gift of "double focus." As we should expect, Auden starts from the premise that love is the animating force of the universe. If this is true, then "Evil is not an existence but a state of disharmony between existences"—there really is no devil:

> . . . for all your fond insistence,
> You have no positive existence,
> Are only a recurrent state
> Of fear and faithlessness and hate,
>
> That takes on from becoming me
> A legal personality . . .

Indicative of the direction in which Auden is moving, the key word here is "faithlessness"; the devil represents mainly doubt, though not of the kind confronting the limitations of human knowledge with a healthy skepticism and, indeed, frustrating the devil; doubt, rather, is here a want of faith in ultimate order, an anxious response to the estrangement from order caused by the Fall, taking the form of an impatient reaching for absolutes. We are told in the notes that the devil's philosophy in all its varieties begins in dualism. Since evil is disharmony, it is any philosophy of one-sidedness that fractures the whole so as to exalt the part, and its manifestations are distortion, oversimplification, inflexibility—all those practices representing flight from the insecurities of existence by a resort to the false certainty of extremes.

Directed since the Fall towards the goal of "Rule-by-sin," the devil's temptations indicate the solemn result of self-consciousness: our ability to do evil consciously. In the poem's words, to sin is to be aware of violating harmony, "to act consciously / Against what seems necessity." And since all creatures are parts of the whole, sin, like evil, entails acting "contrary to self-interest":

> It is possible for all living creatures to do this because their knowledge of their self-interest is false or inadequate. . . . The animals whose evolution is complete, whose knowledge of their relations to the rest of creation is fixed, can do evil, but they cannot sin.
>
> But we, being divided, remembering, evolving beings composed of a number of "selves" each with its false conception of its self-interest, sin in most that we do. . . .[3]

But if self-consciousness makes sin possible, it also makes possible efforts to lessen disharmony and the goal of "Diversity in unity." It is the devil's dilemma that, though sin requires an awareness of our interests, this awareness also works against sin; and the result is that, "torn between conflicting needs, / He's doomed to fail if he succeeds." In championing a particular bias, the devil is undermined by the capacity of a self-understanding being to know his values relative:

> . . . If there
> Are any cultures anywhere
> With other values than his own,
> How can it possibly be shown
> That his are not subjective . . .

While if he plays the god and establishes an absolute, eliminating the awareness of alternatives, he destroys the foundations of his own existence, reducing us to the status of animals, capable of evil but not of sin, "A possibility cut out / In any world that excludes doubt." The devil's only recourse is to try the impossible, "To be both god and dualist," and this means that, while continually active, he must resist pushing his efforts to a self-defeating conclusion and, thus, must run the risk of educating his victims.

All this is a flat summary, with the aid of the notes, of what is briskly and wittily dramatized in the poem. On the level of particulars, the devil's stratagems are varied and shrewd; he is the partisan not only of all extremes but of the full about-face, as in the case of Wordsworth, whose conservatism was the result of failing to find in the French Revolution the "Parousia of liberty." Observe to the devil that the categories of intellect are barren abstractions, "that we, / In fact, live in eternity," and he will shift from the opposing position with unctuous grace:

> . . . when with overemphasis
> We contradict a lie of his,
> The great Denier won't deny
> But purrs: "You're cleverer than I;
> Of course you're absolutely right,
>
> I never saw it in that light,
> I see it now . . ."[4]

The danger of the devil is that he will encourage our individual tendencies to one-sidedness and then convert the correction of disillusionment into the reaction of despair, but our protection lies in the paradox of his position: anchored in our own nature, "he may never tell us lies, / Just half-truths we can synthesize."

Summarizing the implications of this view, Part III marshalls resources for a confrontation with the future. It is the longest and most historically encompassing of the three sections—but not so long as to prevent a clear expression of most of what it has to say in images of landscape and, in particular, in the image of man in endless forms seeking his temporal Way along the slopes of Purgatory. The Renaissance conqueror of nature, "Empiric Economic Man," could "drive himself about creation / In the closed cab of Occupation," but the corresponding images of today show Kafkas of the laboratory puzzling over "the odd behaviour of the law," "The path that twists away from the / Near-distant CASTLE they can see," and the *Völkerwanderungen* by which Americans explore that freedom to change their fate won by bringing to a conclusion the work of the Renaissance. Today, the search for a Way is an obligatory venture over open ground, an individual Quest:

> Each salesman now is the polite
> Adventurer, the landless knight
> GAWAINE-QUIXOTE, and his goal
> The *Frauendienst* of his weak soul . . .

Landscape in this section, in addition to furnishing symbolic settings (and allegorizing Auden's opinions as shaped by youthful experience) defines the relationship between the individual and society: "Maps and languages and names / Have meaning and their proper claims," Auden asserts. He argues that there are "two atlases," one identifying the inner world of self, "the place / That each of us is forced to own," the other the world of public affairs in which we work and act: "Where each one has the right to choose / His trade, his corner and his way."

The New Year actually arrives in this section, accompanied by the reflection that this *"Annus* is not *mirabilis"*: "Our road / Gets worse and we seem altogether / Lost." It had been implied, earlier, by the indecipherable signpost. But if the goal of the Quest is not in sight—the Just City for society, for the individual his fulfillment therein—the section does acknowledge that rebirth of purpose which comes from an experience of union with unconscious life-sources nourishing all our strivings:

> . . . it happens every day
> To someone. Suddenly the way
> Leads straight into their native lands,
> The *temenos'* small wicket stands
> Wide open, shining at the centre
> The well of life, and they may enter.

During such moments, the split in consciousness is healed: immersed in "free rejoicing energy," we have regained the garden where freedom and law are one. Our problem is that we cannot live there: ". . . perfect Being has ordained / It must be lost to be regained." A refusal to be subject to time and continual Becoming brings a drastic change of landscape: "The sky grows crimson with a curse, / The flowers change colour for the worse," the wicket padlocks itself. And Heaven becomes Hell, the state of suffering of all who refuse to accept suffering as a necessity and consequence of living. Mountains in early Auden had been barriers to cross on the way to a life of aesthetic immediacy; but he now contends that we are a mountain people, that we live on Purgatory, where we must suffer and will our salvation, "Consenting parties to our lives."

It is still with a reliance on natural law, however, that he considers our terrain negotiable, for the notes tell us that there is a "Natural Way" and that the attitude of the seeker must be one of faith and doubt: "Faith that Natural Law exists and that we can have knowledge of it; Doubt that our knowledge can ever be perfect or unmixed with error." This long-standing faith in natural law Auden will soon surrender, deciding that "If the commands of God were laws *of* men, then disobedience would be impossible"; they are instead the "call of duty, 'Choose to do what at this moment in this context I am telling you to do.' "[5] At present, however, his category of inquiry is still the evolutionary one of "Man in Society," and "New Year Letter" retains a secular hope in the Just City as a state of equilibrium, continually enlarging, with environment, considering the individual's existential quest mainly in terms of an abstract freedom won by society from nature.

In an article, Auden points out that on the tribal level, where the pressures of nature are intense, freedom means little more than "the privilege to be alive," that it is only when control over natural forces improves, lifting the power of external necessity, that it becomes clear that "the life of the individual and the life of his community are not identical and that freedom is not only the freedom to live, but the freedom to live one of several possible lives."[6] This development may be attributed to "Empiric Economic Man," who in his subjugation of nature brought under the control of moral will what were before events only to be endured as "tribulations":

> . . . he broke
> The silly and unnatural yoke
> Of famine and disease that made
> A false necessity obeyed . . .

And if Blake and Baudelaire were right to decry his neglect of the self, to predict that his dedication to "progress" would end in enslavement to the machine, Auden points out that it is to this dedication, fragmenting society and unsettling tradition, that we owe the truth once apparent only to the few, that "Aloneness is man's real condition," that each must send forth a questing Ego to seek his Way; we can no longer learn our good "From chances of a neighborhood / Or class or party."

Ultimately, Auden locates the root of our troubles in the failure to do "Eros's legislative will." He explains that "The flood of tyranny and force / Arises at a double source," and characteristically (one recalls the Lords of limit), he sees these as extremes towards which the devil tempts, involving a separating of the functions of ego and self. The first is "PLATO'S lie of intellect," which locates truth in the abstractions of reason and makes it the concern of the elect; the other is "ROUSSEAU'S falsehood of the flesh," which in contemporary form is Hitler's "metaphysics of the crowd," described in "Jacob and the Angel" as the "morbid abdication of the free-willing and individual before the collective and daemonic." And responsibility for both of these errors lies with the unwilling Ego, her refusal to use her freedom:

> . . . our political distress
> Descends from her self-consciousness,
> Her cold *concupiscence d'esprit*
> That looks upon her liberty
> Not as a gift from life with which
> To serve, enlighten, and enrich
> The total creature that could use
> Her function of free-will to choose
> The actions that this world requires
> To educate its blind desires,
> But as the right to lead alone
> An attic life all on her own . . .

Such things as Political Romanticism are a consequence of the Ego's despair at then finding its life deprived of necessity, for its response is "suicide," a romantically willed surrender to the furies of the neglected unconscious.

To define the proper relationship between ego and self Auden chooses an image of creative conflict, that of the wrestling bout. In prose echoing the lines quoted above, he declares that the liberals are wrong, reason is not self-sufficient, for we *are* lived by the daemon of the unconscious; but because the daemon cannot know its ends without an agent to discover them, it creates Jacob, "the prudent Ego": "not for the latter to lead, in self-isolation and contempt, a frozen attic life of its own, but to be a loving and reverent antagonist; for it is only through that wrestling bout . . . that the future is born, that Jacob acquires the power and the will to live, and the demon is transformed into an angel." Although the closing prayer of "New Year Letter" is distinctly Christian in its evocations, it seems to represent no commitment other than to this parable, retold in the note glossing the line ". . . the powers / That we create with are not ours." If in some measure the prayer is to an orthodox God, probably, like most of Auden's prayers to this point, it has more in view the conception that "Man is aware that his actions do not express his real nature. God is a term for what he imagines that nature to be." In the phrase "My Father worketh and I work," Auden explains, " 'My Father' is the real nature of man; 'I' his conscious awareness of that nature."[7] "My Father" is the Logos implicit in the unconscious, "I" the ego that must seek, by employing its freedom, to make the Logos flesh.

The twenty "Quest" sonnets, in search of the Logos, invite us into a comic-surrealistic world of story book ordeals and desolate places, ogres and magical transformations, into the fun-house of the unconscious and its private perils, much in the manner of an effective source of imagery, *Alice in Wonderland* (if this had been written by Franz Kafka), or of Kafka himself, who, like Jung and Kierkegaard, is an obvious influence. Like "New Year Letter," "The Quest" is concerned with "the Way," but Auden's category is here "the Individual," and the most relevant commentary on the poems is Jung's remark that "A way is only *the* way when one finds it and follows it oneself."[8] Considered from an existential point of view, the Logos or "Necessary" which is object of the quest is inseparable from individuality, for each individual "The nature of Necessity like grief / Exactly corresponding to his own." Informing this view is Kierkegaard's conception of truth as a subjective and inward relationship that the individual exists *in,* rather than as something knowable or known. Combining Kierkegaard and Jung, Auden sees this relationship as one with the unconscious, and, by placing the quest within a world of the pasteboard surreal—peopled with archetypes drawn from fairy tale and childhood dream—and by using images which metamorphose and disorient, he assimilates this view into his fable technique.

In deference to the subjective nature of the Way, the sonnets deal mainly with the difficulties of properly setting out and with the temptations and misunderstandings leading one astray. They have little to say of success on the quest other than to indicate its inward character and its ultimate dependence upon sources outside the individual's control. Providing a glimpse into the garden which transforms existence, "The Door" suggests that success involves a coming into relation with the unconscious. "The Garden," how-ever (St. Augustine's among others), reveals the important point that the relationship means not, in any normative sense, health, but the integration of personality described by Jung. Mocking the conventions of quest literature, "The Way" observes that no formula will guide us to this end, not even one derived from reversing customary practices. To support this point "The Lucky" and "The Hero" show that success depends on grace and virtues that may seem to others trivial. In "The Preparations," individuals are destroyed by their peculiar natures for regarding as an external matter something requiring a questioning of their natures, while "The City" reveals the danger of reaching a place where nature has been overcome (Cf. "The Capital"), so that moral freedom entails the danger of settling down to "being nobody." Those who arrive, in proper quest fashion, to seek their fortunes here find that the city offers not only what for them is the Necessary but also the freedom to disobey it; they fail the one requirement of the quest, which is that they become themselves. The three "Temptation" sonnets, exploring themes returned to in "The Sea and the Mirror," parallel Satan's testing of Christ. The first temptation is treated as the danger for the artist of using his magic so as to transform the frustrations of reality into fantasy satisfaction, the second as the surrender to nihilism threatening those impatient with the finitude of existence, the third as the temptation to yield for the sake of power to a cynicism distorting one's humanity.

Several of the remaining poems turn upon a distinction between the exceptional and the average, but this is to be understood not pejoratively, as in Jung, but with the humility of Kierkegaard's contention that the Knight of Faith may be unrecognizable, that, as Auden puts it, "Only God can tell the saintly from the suburban." Like both of these writers, Auden distin-guishes between the true individual, conscious of his choices, and those for whom convention and conditioned response constitute all of self so that they have no being save in what Kierkegaard calls the "Crowd" or "the Public." To be exceptional enough to undertake the quest means simply to be reflective, however, and his concern in the poems is that this today is the position of each of us. "Today a man has only two choices," Auden writes: "he can be consciously passive or consciously active. He can accept deliberately or reject deliberately, but he must decide because his position in life is no longer a real necessity."9 The Quest, then, is something we are all called upon, but for "The Average" the Way will lie in an acceptance of ordinary relationships, and the attempt to fill an exceptional role will frustrate self-realization. The point of "The Presumptuous" is that to be exceptional is to obey a call, what Jung calls a "vocation" and Kierkegaard "the voluntary"10—notions envision-ing the individual unfree to take a normal course, compelled out of the common way into a position conducive to his unique development. Those in the sonnet fail because, succumbing to the dangers of imitation, they choose a perilous course which for them is not compulsory.

If one recalls the old ideal of the "Truly Strong," this new notion of the exceptional will serve to underline the rejection of health as a criterion of value and help to explain why almost all the well-known figures in *Another Time* are carefully shown to have derived their creativity from abnormal circumstances. Pascal's view of man's destitute condition is traced to a lonely and loveless childhood; Matthew Arnold's moral denunciations are a servitude to his father and also an unconscious assault upon him; Edward Lear blossoms into nonsense by tapping the resources of his "Regret." These explanations are all baldly put forth and no doubt they oversimplify, but they reflect an interest in the circumstances from which unique accomplishments arise rather than an effort to explain away creative achievement by equating it with neurosis. In his own formulation of "the voluntary," Auden now writes, in an arresting statement, that "the true significance of a neurosis is teleological." He no longer means that it is a warning to change ways but, instead, that a child *seeks* a traumatic experience: "in order to find a necessity and direction for its existence, in order that its life may become a serious matter . . . a neurosis is a guardian angel; to become ill is to take vows."[11]

Despite an occasional use of Christian symbolism, "The Quest" reveals no unmistakable commitment to Christianity. The epilogue to *New Year Letter,* dated in *Collected Poetry* "Autumn 1940," is less ambiguous. Describing the reluctant return of the ego from sleep to the hostile, death-filled world in which choices are necessary, it raises a question at the heart of "The Quest" and upon which a purely "Ethical" view founders. In a world of war, with escape no more possible than indifference, how, willing though we may be, "can / We will the knowledge that we must know to will?" The poem makes no answer but, as prerequisite to an answer, it asks us to acknowledge "One immortal, one infinite Substance" and "the Word which was / From the beginning."

If we are not to misunderstand Auden's commitment to Christianity, we must grasp the point that the considerations finally impelling it were not intellectual ones. His personal experience, he tells us, was a genuine "conversion," something in which "suffering plays a greater part than knowledge." That our life is a gift, our powers not our own, he had always contended. From where one responds to this feeling by equating our powers with "love" and assigning one's awe to the unconscious, the way is not long, although it may be circuitous, to the conviction that existence stands in direct relationship to God—that our experience of dependence and obligation testifies that it is in God that our lives are grounded. Auden's acceptance of Christianity was an acceptance of self, an acknowledgment of feelings long present, which, as an "enlightened" mind, he had refused to express in an orthodox form— orthodoxy could too easily be seen as a rationalization: "Like so many of my generation who have been saved from many kinds of hypocrisy by the Freudian or Marxist premise that all thinking is 'interested' thinking, I forgot that this rule applies just as much to denying as it does to affirming."[12]

The personal experiences prompting conversion also, however, enforced a point that world conditions were suggesting independently and towards which his thought had been moving for some time. The same year *I Believe* was circulating his "fairly optimistic" opinion that badness in individuals was mainly the result of bad environment, Auden announced in a review the conviction that Democracy was hard, that it would only work "if as individuals we lead good lives." "I do not think that democracy can be sustained or defended," he argued, "unless one believes that pride, lying, and violence are mortal sins, and that their commission entails one's damnation."[13] This view is reflected in the insistence of "New Year Letter" that the devil can damn and that democracy begins with free confession of sin. But "sin" and "damnation" in what sense? And on what basis do we trust that the wrestling bout between ego and self will issue in law or equilibrium? As far as "reasons" ever motivate conversion, Auden's reason was that the failure to deal decisively with fascism short of war had shown that the liberal values so widely taken for granted were really dependent upon a sustaining foundation in Christianity. Why was it, he asks, that not only the Right but also the Left was deceived into thinking National Socialism in the interests of Capitalism? "Europe consented to Hitler," he answers, "because it had lost the sense of law which makes the recognition of an outlaw possible." Hitler carried to its logical conclusion every relativistic assumption of liberalism:

> He was neither understood nor resisted because millions of people had really accepted the same view of life, viz., that there is nothing which is unconditionally required, nothing for which one is in some sense or another eternally damned for doing or not doing, and therefore no reason for condemning or preventing the behavior of another unless it directly interferes with with [*sic*] oneself, that if one were Hitler in fact, one would do exactly the [same].[14]

Notes

1. *Auden: An Introductory Essay* (London: Chatto & Windus, 1951), p. 160. Like the London edition of *New Year Letter* (Faber and Faber, 1941), *The Double Man* (New York: Random House, 1941) gives notes to the poem not reprinted in *Collected Poetry*.

2. *Counter-Statement* (Chicago: University of Chicago Press, 1957), p. 139.

3. Prose quotations pertaining to the devil are from the "Notes" section, *New Year Letter*.

4. The Faber and Faber text of "New Year Letter" gives an erroneous end-quote after the phrase "cleverer than I." This probably accounts for Francis Scarfe's mis-attribution of the devil's speech to the poet himself, and his consequent misreading (*W. H. Auden*, Monaco: Lyrebird Press, 1949, pp. 43–44). Curiously enough, Richard Hoggart (*Auden*, pp. 163–64) makes the same error and ascribes to Auden a disposition in favor of heart over intellect inconsistent with the poem's principle of "symmetry."

5. *The Living Thoughts of Kierkegaard*, ed. W. H. Auden (New York: David McKay,

1952), intro., p. 16. For Auden's first statement on the untenability of a theory of natural law, see "The Means of Grace," *New Republic,* CIV (June 1941), p. 766.

6. "The Means of Grace." The distinction referred to in this paragraph between temptations and tribulations is given in *New Year Letter* ("Notes," p. 132) as follows: "As far as I know, Kierkegaard was the first to distinguish accurately between *tribulations,* all the troubles that come upon us from without and can't be disposed of by acts of will but can only be endured, that is, treated aesthetically; and *temptations,* all the internal conflicts that must not be endured but solved in action by the will, that is, treated ethically. Further he was the first to include among tribulations, not only physical disasters like flood, fire, and famine, but also all images, impulses, feelings of guilt that rise from the subconscious."

7. "Christian on the Left," *Nation,* CXLIX (Sept. 1939), p. 273. The passage on the prudent Ego is from "Jacob and the Angel," p. 293.

8. *The Integration of the Personality,* trans. Stanley Dell (London: Kegan Paul, Trench, Trubner & Co., 1949), p. 32. This book is an important influence on "New Year Letter" as well as on "The Quest."

9. "Criticism in a Mass Society," in *The Intent of the Critic,* ed. Donald A. Stauffer (Princeton: Princeton University Press, 1941), p. 134. Auden writes in "The Wandering Jew" (*New Republic,* CIV, Feb. 1941, p. 186): "To become exceptional—that is to say, to become reflective—is to discover that the Necessary itself, to the human vision, appears arbitrary."

10. "A man cannot embark upon 'the voluntary' (the requirements of which are higher than the universal requirements) unless he has an *immediate certainty* that it is required of him *in particular.* From the point of view of the universal requirements, 'the voluntary' is in fact presumption. . . . In order really to be a great genius, a man must be an exception. But in order that his being exceptional should be a serious matter he himself must be unfree, forced into the position. There lies the importance of his dementia. There is a definite point in which he suffers; it is impossible for him to run with the herd. Perhaps his dementia has nothing whatsoever to do with his real genius, but it is the pain by which he is nailed out in isolation—and he must be isolated if he is to be great; and no man can freely isolate himself; he must be compelled if it is to be a serious matter." This passage from Kierkegaard's *Journals* is quoted in the "Notes" to *New Year Letter* (pp. 88–89).

"It is what is called vocation: an irrational factor that fatefully forces a man to emancipate himself from the herd and its trodden paths. True personality always has vocation and believes in it, has fidelity to it as to God. . . . This vocation acts like a law of God from which there is no escape. That many go to ruin upon their own ways means nothing to him who has vocation. He must obey his own law, as if it were a demon that whisperingly indicated to him new and strange ways." This appears in Jung, *The Integration of the Personality,* p. 291.

11. "The Wandering Jew," p. 186.

12. Auden, "Foreword" to Emile Cammaerts, *The Flower of Grass* (New York: Harper & Brothers, 1945), p. xii. For the comment on "conversion," see Howard Griffin, "Conversation on Cornelia Street: Dialogue with W. H. Auden," *Accent,* X (Autumn 1949), p. 52.

13. "Democracy Is Hard," *Nation,* CXLIX (Oct. 1939), p. 386. Perhaps it is Democracy to which Poem XXIII from *Another Time* ("Not as that dream Napoleon") is addressed.

14. "Where Are We Now," *Decision,* I (Jan. 1941), pp. 49–50, 51.

The Poet in Wartime: Yeats, Eliot, Auden
[From *Saving Civilization: Yeats, Eliot, and Auden Between the Wars* ("September 1, 1939," "In Memory of W. B. Yeats," and "At the Grave of Henry James")]

LUCY MCDIARMID

Although Auden found Yeats's "parish of rich women" an embarrassment, part of the dead poet's "silliness," he was soon to meet his own equivalent of Lady Gregory in Elizabeth Mayer, the Beatrice to whom *New Year Letter* was dedicated. She is mother and muse and also—just as important for a thirty-three-year-old immigrant in a new city—hostess. If Yeats had described her she would certainly have been Castiglione's Duchess. Like Lady Gregory ("mother, friend, sister, brother") she is a benevolent maternal presence who rescued the poet at a time when he felt isolated and rootless. And, like Lady Gregory's, her house—on a considerably smaller scale than Coole mansion, a mere "cottage" on Long Island—provided social and aesthetic order, a little society within a society. The music of Buxtehude, played on Christmas Day,

> made
> Our minds a *civitas* of sound
> Where nothing but assent was found,
> For art had set in order sense
> And feeling and intelligence,
> And from its ideal order grew
> Our local understanding too.[1]

The *civitas* of kindred spirits, like the "intellectual sweetness" of the harmony Lady Gregory created at Coole, is sharply distinct from the public community where there are "visible hostilities" like the war in Poland. The "same sun," says Auden, with his usual habit of observing the globe from a heav-

Reprinted from *Saving Civilization: Yeats, Eliot, and Auden Between the Wars* (New York: Cambridge University Press, 1984) by permission of Cambridge University Press and Lucy McDiarmid.

enly body's point of view, lights up the Polish war and the Long Island *civitas*. In the private life, at least, there is "assent," and a community "set in order" by Buxtehude, under the warmth of Elizabeth Mayer. She is a sun to her own smaller world, casting on the lives about her a "calm *solificatio*." That locution, at the end of the poem, delineates the realm in which the sun can look down on order and love.

Like Eliot's *voix d'enfants* [and] the fishmen in the bar, like "tutti" [in Auden's *For the Time Being*] at the manger, this is a *civitas* of sound, a musical harmony offered as a model for social harmony. But it is not, as the Augustinian word so emphatically reminds us, the whole *civitas terrena*. Acutely aware that the Buxtehudes and Elizabeth Mayers of the world do not save civilization, Auden emphasizes that aesthetic order does not "cause" social order: "Art is not life and cannot be / A midwife to society." What Auden states in *New Year Letter* in 1940 is typical of the claims and apologies all three poets [Yeats, Eliot, and Auden] were making in poems written around the beginning of the Second World War: [art] provides a world that can be perfectly ordered, or "saved," but this aesthetic order is dependent on the artist's rejection of an activist, *engagé* role. In a number of major poems about the role of the artist, poems inspired by present or imminent war, the artist is shown as successful in creating order and beauty, but the necessary precondition for that success, in the realm of art, is the rejection of all demands that art act in the public world.

There is a slight shift in this idea from Yeats to Eliot to Auden that reflects the increasing ontological independence of poetry from society in the poets' literary criticism. The "saved" world of the work of art becomes more separate from the unsaved civilization around it with each generation of poets. In "Long-Legged Fly" and "Lapis Lazuli" Yeats implies a remote causal connection between art and the world of political action. In *Little Gidding* Eliot presents art and history as parallel, non-intersecting planes, neither one absolute. In "In Memory of W. B. Yeats" and "At the Grave of Henry James" Auden insists on the dangers of confusing the two realms, to such an extent that his denial of relation between them is as strong as his positive statements about art.

In "Long-Legged Fly" Yeats backs into a definition of the artist's relation to saving civilization; the poem's this-is-the-house-that-Jack-built structure moves backward, in what Whitaker calls "causal regression," from history as effect to art as cause.[2] The structure embodies a rejection of political engagement, as the poem retreats from the urgent crisis of the first stanza, a crisis that demands political action ("That civilization may not sink"), to the second stanza's more muted apocalypse ("That the topless towers be burnt"), to the final stanza's act of creation ("There on the scaffolding reclines / Michael Angelo"), in the remote, sacred space where the civilization saved at the poem's opening is made in the first place. The a-historical sequence—Caesar, Helen, Michael Angelo—emphasizes the insignificance of chronology, and the simultaneous but differentiated existence of these representative figures and their activities. Creation and wars are always happening: the great battle always being fought, the topless towers always about to be burnt, works of art always being brought to life. By the third stanza the "great battle" of the first has lost its feeling of urgency; certainly to skip from Julius Caesar to Troy to Michael Angelo baffles any sense of the historical moment. The dominant impression at the end is of the artist's imperviousness to everything outside his work.

Although "Long-Legged Fly" epitomizes the way all three poets see the coexistence, and the separation, of historical crisis and artistic creation, it does not show the artist's sense of being pressured by external events. Yeats implies a kind of pressure on Michael Angelo by uttering the rhetorical imperative, "Shut the door of the Pope's chapel." The poem sets up the ideal isolation for the artist, but does not say what it would feel like to be interested in the Sistine Chapel ceiling and the world on the other side of the door as well. The overflowing life pressing in on the artist in the form of children outside the chapel is reminiscent of the fish, flesh, and fowl surrounding the speaker of "Sailing to Byzantium," or the schoolchildren around the sixty-year-old smiling public man. They are a potential disturbance, but not a temptation to make art do something it cannot.

That pressure does occur in "Lapis Lazuli," where it is not Caesar who must act "That civilization may not sink," but poets. The poem is generated out of the hysterical women's demand that artists act in the realm of history. *They* are the children on the other side of the chapel door, disturbers of artistic serenity. And it is the poets whom they burden with the "great battle" to save civilization: ". . . if nothing drastic is done / Aeroplane and Zeppelin will come out. . . ." Like "Long-Legged Fly," the poem moves from the urgencies of history to a remote aesthetic height. Once the chapel door is shut, or the hysterical women ignored, the end of the world seems somewhat less important, and less likely. No battles rage or cities burn at the end of "Long-Legged Fly," and the imminent bombardment of "the town" in "Lapis Lazuli" turns into an aesthetically viewed "tragic scene." In both poems the artist is a "first cause" of history: he builds the civilization that needs saving. His role is defined by its differentiation from the political roles of Caesar and those who take "drastic" action. His supply of beautiful objects and war's destruction are infinite and continuous: "All things fall and are built again." Michael Angelo keeps on creating so that beautiful girls will feel the sexual impulse, more men risk cities for their beauty, and more Caesars defend cities. The pattern is "Nineteen Hundred and Nineteen," calmed down; no illusions are lost, no one expects to save civilization, or "mend / Whatever mischief seemed / To afflict mankind" with art, and civilization does not grind to a halt because of war. Both poems show the limits of what the artist's actions can do, but also the long-range effects of those actions.

The pressures of history do not disappear so easily in poems by Eliot and

Auden. In the place of Yeats's systematic distancing, there are insistent reminders. War is present throughout *Little Gidding,* as the "world's end," the Blitz, the English Civil War, or the descending dove. The fires left by the German bombers are viewed as purgatorial flames, but they do not cease being actual fires in the streets of London. Violent death is present in muted form at the end, as "a step to the block, to the fire, down the sea's throat / Or to an illegible stone." Perhaps in the last line, "And the fire and the rose are one," the contemporary war has been as symbolized away as the "tragic scene" at the end of "Lapis Lazuli," but the fire retains its sense of secular destruction. It is pervasive in a way Yeats's wars, in "Lapis Lazuli" and "Long-Legged Fly," are not. War may be seen from different perspectives, religious or historical, but it remains a fact to be reckoned with, even at the very end.

In Auden's elegy for Yeats the fact of war is not even muted. Auden saves for the poem's final section a vivid reference to a singularly unsaved civilization. The violence of history is not transformed to an aesthetic "scene" or "pattern." It persists in unpalliated form as nightmare:

> In the nightmare of the dark
> All the dogs of Europe bark
> And the living nations wait
> Each sequestered in its hate.

In "At the Grave of Henry James," written in 1941, the same war is a less dramatic but more pervasive pressure:

> Now more than ever, when torches and snare-drum
> Excite the squat women of the saurian brain
>   Till a milling mob of fears
> Breaks in insultingly on anywhere
> ....
>
> Are the good ghosts needed with the white magic
> Of their subtle loves.[3]

These squat women sound like a more subjective—and fatter—version of the hysterical women of "Lapis Lazuli," but the hysterical women are mentioned once and never return. As a "resentful muttering Mass," a "vague incitement," a "wind that whispers of uncovered skulls / and fresh ruins," the anxieties these women represent persist to disturb the poet. It is against this background that Auden prays to so calm and remote a figure as James.

The undeniable fact of war in *Little Gidding* and in Auden's poems does not make art a less potent force than in Yeats's poems, but it does separate the political and aesthetic realms more definitively. The Chinamen listen to music while still gazing down on the tragic scene, and Michael Angelo is the first cause of Caesar. In *Little Gidding* Eliot does not put poetry into relation with history; he is more concerned to show that neither realm is absolute, that the significance of poetic events, as of historical ones, must be understood *sub specie aeternitatis*. Whether in the refining fire's dance or through the "purification of the motive / In the ground of our beseeching," both literature and history, equally creations of the human will, derive value from another source. They are analogous realms, but not causally linked. Auden's denial of connection is explicit: "poetry makes nothing happen." This is not a statement of frustration or futility, but merely of limitation. Like Yeats's insistence that tragedy cannot be affected—"Though all the drop-scenes drop at once / Upon a hundred thousand stages / It cannot grow by an inch or an ounce"—like the denials of Eliot's ghost in the second part of *Little Gidding,* Auden's denial is a necessary precondition for making claims for art's powers. All these statements of ontological differentiation precede the liberation of art from circumstance. Freed from direct dependence on history, art is freed from responsibility for saving civilization. So liberated, it is enabled to express its own powers to the fullest. Yeats can say that all things are "built again," Eliot can refer to "every phrase and sentence that is right," and Auden can call on the poet in resounding, enthusiastic imperatives:

> Follow, poet, follow right
> To the bottom of the night,
> With your unconstraining voice
> Still persuade us to rejoice.

The poets are aided in acceptance of art's limitations, and in the affirmation of its powers, by identifying with figures of ascetic denial, "dead masters" in religious or contemplative retreat from the world. When they conceive of small, temporary communities, the poets imagine women in charge: Lady Gregory, the Virgin Mary in "At the Manger," Elizabeth Mayer—all motherly, nurturing, domestic. But the dominant figures in the world of art, the only realm they can imagine saved without qualification, are male, stern, and priestly; men disengaged enough to please Benda. Henry James, as he appears in Auden's poem, is a paradigm for these figures. He is prayed to as the patron saint of disengaged writers, a holy celibate whose dedication to art was a religious vocation:

> . . . your heart, fastidious as
> A delicate nun, remained true to the rare noblesse
> Of your lucid gift, and, for its own sake, ignored the
> Resentful muttering Mass.[4]

The world James retreats from—or "ignores"—is a popular audience, whose "hatred of all which cannot / Be simplified or stolen is still at large." No Michael Ransom, reluctant hero of the thirties, James with his fastidious sensibility seems to have found easy the artist's sacrifice of the world. The eremitic devotion is harder for Auden, who needs James's authority and personal example to control his own tendency to be distracted from his vocation by more immediate but corrupt satisfactions: "Preserve me, Master, from its vague incitement; / Yours be the disciplinary image that holds / Me back from agreeable wrong. . . ."[5] "Agreeable wrong" is the wish to be Marie Lloyd, to hear your poetry sung and marched to, to entertain the mob. The chief sin for which Auden needs forgiveness is what Benda calls "the tendency to action, the thirst for immediate results, the exclusive preoccupation with the desired end"—the sin, in short, of wanting to save civilization.[6] Although Auden cannot acquire James's innocence, he can at least acknowledge his fault and, like Eliot's compound ghost, pray for purgation:

> Master of nuance and scruple,
> Pray for me and for all writers living or dead,
>   Because there are many whose works
> Are in better taste than their lives; because there is no end
> To the vanity of our calling.[7]

When, in the final stanza, Auden refers to God in the words of the *Book of Common Prayer,* as the "author and giver of all good things," he attributes ultimate creative power to a source beyond "all writers living or dead."[8]

With each generation, the anti-activist stance is won through greater struggle. The Chinamen of "Lapis Lazuli" look on the tragic scene with apparent composure, and their eyes "are gay." They do not have to become gay, or meditate for half an hour, or recite mantras. They are obvious models of detachment because the attitude comes naturally to them; the East, as Yeats wrote, "has its solutions always and therefore knows nothing of tragedy."[9] With a Western figure some distraction clouds the picture: Michael Angelo is separated from the profane world on a scaffolding in a sacred spot, the Pope's chapel. The "vague incitement" of the world is just outside the door, in the children pressing in on his privacy, so the poet must command, "Keep those children out." The creative solitude common to the Chinamen and Michael Angelo is shared by Milton, as Eliot makes a glancing reference to him in the third part of *Little Gidding.* The adjectives Eliot uses—Milton is "one who died blind and quiet"—imply a calm retreat from the world, but the context suggests resignation and loss. To invoke Milton after a reference to Charles I and "three men, and more, on the scaffold" is to call to mind the politics in which Milton was *engagé.* Milton's quiet was the result of giving up the struggle to save civilization, and devoting himself to ordering language.

The most complex as well as the most authoritative of these dead masters is Yeats himself, an ambiguous, arrogant figure, one who understands "the day's vanity, the night's remorse" and is well qualified to forgive and bless the pride of younger poets. In *Little Gidding* and "In Memory of

W. B. Yeats" he shows Eliot and Auden how to be a poet—or rather, they use him to define their roles—by insisting that poetry is not absolute. As a ghost he is "compound" with Dante, among others, another authoritative master who sacrificed saving civilization for making art. Like James, he warns against "agreeable wrong," the ephemeral satisfactions of popularity ("Last season's fruit is eaten / And the fullfed beast shall kick the empty pail") and fame ("fools' approval stings, and honor stains"), and the pain of public engagement without power, and moral idealism mixed with moral culpability:

> . . . the conscious impotence of rage
> At human folly, and the laceration
> Of laughter at what ceases to amuse.
> And last, the rending pain of re-enactment
> Of all that you have done, and been; the shame
> Of motives late revealed, and the awareness
> Of things ill done and done to others' harm
> Which once you took for exercise of virtue.

The language is the language of Yeats, but the tone is the tone of Cotton Mather. For this hellfire-and-brimstone Yeats, a sterner "disciplinary image" than Henry James, the only salvation for the exasperated spirit of poets is the refining fire, the humility of "moving in measure." The sacrifice of originative power for religious purification is reminiscent of the end of the James poem, where God is addressed as "author."

The Yeats evoked in Auden's elegy also needs forgiveness. His sin is reactionary politics, and he is pardoned by Time not for any act of self-abnegation but "for writing well." This Yeats is not such a preacher as Eliot's or so remote and detached as his own Chinamen or Michael Angelo. He blunders through to a position of literary authority:

> You were silly like us: your gift survived it all;
> The parish of rich women, physical decay,
> Yourself; mad Ireland hurt you into poetry.
> Now Ireland has her madness and her weather still,
> For poetry makes nothing happen: it survives
> In the valley of its saying . . .

He is not only sinful and arrogant, he is unself-conscious. His poetry survives his political interests not through humility or sensibility, but through sheer talent. Poetry itself has a survival instinct, and great poetry creates its own world even when poets try to force it into other worlds: "it survives, a way of happening, a mouth."

Guilty of activism, of abusing art, the poets in these war lyrics confront all the urgency of a war they cannot affect, and define their own function by denial. Having acknowledged the reality of war, the perpetual battle to save civilization; having confronted the ineffectiveness of art in the world where those battles take place; having said *"mea culpa"* for the vanity of their calling, and submitted to the stern disciplinary image of a dead artist who also restrained his inclination to save civilization, the poets rejoice in the world that they can order perfectly, the work of art. It is a physical space that seems to expand as the poets devote themselves to it. It exists in its own private spot, fertile, pure, far from the poisoned wells of the public realm. It is a landscape in the imagination ("I / delight to imagine them seated there"), purified by snow or water ("a water-course or an avalanche") and fecund: ". . . doubtless plum or cherry branch / Sweetens the little half-way house / Those Chinamen climb towards. . . ." It exists in the Sistine Chapel, near the ceiling. It is free from aeroplane, Zeppelin, and Caesar as only the world created by art can be. It is the ideal harmonious *civitas,* the good community Eliot describes in *Little Gidding:*

> (where every word is at home,
> Taking its place to support the others,
> The word neither diffident nor ostentatious,
> An easy commerce of the old and the new,
> ....
>
> The complete consort dancing together)

The words of a phrase and of a sentence can, under the poet's direction, combine and support each other as no group of human beings ever could, for all the poet's wish. They behave here like Auden's refugees, handing the bricks, supporting the others. This group is the crowd of words transformed into a community, as the crowd flowing over London Bridge could never be. With each man fixing his eyes before his feet, no one was "at home" or had any interest in the others at all. Dancing together, the words are like the children singing under the dome or the fishmen in the bar, or "tutti" at the manger, or Lady Greogry's group at Coole Park; except, of course, that they are not human, and can neither give nor sympathize, though under the poet's control they can dance.

In an early draft of this passage Eliot had written,

> So every phrase
> When it is ᵗʰᵉ right, ᵒⁿᵉ when every / word has power
> To sustain the others, to do its part
> In subservience to the phrase—[10]

Even more than the final version, these lines insist on the social relations of the words; "sustain" sounds more social, and less aesthetic, than "support," and "to do its part / In subservience to the phrase" seems to impute a power of volition to the word. Like the "individual talent," it surrenders to a larger collective entity. Like Auden's description of a poet creating a poem ("every occasion competes with every other, demanding inclusion and a dominant position to which they are not necessarily entitled"), Eliot's language implicitly defines the poet as the creator of a verbal society, a perfect world where each does "its part."

Auden's "saved" poetic world is delimited by the encompassing world of history; he insists on their autonomy and their coexistence. History may be a cold, dark, bleak, frozen landscape, with hatred, disgrace, and isolation, but art—as the poet brings it into being—can be fertile and healthy:

> Follow, poet, follow right
> To the bottom of the night,
> With your unconstraining voice
> Still persuade us to rejoice;
>
> With the farming of a verse
> Make a vineyard of the curse,
> Sing of human unsuccess
> In a rapture of distress;
>
> In the deserts of the heart
> Let the healing fountain start,
> In the prison of his days
> Teach the free man how to praise.

The imperatives directed at the poet require him not to make the dark cold surroundings disappear, or to transform them magically, but to face them and act in spite of them. "Still" means "nevertheless" as well as "always." The poet persuades with full awareness of his context. In the act of persuading and singing in spite of circumstances, the poet creates his own world. Like the river's valley in the second part, the poetic landscape here comes into being gradually as the poet invents it. But the surrounding world cannot be wished away, or even distanced. Balancing creative energy against binding circumstances, Auden insists on the abiding reality of "unsuccess" and "distress." The reality of the good, saved world is assured, but it must endure in the midst of the desert and frozen seas which the poet can never change.

Notes

1. Auden, *Collected Poetry* (1945), 266.
2. Thomas R. Whitaker, *Swan and Shadow: Yeats's Dialogue with History* (Chapel Hill, N.C., 1964), 127.

3. Auden, *Selected Poems* (1979), 121.

4. Ibid., 122.

5. Ibid.

6. Julien Benda, *The Treason of the Intellectuals,* trans. Richard Aldington (New York, 1928), 46.

7. Auden, *Selected Poems* (1979), 123.

8. My understanding of this stanza was much illuminated by Richard Johnson's talk, "Original Sin and the Sin of Originality," delivered at the Auden Symposium at Swarthmore College on 13 October 1979.

9. Yeats, *The Letters of W. B. Yeats,* ed. Allan Wade (London: Rupert Hart-Davis, 1954), 837.

10. See Helen Gardner, *The Composition of* Four Quartets (Oxford, 1978), 219.

[From *Auden's Poetry* ("The Sea and the Mirror")]

Justin Replogle

In *For the Time Being* [1944] characters flounder in a collapsing Ethical world. These in *The Sea and the Mirror* (1945) sail from the collapse of an Aesthetic world. Inevitably, therefore, nearly everything in *The Sea and the Mirror* carries a message about art as well as about life. In fact, by writing about both at once Auden resolves temperamental conflicts for years unresolved. Thus the work is a very important one. It contains the best poetry Auden had yet written and marks a turning point in his entire development. His doubts about the value of all art, and bigger doubts about the kind he should make himself, his conflicting feelings about the attractions of life—in short, many of the opposing affinities that had split his temperament for years come into the open here to be examined and unified. . . . [This essay] shows how in *The Sea and the Mirror* the pattern of Auden's philosophical development unfolds. *The Sea and the Mirror* contains another dialectical landscape where men journey from one frontier to the next, sometimes without crossing any. Launched out over seventy thousand fathoms, a whole shipload of characters from Shakespeare's *The Tempest* make their slow collective leap from Prospero's past and their own. On the far side of their watery abyss, one or two believe, Religion shimmers dimly in the distance. For others the distant shore is Ethical. Still others (and all but Antonio, in one sense) carry with them a private Aesthetic isle, from which they will never depart.

According to *New Year Letter,*

> Hell is the being of the lie
> That we become if we
> . . . claim
> Becoming and Being are the same. . . .
> (*CP*, p. 292)

The Sea and the Mirror is one illustration of that bare philosophical definition. The Aesthetic life always moves, even if surreptitiously, toward a world of

Reprinted from *Auden's Poetry* (Seattle: University of Washington Press, 1969) by permission of University of Washington Press and Methuen & Co.

Being where men, all mutability gone, might sing like golden nightingales in a life that moves but never changes. Since real men can never avoid being human, few ever sail very near such a place, but the fictional Prospero had sailed all the way, and on his enchanted isle had fashioned an Aesthetic paradise more perfect than any Yeats dared dream of. As a critic, Auden likes to show how the plots of almost any sort of literature can be turned into existentialist parables. *The Tempest*'s final scenes yield easily. There Auden found all but two of Shakespeare's characters traveling a dialectical path from Aesthetic to Ethical or Religious existence. The two exceptions, Ariel and Caliban, the patron sprite of Aesthetics itself and his brutish counterpart, disorganized reality, fill out the fable. Shakespeare's cast on their final journey perfectly suited Auden's interests. In *The Sea and the Mirror* the old artificer Prospero speaks first, renouncing his Aesthetic life, bidding Ariel farewell. He, better than anyone, understands the sinfulness of confusing Being and Becoming. Attracted to magic since childhood, he defines it as "the power to enchant / That comes from disillusion" (*CP*, pp. 353–54). Aesthetics, in other words, by trying to create a garden of Being in a desert of despair, attracts those too weak to face the depressing realities of human existence. Seeking to escape these, talented unfortunates build around themselves an imaginary world of their own, perfect, organized, lacking the wildness of freedom, choice, and the erosion of time. In the center of these Aesthetic constructions, Godlike, sits the Aesthetic creator himself. So Prospero has built his enchanted isle, and in the fullness of his pride, completed his imitation of God by creating man, who would tender him "absolute devotion" (*CP*, p. 356). Unfortunately, like other men's, Caliban's devotion has been somewhat less than absolute. In fact Caliban's unruly reality is the only flaw in an otherwise perfect Aesthetic design. Thus even Prospero cannot entirely escape his human legacy. No man can, as Caliban points out later. The only perfect Aesthetician is God.

Considerably wiser now, Prospero, his magic books thrown in the sea, has renounced Being to embrace Becoming: "At last I can really believe I shall die" (*CP*, p. 352). His future life, he hopes, will follow what Kierkegaard called the path of "incessant becoming [which] generates the uncertainty of the earthly life, where everything is uncertain."[1] "I awake, and this journey really exists," Prospero exclaims with the new delight of the twice-born: "And I have actually to take it, inch by inch, / Alone and on foot . . . / Through a universe where time is not foreshortened . . ." (*CP*, p. 358). Prospero's destination, he hopes, will be not Ethical but Religious existence. Like Kierkegaard's knight of faith, he travels perilously suspended above one of the philosopher's favorite metaphors, the seventy thousand–fathom abyss Religious aspirants must leap. And in mid-leap, because "the entire essential content of subjective thought is essentially secret . . . and [therefore] cannot be directly communicated,"[2] Prospero can explain himself only fitfully: "Sailing alone, out over seventy thousand fathoms—? / Yet if I speak, I shall sink without a sound / Into unmeaning abysses" (*CP*, p. 358). He knows too, as Kierkegaard says, that "suffering is posited as something decisive for a religious existence,"[3] and therefore that he must overcome his Aesthetic habit of making pleasing designs out of painful facts. He at least has hopes that he can ". . . learn to suffer / Without saying something ironic or funny / On suffering" (*CP*, p. 358).

At first Prospero seems to be the wholly good man. But, pressed forward by his philosophical doctrines, Auden knocks him down in the next poem. The image of benign Prospero, built up through so many skillful lines, shrivels beneath Antonio's laconic scorn. With a contempt so diffident he scarcely bothers to utter it, Antonio mocks the very wisdom, humility, and good nature so attractively revealed but a moment before. In their place Antonio sets self-delusion and pride. Prospero moves in circles, he declares. The abandoned island, fading in the distance, fools only the nearsighted. Escape from Aesthetic enchantment has been an illusion. Prospero's magic wand, so ceremoniously broken, will rejoin, his sea-drenched books "soon reappear, / Not even damaged" (*CP*, p. 361). Even now the old Aesthetic conjuring begins; in fact it has never stopped. The forsaken island, the voyage, the characters paired off, raised or lowered, their futures bestowed— everything, the whole pattern of events, has been arranged by Prospero. And even now, dotted about the deck, kissing against the sails, the characters act out their parts in accord with Prospero's Aesthetic designs. "Yes, Brother Prospero, your grouping could / Not be more effective," Antonio mockingly observes (*CP*, p. 360). One Aesthetic existence left behind, Prospero now fashions another, and will never cease, Antonio insists: ". . . whatever you wear / Is a magic robe," he tells Prospero. You can "Never become," he says (*CP*, p. 361). The attraction of Being is too strong.

Antonio is spokesman for whatever makes human imperfection certain. In theological terms he announces necessity, God's design. Men must remain human. None escape. Without Antonio, Prospero's beneficently arranged world would seem peaceful and happy, the wrongs righted, the wounds healed, enemies reconciled, the young in one another's arms. Human perfection might seem just a few leagues off, rising in the distance across the seventy thousand fathoms. But such longed-for shores remain nothing more than a persistent human dream, Auden's philosophy insists. Imperfection and sin remain always, part of the human pattern: ". . . every step we make / Will certainly be a mistake," the speaker in *New Year Letter* declared (*CP*, p. 294). Even Prospero's cautious optimism goes too far, and Antonio's eagle eye notices the crack in every image, no matter how dazzling its surface appears. The dropped clue, the overlooked symptom, the telltale shred of pride instantly reveal to him the flaw in every human act and motive, even the best. Antonio's message is, nothing is right, or, rather, nothing has changed. If for God, everything that is is right; for man everything is wrong. Antonio plays the role of devil or genuine knight of faith. The two are mirror images, one almost perfectly good, the other almost perfectly evil. Neither is as perfect as God or as imperfect as ordinary mortals. *"Your all is partial, Prospero; / My will is all my own . . ."* Antonio declares (*CP,* p. 361), and he compares himself, in much the same way, to each of the other characters in turn. More than other men, devil and knight of faith sail alone outside the ordinary human condition, yet far from the divine too. *"Your need to love shall never know / Me,"* Antonio announces to Prospero; *"I am I, Antonio, / By choice myself alone"* (*CP,* p. 361). And the substance of this declaration, too, is repeated to each of the other characters. In the grand cosmic design, devil and knight of faith have a common purpose. The devil will "push us into grace," *New Year Letter* states (*CP,* p. 277), and the knight of faith can do the same thing. Our tiniest fault, exposed by the devil's cynical scrutiny, urges us forward to greater improvement. So does the impossibly high example set by the knight of faith. Impossible perfection is our goal, cries the knight of faith; perfection is impossible, whispers the devil. Responding to either, we redouble our effort (or fall at once, as all do in the end, devil and knight of faith included). Antonio, the voice of the nearly inhuman, reminds all men of their humanity, and therefore of their pride, delusions, and imperfections. So Prospero's image, shriveled as it is beneath Antonio's fastidious scorn, shrivels only to life size from its formerly too-large dimensions. Everything Antonio says is true, but his accusations do not set Prospero among the worst—merely among his fellow human beings. His imperfections are human limits, the necessity no one since the Fall can entirely escape. Prospero emerges after Antonio's deflation still the best of men, but always a man.

The other characters either remain fully enmeshed in their Aesthetic lives or believe themselves now to be moving on toward the Ethical or Religious. So far, Miranda and Ferdinand languish in a world of nearly perfect Being, a love that excludes external reality, though Prospero has already remarked on its impermanence (*CP,* p. 356). Trinculo and Stephano both find the real world too much and withdraw as best they can into Aesthetic realms of their own creation. Stephano's belly becomes his pleasure dome—bride, daughter, mother, and nanny combined. Trinculo, a more pitiful case, escapes into a landscape of satisfying childhood fantasy, just as Rosetta will do in *The Age of Anxiety,* a place of "Quick dreams" where "I / Was Little Trinculo" (*CP,* pp. 371–72). But long since his garden of Being has turned hellish, as *New Year Letter* informs us all gardens must. Trinculo's hold on existence is slipping, and in fact apart from Prospero and Antonio only Sebastian, Alonso, and Gonzalo confront human existence squarely enough to allow Auden to develop extended philosophical issues in their speeches. Both Sebastian and Gonzalo have just recently emerged from "The lie of Nothing" to the "Just Now" (*CP,* pp. 370, 371), and Gonzalo talks about this escape from the Aesthetic at some length. In the past, instead of trusting "the Absurd" and singing "exactly what I heard," this man of little faith had made songs more pleasing to his Aesthetic ear. "Jealous of my native ear, / Mine the art which made the song / Sound ridiculous and wrong . . ." (*CP,* p. 364). This is nothing more than Gonzalo's own repetition of Adam's fall, with Gonzalo, like Adam, believing himself free "to choose his own necessity." Gonzalo's pride ("self-reflection") ultimately makes his "Consolation an offence" (*CP,* p. 364), following a pattern Kierkegaard describes. "For what is an offense?" Kierkegaard asks, and answers, "it is an envy. . . . The narrow-mindedness of the natural man cannot welcome for itself the extraordinary which God has intended for him; so he is offended."[4] But now "restored to health," his "subjective passion" once more vigorous, Gonzalo hopes he can move toward a Religious existence, a man whom "The Already There can lay / Hands on" (*CP,* p. 365). Pride, the cause of Gonzalo's (and all men's) fall, is just what Alonso warns against in an open letter to his son. Singling out for special emphasis the archetypal rudiments of pride, he tells how they grow out of that perennial wish: to escape the human condition. In believing escape from Becoming to Being possible, each man repeats Adam's mistake, imagining necessity to be entirely his own creation. Both mind and body can seduce, and Alonso warns against both. In one ear the Aesthetic "siren sings" of "water . . . / Where all flesh had peace," he tells his son, and in the other of ". . . a brilliant void / Where [the] mind could be perfectly clear / And all . . . limitations destroyed . . ." (*CP,* p. 367). But whether the Aesthetic bower of bliss originates in intellectual or physical pleasure, it will soon crumble and grow hellish.

The Sea and the Mirror is other things besides a philosophical or religious allegory. In fact, its characters, isolated in their monologues, do not really act at all, and perhaps a work without action should not be called an allegory. But action is implicit. The characters merely step out of *The Tempest* plot long enough to speak in *The Sea and the Mirror,* and their speeches turn that borrowed and off-stage action into an allegorical journey. Yet the work makes good sense without being read as a Kierkegaardian allegory, and the separate remarks about life and human nature in most speeches can be understood without a Kierkegaardian gloss. Taken as a non-Kierkegaardian commentary on art, rather than on the Aesthetic life, *The Sea and the Mirror* will yield a similar, though smaller, message. (For that matter, readers who have never heard of Shakespeare can understand much of it too). Nevertheless *The Sea and the Mirror* is filled with the Christian view of man Auden fashioned with the help of Kierkegaard, and Caliban's dazzling speech presents this matter explicitly. Facing an audience of the Aesthetically and Ethically complacent, Caliban hopes to jolt them forward onto the Religious Way. After brilliantly lecturing for a time on the relationship of these triadic terms, he becomes more hortatory. Trying to escape from Becoming to Being, he tells his audience (most of whom have come to the theater to do just that), will lead to hell, and he takes evangelistic delight in illustrating this abstract theology with topographical details. "Cones of extinct volcanoes . . . plateau fissured by chasms . . . pitted with hot springs" await foolish sinners who hope to

evade their human necessity (*CP,* p. 395). Simply understanding their predicament is not enough, he cautions. Since sin is not mere ignorance, Kierkegaard had stressed, wisdom is not salvation. Men *choose* to sin, and therefore
must *act* to save themselves. So Caliban warns his audience of the "delusion
that an awareness of the gap is in itself a bridge" (*CP,* p. 400). Knowledge of
dialectic is no substitute for leaping. But after raising an "admonitory forefin-
ger" for many pages, Caliban must begin to reverse himself as he approaches
the heart of his message. The paradox there, avoided for so long, must now
be faced, and his finger-wagging reproaches now must in one sense be
withdrawn. After showing for most of his speech that neither of "the alternative routes, the facile glad-handed highway or the virtuous averted track,"
lead to anything but a "dreadful end" (*CP,* p. 399), he is now compelled to
explain that these Aesthetic and Ethical roads must, in fact, be taken, and
their hellish directions gladly followed right to the certain despair at their
dead ends. Here too the way up is the way down, the way in is the way out,
the way back is the way forward, so that if neither Aesthetic nor Ethical roads
lead directly to the Religious, both lead there indirectly, and the indirect
route is the only one there is. Only when all secular routes have been tried
and found wanting can the Religious leap be taken. When "There is no way
out . . . it is at this moment that for the first time in our lives we hear . . .
the real Word which is our only *raison d'etre.*" Not that with a Religious leap
men can escape human existence. Even the most successful leap only to fall
back into a secular world in one sense completely unchanged: ". . . everything, the massacres, the whippings, the lies, the twaddle, and all their
carbon copies are still present," Caliban reports, all "more obviously than
ever." But in another paradoxical sense everything *is* changed by a Religious
leap. Only after Religious illumination do we fully understand that "it is not
in spite of [massacres, whippings, and lies] but with them that we are blessed
by that Wholly Other. . . ." This is the Christian paradox at the heart of *The
Sea and the Mirror* and all Auden's long works in the 1940's, and here as in all
the others, Auden chooses to stress one side of it, the need to accept secular
life. For all its sinfulness the Aesthetic-Ethical world of human existence
must be lived in fully before Religious leaps can be made, and, if they are
made after the inevitable fall backward. Men's greatest reward is not to
transcend secular life but to experience its blessedness. That is the ultimate
Religious illumination, Caliban says in conclusion, the recognition that "it is
just here, among the ruins and the bones, that we may rejoice in the per-
fected Work which is not ours" (*CP,* p. 402).

Notes

1. Kierkegaard, *Concluding Unscientific Postscript,* trans. David F. Swenson and Walter
Lowrie (Princeton, N.J.: Princeton University Press, 1944), p. 79.

2. Ibid., p. 73.

3. Ibid., p. 256.

4. Kierkegaard, *Fear and Trembling* and *The Sickness Unto Death,* trans. Walter Lowrie (Garden City, N.Y.: Doubleday, 1954), pp. 216–17.

Through the Looking Glass
[Review of *For the Time Being*]

Harry Levin

Poetic justice, with its attendant ironies, must have presided over the mutually rewarding interchange that sent T. S. Eliot to England and brought W. H. Auden to this country. Eliot, whose preaching has never quite rationalized his practice, has retained a peculiarly individual talent. Auden, whose iconoclasm has merely tested his loyalties, has not broken with tradition. Craftsmanship is a surer link than manifestos and genuflections, and Auden's skill is linked with the odes of Dryden and the patter of Gilbert, with the varied masters and characteristic journeymen of English prosody. He has taught much, and can teach more, to our native poets: few of them have really mastered the technical requirements of their craft, and those who have spend most of their efforts reminding us of the fact. A book which—despite its temporizing title—takes in its stride the ballade, the villanelle, the sestina, sapphics, elegiacs and *terza rima,* while making words a vehicle for ideas instead of the contrary, is more than a current event; it is an enduring delight. When poetry is as topical and colloquial, as pregnant with issues and idioms as Auden's, it cannot be transplanted without undergoing some abstraction of matter, some intensification of manner. Imagery becomes less immediate, diction more macaronic. Gorgeous dames have Oxford accents and juke-boxes play Handel. The old familiar-exotic contrast between a concrete little England and the big abstract globe gives way to the broader antitheses of art versus nature and naturalism versus supernaturalism. But the *discordia concors,* whereby they are resolved, is still the dominant mode; Auden and Eliot can still meet, if not on the common ground of the vernacular and contemporary, then in the rarefied atmosphere of the literary and philosophic.

The perpetual aspiration of poetry toward the condition of drama, which Eliot has bravely expounded and weakly exemplified, finds further expression in the two long poems that compose Auden's latest volume. Since his province is not dramatic characterization, but lyric speculation and satiric generalization, he has wisely allowed Shakespeare and the gospels to provide the text for his comments. "The Sea and the Mirror" is a commentary on "The Tempest"

Reprinted from *New Republic* 111 (18 September 1944).

and "For the Time Being" is a Christmas oratorio. Taken together, as mystery and masque, they represent the alpha and omega of the theatrical cycle. The last comes appropriately first, for Shakespeare's ending is far too happy to be conclusive: it suggests disparities between literature and life which neither Prospero's magic nor the audience's make-believe can altogether reconcile. By singling out the unreconciled character, by harping on the discordant note, Auden bespeaks our attention for "The drama that Antonio / Plays in his mind alone." But it is Caliban who provokes Auden, as he did Browning and Renan, to the most interesting afterthoughts. The servant-monster, gesturing with the hands of Sweeney and speaking in the voice of Henry James, expresses the paradoxical "relationship between the real and the imagined." If he is nature, art is his mirror, and Ariel is the artist's tricksy genius, "the spirit of reflection." If Ariel is the idealized image of Caliban, Caliban is the gross echo of Ariel, and metaphysical reality lies behind the proscenium—on the other side of the mirror. Life is ultimately envisaged, not as Plato's cave nor Bede's sparrow, but as "the greatest grandest opera rendered by a very provincial touring company indeed"—a mock-heroic metaphor which Trotsky once applied to the social-revolutionary government.

> It's as if
> We had left our house for five minutes to mail a letter,
> And during that time the living room had changed places
> With the room behind the mirror over the fireplace . . .

Thus the oratorio picks up the whimsical theme of the commentary, and carries it through a series of resourceful modulations to a music-hall finale, setting the Flight into Egypt—"the Land of Unlikeness"—against a real-estate development of the Waste Land. The perplexities and strivings of the intellectual, the man with the mirror, are profoundly grasped and impressively orchestrated: "How can his knowledge protect his desire for truth from illusion?" The response, prompted by the occasion, is the Good News from Bethlehem, refulgent against the bad news of modern civilization. Herod, the very pattern of a modern liberal, is outheroded by Simeon, prototype of the convert. Auden, like most intelligent believers, affirms a positive faith by a kind of double negation, a denial of doubt, a questioning of skepticism. He is more adept at burying Caesar than at praising Christ, more anxious for a Messiah than confident in the Revelation. When his libretto calls for a paradisiacal strain, he touches the quavering reed-organ of revivalism: "There's a Way. There's a Voice." The medieval nativity plays, *sancta simplicitas,* could mix slapstick with piety; but the mixture of satire and theology, as Dostoevsky shows, is diabolically complex. Sin is notoriously easier to dramatize—or believe in—than grace; hence Freud is a more pertinent guide than Beatrice. The rhyming clichés of the romantics, "love" and "dove," are displaced by the Freudian be-all and end-all, "womb" and "tomb."

The cult of Mary is treated as the supreme mother-fixation, and Joseph is seen as a comic degradation of the superfluous husband. Nostalgia conjures up expressionistic visions of the sea-changed past and the air-conditioned future. Belief is a god in the machine, who sublimates private and public problems, and by whom Imagination is redeemed from "promiscuous fornication with her own images."

That this is all done with mirrors, that poetry which aspires to prophecy is even more paranoid than art for art's sake, the skeptical reader can neither affirm nor deny. But he cannot help observing a narcissistic tendency to escape through the looking-glass into an island kingdom or desert exile. Auden's parenthetical remark "(there is probably no one whose real name is Brown)" seems very revealing; it reveals the "contrived fissure" between the poet and his audience. His function—for we have almost lost sight of Shakespeare's definition—is to hold the mirror up to nature, not to denaturalize Caliban or supernaturalize the White Knight. "Our wonder, our terror remains," to be sure, but it is more fully explained by today's headlines than by Auden upon Setebos. Though so sincere and talented a writer is not fairly to be compared with Aldous Huxley, their self-conscious pilgrimages from modernism to mysticism run curiously parallel. And latterly their insight into our follies and weaknesses has been made the sudden pretext of an evangelical appeal which, for those of us who do not happen to be going their way, is more embarrassing than convincing. Huxley was always a glib faddist, whereas Auden drew energy from his social convictions. To have exhausted them so quickly, while the circumstances they faced are more pressing than ever, does not heighten the plausibility of his present credo. To be stalemated by the false dichotomy between a subjective Us and an objective Them, a sentimental notion of culture and naïve prejudice against science, is hardly the way to protect a desire for truth from illusion. It is what we have learned to expect from our academics and clericals, our all-too-humanists and quack angelic doctors. But we still expect something more truly humane from a poet whose writing has been so lucent and polished a mirror of the time being.

[From *Changes of Heart*
(*The Age of Anxiety*)]

Gerald Nelson

The Age of Anxiety is a quest poem, perhaps Auden's most elaborate one, yet the quest is false.[1] Its characters search within themselves in an attempt to gain self-knowledge, yet their search is doomed from the very beginning because it is induced by external stimulants. *The Age of Anxiety* is a poem that "means" only in the negative sense. The characters search, but do not; their vision is, but is not; the language and ideas are theirs, but are not. They are the damned who refuse to recognize their damnation; they are in Hell but believe themselves to be only in Purgatory. A more legitimate complaint about *The Age of Anxiety* than those about its tone would seem to be that Auden tries to give a picture of the modern human condition which denies possibility but refuses to call it impossible.

In a cursory examination, *The Age of Anxiety* appears to be a dramatic amplification of Auden's earlier poem, "September 1, 1939." . . .

. . . In "September 1, 1939," the bar appears to be a temporary stop, a place to rest and gain the strength necessary for the battle, much like Prospero's island. In *The Age of Anxiety* the bar is all there is. The time is one of real war, and the bar has become an end in itself, instead of merely a false stopping place. It offers the possibility of escape into illusion, it gives its customers the possibility of believing that things are not what they are, that life is not life. *The Sea and the Mirror* began with its characters about to leave the illusion of their island, about to enter into life. There is hope in that work, because, in spite of the odds, there is hope in the characters. Naïve, sophisticated, or humble, they are earnest about their lives. In *The Age of Anxiety* any attempt to leave the island is hallucinatory, induced by liquor. The voyages of the characters are taking them further from life rather than drawing them deeper into it. They cannot be earnest, and as a consequence their quest is mock, an attempt which can end only in foolishness and failure. Quant, Malin, Rosetta, and Emble do not want reality; they want escape, yet this is impossible.

Quant, as has been mentioned earlier, begins the action of *The Age of*

Reprinted from *Changes of Heart: A Study of the Poetry of W. H. Auden* by permission of Gerald Nelson and the University of California Press. © 1969 by the Regents of the University of California.

Anxiety by addressing his image in the mirror. This is typically (as well as stereotypically) a drinker's action. Facing the self that is not the self, the double, the "dear image" of the mirror, is much easier than forcing one's attention on the real self. It is possible to hold back the real problem by simply commenting on appearance. The mirror can always lie by offering man the chance not to believe that what he sees is himself; it enables him to believe that the real self might be "the poet disguised."[2] Quant is an aging, homosexual widower whose lack of legitimate experience has rendered him impotent in relation to life. His only responses are simpering self-admonitions ("Why Miss ME, what's the matter?") or limp excuses. The mirror interests him because it offers him the easiest way of facing himself.

Malin, the second character to appear, is the dominant character of the work. He is on leave from the Canadian Air Force where he is a medical intelligence officer, and in the world of *The Age of Anxiety* he is both the would-be doctor and the leader. His name is important, for he is—in terms of the war outside—a malingerer, and there is more than a hint of the satanic in his make-up.

Rosetta, a department store buyer, is the most human of the characters, and in her long soliloquy at the conclusion of Part V she comes very close to a moment of genuine self-realization. The fourth character, Emble, is a young sailor. He is the would-be prince, and much of the action in *The Age of Anxiety* leads up to his prospective sexual union with Rosetta. His failure in this—he achieves only the oblivion of sleep—is the act which (ironically) climaxes the work.

Part I, entitled "Prologue," introduces the scene and the characters. Each character begins by thinking "out loud" in soliloquies meant to reveal character. Quant, for instance, looks at himself with false admiration and is even a bit awed at his imaginary idea of his own mystery. Malin, coolly intelligent, examines the theoretical nature of man. Rosetta, unhappy with herself and her present, endeavors to create an imaginary and happy past. And Emble, feeling himself isolated from his fellows, passes his youthful judgment on their follies.

. . . .

Part II of *The Age of Anxiety*, "The Seven Ages," serves as the first act. Malin dominates this section, acting as a guide and, through his introductions to each of the ages, controlling the characters' reactions. He describes each age and sets the tone for response. The others give substance to his theories, drawing on experiences from their own pasts, presents, and hypothetical futures. The effect of this technique is to cast Malin as the Tempter. He speaks not of himself but of universals, forcing his companions not only to reveal themselves but to see their own lives merely as examples which prove his theories. He is the false or, at best, one-sided hero. He knows something that is, or seems to be, true about life, but his knowledge is not connected to his life. He is able to describe, yet he does not, like Caliban, stand "down stage" with his companions. He is a disconnected priest, separated from his flock.

At the beginning of "The Seven Ages," he asks us to "Behold the infant"; we feel him to be looking at us as if *we* were that infant, while his own infancy remains inviolable or seems even nonexistent. What he says is, for Auden, true; it is the *manner* in which he says it that puzzles. He describes the state of infancy in almost Wordsworthian terms. The child is "helpless in cradle and / Righteous still"; yet, and Auden here is closer in thought to Freud than to Wordsworth, he already has a "Dread in his dreams." The child knows nothing of the leap before him, yet "He jumps and is judged: he joins mankind, / The fallen families, freedom lost, / Love becomes Law."[3] From innocence to experience is such a simple step—merely the process of becoming conscious, and then self-conscious. The innocent becomes the guilty, "A foiled one learning / Shyness and shame, a shadowed flier." This familiar Audenesque picture of the flier concludes Malin's description of the state of being in the first age, the "Fall" of each man, and sets the scene for the responses of the other characters.

. . . .

The second age of man, as Malin describes it, is youth. No longer a child let loose among unfriendly giants, the youth moves out into life. This is the age when man first realizes that "He has laid his life-bet with a lying self." Yet his naïve belief in himself and in his place in life is boundless. He knows that he is special and that the great hold a "promised chair / In their small circle" for him. He must only reach it. He is in love with himself not as he is, but as he knows he will be—with his becoming, not his being. If childhood is as the characters indicate it to be, the age of discontent with the present, youth is the age of belief in the possibility of the future. . . .

The next age is that of sexual awakening, when man must cut off his dream images as "he learns what real / Images are." He may have dreamed of love, but here he encounters the actual presence of another, and, in the process of "learning to love, at length he is taught / To know he does not." This is a bitter notion, but in the world of *The Age of Anxiety* there is no such thing as love. Sexual attraction becomes ludicrous as, "Blind on the bride-bed, the bridegroom snores." . . .

The fourth age takes us back to the circus imagery of *The Sea and the Mirror*. There Auden used the circus as a form of art too close to life to have any purgative effect on the audience. Here he uses it as life itself, ordinary life with the illusions of personal fulfillment taken from it. Our life in this world is, as Rosetta terms it, an "Impermanent appetitive flux," and the world itself no more than a "clown's cosmos." . . .

Malin presents man in the fifth age as "an astonished victor, . . . at last / Recognition surrounds his days." He feels as though he has made his peace with the meaning of life. His anxiety seems to lessen as "He learns to speak / Softer and slower, not to seem so eager." He no longer feels trapped in the circus ring and ruled by a mob; he now finds the world a dull, bland place.

Emble, however, caught up in his own youth, refuses to move so swiftly into stagnant middle age. He demands to know why Malin and the others must "Leave out the worst / Pang of youth." What youth wants most is to know what will happen. Afraid of time, youth asks, "Shall we ever be asked for? Are we simply / Not wanted at all?" Emble is the only one of the characters who is still bound by youth; as Auden describes him earlier, he suffers "from that anxiety about himself and his future which haunts, like a bad smell, the minds of most young men."[4] He is disturbed by time in a different way from Quant or Rosetta, for he is still young enough to demand a future from the world—he wants an answer from Caesar, from the world. . . .

. . . The fifth age is the most depressing because it is Quant's. He dominates it and tries to eliminate all hope. His attitude is that if man cannot adjust to mediocrity, it is too bad. That is all there is. If man asks for more, the world only gets worse.

So, by the sixth age, man, the anxious, mediocre creature, begins to show his age. The road to mediocrity is almost complete, and now man can only pine "for some / Nameless Eden where . . . the children play . . . / Since they needn't know they're not happy." Impotent, aged, and successful, Malin's man of the sixth age is past the point of worrying and almost past the point of caring.

By the time Malin reaches the seventh age, his hypothetical man is tired out; "His last illusions have lost patience / With the human enterprise." The other characters have passed the point of personal involvement; none of them is ready to die just yet. So they examine the future, both their own and that of general man. Rosetta says that for all men "Poor and penalized [is] the private state." Emble adds a personal note: "Must I end like that?"

With the conclusion of "The Seven Ages," Auden's intent in *The Age of Anxiety* begins to emerge. He wishes to give us a picture of the damned in a world gone mad. Malin, the prospective priest, seems no priest at all, but a malicious psychoanalyst. He knows what is wrong with life but not how to cure it. He is able to bring the other characters out, to get them to confess their failings and hostilities, but he is unable to offer them a better way. . . .

The next phase of their journey is through space rather than time. They have seen, through Malin's guided tour, that man's movement through life leads only to death, not to happiness. Perhaps contentment lies in the other direction, in finding the "Regressive road to Grandmother's House." By travelling through life as though it were a landscape, man might find "that state of prehistoric happiness," "The Quiet Kingdom."

The first act of their play ends with the authors/actors dissatisfied with what they have discovered. Having tried to examine what the past, present, and future mean to each of them, they have seen nothing save the horror of the process of aging until death. The journey through "The Seven Ages" was a realistic one, composed by a group of people sitting and talking about their separate real or imagined experiences. "The Seven Stages," the second act of the play done by the characters of *The Age of Anxiety,* is completely nonrealistic. In order to perform it, the characters try to submerge themselves into a group organism. As Auden says: "The more completely these four forgot their surroundings and lost their sense of time, the more sensitively aware of each other they became, until they achieved in their dream that rare community which is otherwise only attained in states of extreme wakefulness. But this did not happen all at once."[5] "The Seven Ages" was an attempt to find the perfect time of life, the age of innocence, fulfillment, or peace at which a man could be content to stop. "The Seven Stages" is an attempt to find home, the place where man can stay. Just as there was no time, there is no place. . . .

In the first stage of the characters' journey, each of them is alone, isolated with his own thoughts: "At first all is dark and each walks alone." This is the way that every journey—symbolic or real—begins, and, although the characters do not realize it yet, this is the way that each false journey ends. Their journey, then, because it is a false journey, is a journey to nowhere. . . .

This first pairing initiates the second stage of the journey and is important to the journey as a whole because it shows both the possibility and the futility of hope. Malin and Quant, the old, really have no hope; they are past caring or believing. However, Emble and Rosetta, the young, do have hope, for Emble in particular still cares, still believes that a meaningful journey is possible. As a young man, he considers himself to be among the exceptional, who differ from the ordinary, and he clings to his journey as a means of distinguishing himself. It is evident, however, that his is a journey towards what is not, and his desire to make the journey seems to come more from a fear of failure than from a genuine desire for the quest. His is a feeling of youthful insecurity disguised in the glamour of being different. As this second stage of the journey ends, it becomes apparent that there is no escape from self, either through the romance of youth that Emble and Rosetta typify, or through the resignation to age that we see in Malin and Quant.

As the couples turn inland, Emble and Rosetta by plane, Malin and Quant by train, the third stage of the journey begins, and a different path to escape is explored. Here, once again, is Auden's favorite separation of the exceptional and the ordinary. To Rosetta and Emble their trip by private plane renews the possibility of escape, for they feel that by skill they have escaped the "public prison" of human life. . . .

In juxtaposition with the flight of Emble and Rosetta is the train journey of Quant and Malin. Just as Emble and Rosetta find they cannot escape life by flying above it, so Quant and Malin find they cannot escape it by ironically immersing themselves in it. In spite of the knowledge that they are surrounded by "melancholics mewed in their dumps," "short blowhards," or all "the successful smilers the city can use," they still despair of the possibility of any kindness in the world and feel that the only available guide is no more than a "mad oracle."

High or low, by attempted escape or attempted immersion, the characters complete the third stage of their journey still failures as they arrive in the city. Malin speaks for them all in commenting on the city. It is an ugly place, the seat of a "facetious culture" with its "Publishing houses, pawnshops and pay toilets." The people are no better than the place in Malin's eyes, and all he really wants to know about them is "How are these people punished?"

From the city they take a trolley car northward to "the big house," which is the end of the journey's fourth stage. Rosetta's fantasy since her unhappy childhood has been of the mansion in which she wishes she had been reared and to which she feels she will return. It is no wonder, then, that it is she who exclaims on sighting "the big house," "In I shall go, out I shall look."

While she is within, the others wait, examining the outside. Quant says, "The facade has a lifeless look." The house is, of course, the human body, with its "book-lined rooms at the back" serving as the brain and "the guards at the front gate [who] / Change with the seasons" serving as the senses. Man, as he contemplates his house from the outside, is a sorry creature; he cannot even conceal his failings, for the outside world watches his "ruined kitchen-maids / Blubber behind the bushes."

Within the house it is no better, as Rosetta reports on her return. In her desire to see life and the world in their proper perspective, inside the big house of her dreams Rosetta has unwittingly forced herself to see life as it is, complete with all its agony and ugliness. Of her vision she says, "I would gladly forget; let us go quickly." In Rosetta's experience, "The significant note is nature's cry / Of long-divided love," for although she does not understand it, Rosetta has seen Auden's version of the world without Christ. It is a world of "malice" and "greed" where "things" are "thrown into being," and the cry of "long-divided love" is the separation of man from God, the existence of Eros without Agape.

After a short race, the characters arrive at the "forgotten graveyard," which is the end of the fifth stage. The graveyard is a "still / Museum [exhibiting] / The results of life." Yet, even here life begins again, for around the dead "Flittermice, finches / And flies restore / Their lost milieu." These "occasional creatures," the opposite of poor, desperate, unoccasional man, "Blindly, playfully" bridge "death's eternal gap" with their simple "quotidian joy." The difference between man and the rest of nature is put quite plainly. Man does not bridge the "gap" playfully, he does not breed in graveyards, or at least he would like to think he does not.

Once again, the characters pair off, this time Rosetta with Quant and Emble with Malin. . . . Emble and Rosetta feel they want each other and feel guilty about it; Malin and Quant recognize the desires of Rosetta and Emble, yet feel the demands of their own desires as well. All that remains for the characters to do is to face this new pairing and its concomitant absurdity.

This they begin to do as they confront the temptations of the hermetic gardens. Emble is willing, perhaps, to try the possibilities, illusions, and realities of the gardens, and, out of desperation, even Rosetta is willing; but Quant and Malin are not: "They become uneasy and unwell." The charm of the gardens, offering the possibility of action, seems to the characters to be an accusation, a ridicule of their impotence. . . . Gathering their guilt and the resultant imaginary physical ills, "they plunge into the labyrinthine forest and vanish down solitary paths, with no guide but their sorrows, no companion but their own voices," as they begin the seventh and final stage of the journey. They wander through the forest, despairing of their ills, begging mercy. Finally they meet at the forest's edge where they are confronted by the desert, which represents the completion of the first half of the seventh stage.

Their journey of escape is almost done. They began with water, a symbolic birth, and they must end with sand, a symbolic death. However, the desert means more to Auden in this context than merely death. In their fear of the wastes of the desert the characters see mirrored all their fears of living: to cross the desert is to make the journey through a lifetime in the world. . . . [Quant] asks the central secular question of The Age of Anxiety: "Do I love this world so well / That I have to know how it ends?"

As they stand, caught by this question and the sudden fear that there really is no meaning, no positive solution to the problem of existing, their journey completes itself before their eyes: the desert turns into the real world "from which their journey has been one long flight," and their quest for escape ends in a hallucinatory exaggeration of the horrors of reality. What they see, as Emble identifies it for them, is "A grinning gap, a growth of nothing / Pervaded by vagueness."

So, their mock quest completed, their worst fears realized, they end their play, wake up, and leave the bar. . . .[6]

The remaining three sections of The Age of Anxiety follow the characters from the bar to their homes. They do not have exact memories of their journey through the seven stages, and instead of the despair they felt at the conclusion of the journey, they now have a vague urge for companionship. They all accept Rosetta's invitation, actually extended only to Emble, to go to her apartment for a final drink. While in a cab on the way to her apartment, they compose the lament which constitutes Part IV of The Age of Anxiety, "The Dirge."

Having completed their journey through the life and country of man, and having found no hope inherent in either man or nature, they have come to the conclusion that life could not have continued so long "had not some semi-divine stranger with superhuman powers . . . appeared from time to time to rescue both [man and nature], for a brief bright instant, from their egregious destructive blunders." It is the absence of such a "savior" in their present day that they lament. . . .

Part V of *The Age of Anxiety* is entitled "The Masque." It is in this section that the action of the work is climaxed. In a long introductory paragraph, Auden says of his characters and, by extension, of all mankind:

> Had they been perfectly honest with themselves, they would have had to admit that they were tired and wanted to go home alone to bed. That they were not was in part due, of course, to vanity, the fear of getting too old to want fun or too ugly to get it, but also to unselfishness, the fear of spoiling the fun for others. Besides, only animals who are below civilization and the angels who are beyond it can be sincere. Human beings are, necessarily, actors who cannot become something before they have first pretended to be it; and they can be divided, not into the hypocritical and the sincere, but into the sane who know they are acting and the mad who do not.

One of the ideas Auden is particularly concerned with in the long works of the forties is the relationship between actor and character, or man and his mask. He feels that it is most human to pick a guise to wear or to choose a particular role to play in life. . . .

In the earlier sections of *The Age of Anxiety,* the characters tried to escape the problems of life through a make-believe quest. To Auden's mind, this is psychologically dangerous for, as he showed at the conclusion of "The Seven Stages," the real world cannot be escaped or altered by such an attempt. Yet even so, the dream of escape is not nearly so dangerous as believing that one can change the real world by merely willing change; after all, the dream can always be forgotten or hidden, but the real world cannot. We see the dangers of trying to bring man's will to bear on reality in the doomed attempt of Rosetta and Emble to realize the "sweet shared secret" of their dreams.

The tone of "The Masque" is intentionally satiric. In spite of their hopes, the characters know that they are acting; they are only momentarily deluded, not mad. They are making one last attempt to believe that Eros is "the answer" and that it is manifested in sexual intercourse. . . .

. . . Following Quant's libation (pouring the dregs of a glass on the carpet), invocation of "the local spirits" . . . all the characters join together in a chorus which describes the glory that the union of Emble and Rosetta will bring to the world.

With this hope for a redemption in sexual terms for the agonies of the world, Quant and Malin exit, accompanied by Rosetta. Once she has seen them to the elevator, she returns to her apartment and finds Emble passed out on her bed. She realizes that he is not at fault, that he did try ("You danced so bravely") as long as the illusion of romance was just that and nothing more. The trouble came, she feels, when she tried to make the mock marriage into a real one, when, instead of making believe she was his "dish," she began to wish that she really were.

In her soliloquy, Rosetta casts herself as the Wandering Jew in opposition to Emble's Christian Knight. . . .

From this point on, the subject of Rosetta's soliloquy is no longer Emble and herself, but herself alone. She sees no hope in self-delusion, for no matter how hard she tries to run, God the Father, like the Hound of Heaven, will pursue. Her lies have been multiple, her life imaginary, yet the real has never really been hidden from the guilt she feels is God.

. . . .

The "Epilogue" which comprises Part VI and concludes *The Age of Anxiety* is composed of alternating choruses of "an impromptu ballad" which Quant sings to himself while walking home, and the thoughts of Malin as he rides the subway home. Quant's snatches of song seem to make up a cynical commentary on man's foibles through history. His song is a war ballad which makes fun of the inhumanity of the various committees and subcommittees of "the Victory Powers" as they foolishly chop up the holdings of the defeated, such action being brought to the attention of the public by "Commentators who broadcast by the courtesy of a shaving cream."

The thoughts of Malin as he proceeds homeward are as different from Quant's flippancies as Rosetta's attempt at self-examination is from Emble's blocking out of consciousness. Malin begins by accepting the foolishness of the characters' quest. . . .

He is dulled into believing that in this life on earth there is meaning only in the sense that there is no meaning. We do not learn from the past, and the future merely depresses. . . .

At the core of this despair in man's ineptitude is the knowledge that we know nothing: "We're quite in the dark." There is one way out, but it is that of which we are most ignorant. Man tries to use reason to find the connection between his life in time ("The clock we are bound to obey") and his hope that his life will not end ("the miracle we must not despair of"), but this "secret" belongs to neither reason nor imagination; it's "too obvious and near to notice" and is "reserved / For the eyes of faith to find."

At this point in Malin's thought, his subway train comes out from underground onto the Manhattan Bridge. The sun has risen, it is day. Malin wraps up the thoughts and activities of the night.

What all the characters had set out to do was to escape the world as it is, to find some safe truth or "lost dad" or "colossal father" who would say: "It's all right, don't worry." Instead they found only worse horrors, more falseness, and finally the world again, unchanged, its ugliness merely intensified. . . .

It would seem to be our very humanity which causes our distress, our refusal to admit that "We belong to our kind, / Are judged as we judge." For in trying to escape time and space, we do not realize that both of them constantly "respond in our own / Contradictory dialect." Everything is, in short, our fault and not our fault. . . . "In our anguish we struggle / To elude Him, to lie to Him, yet His love observes / His appalling promise. . . ."

He, of course, is Christ, and Malin's waiting unawares is a far cry from Rosetta's recognition of the need to take the hands of her "poor fat father." We are back with the narrator of *For the Time Being* or with Caliban in *The Sea and the Mirror* as Malin, no longer satanic but sadly priest-like, offers salvation but not happiness. . . .

In comparison with the tightly knit structure of *The Sea and the Mirror* or even *For the Time Being, The Age of Anxiety* seems to be a work without movement or purpose. The things that *do* happen in *The Age of Anxiety* are mitigated by the fact that the characters do not really grow. One has the feeling that the "moments of truth" experienced by Rosetta and Malin have happened before and will happen again, as of course they have and will. This is Auden's point in *The Age of Anxiety*. He wants to give a picture of the modern world in action, and to show through the futile, repetitive action of his characters the futility of man's attempts either to escape or to resolve the problems of this world. At the same time, as in both *The Sea and the Mirror* and *For the Time Being,* Auden feels obliged to offer an eventual way out: the recognition of the existence of the Divine as a presence and a world separate from oneself and this world. This attempt, which works so well in the Caliban/Ariel relationship in *The Sea and the Mirror,* and somewhat less well in the Simeon/Herod juxtaposition in *For the Time Being,* seems to fail completely in *The Age of Anxiety.* Perhaps this is because Auden stacks the deck against his characters. Malin, who articulates "the message," is unable to make use of what he says. He is damned to the point where not only can he not act, but after speaking he must return to his normal life to forget, until the next drunken evening, what he has thought and said. This process is not the one described by the Narrator of *For the Time Being* when he discusses the manner in which we forget Christ save when reminded of Him at Christmas and at Easter; what happens to Malin is not induced by experiencing either the Incarnation or its reenactment. Malin, through the artificial heightening of his anxiety by drink, has felt the emptiness of his life more strongly than he normally does and so, as a consequence, becomes religious. But, as he himself so deliberately points out, what he feels is only "the flash / Of negative knowledge." He disgusts himself and knows what he is not rather than what he is. His religion is a momentary feeling of necessity, not a permanent change of heart or direction as Caliban's is. He is not a priest, but he is not an antipriest either; he is simply a lost, befuddled man, able to bear living as long as he does not think. He is the type of Christian who falls back on faith as the need arises, but never sees it as a way of life.

Malin is the "voice" of *The Age of Anxiety.* Through him, more than through any other character, Auden speaks. What Malin says is important. It is important to recognize Christ, to recognize that "He speaks / Our creaturely cry." But it is more important to do something with this recognition. Momentary conversion while drunk means nothing, the guilt of the hangover vitiates all. To Auden, Malin is *not* a good man. His despair, his feeling of ineptitude render him impotent, incapable of genuine commitment. He lives in the dark, "too blind or too bored" to really advance.

Yet perhaps the failure of Malin is necessary to compensate for the success of Caliban, for in *The Age of Anxiety* Auden is trying, once and for all, to get rid of the minister/teacher persona of his earlier poems. More like Tennyson now than Shelley, he wants to make clear the feeling he has that no one knows precisely what life, or afterlife, is all about; that there is no such thing as knowledge, that there is such a thing as faith. In order to do this, he shows us his "old" reason foundering on the rocks. The characters he gives us are modern human beings looking at the abyss and stumbling back into ordinary, frustrated lives. They are all variations on "Auden of the thirties." They search, they grope, until one—Malin—chances upon the Truth. There is, as yet, no Way or Life. These Auden gives us later.

Notes

1. For an extensive examination of various types of quests, see Auden's "K's Quest," *The Kafka Problem,* ed. Angel Flores (New York: New Directions, 1946).

2. Auden says elsewhere in regard to the relationship of the mirror to art: "Art, as the late Professor R. G. Collingwood pointed out, is not Magic, i.e., a means by which the artist communicates or arouses his feelings in others, but a mirror in which they may become conscious of what their own feelings really are: its proper effect, in fact, is disenchanting. "By significant detail it shows us that our present state is neither as virtuous nor as secure as we thought, and by the lucid pattern into which it unifies these details, its assertion that order is *possible,* it faces us with the command to make it actual." W. H. Auden, "The Poet of the Encirclement" (a review of *A Choice of Kipling's Verse,* ed. T. S. Eliot), *The New Republic,* October 25, 1943, pp. 579–81.

3. For another version of this Eros-Logos relationship, see Auden's poem "Law Like Love" in *Collected Poetry* [1945], pp. 74–76.

4. *The Age of Anxiety* (New York: Random House, 1947), p. 6.

5. Ibid., p. 57.

6. Auden, in "K's Quest," describes what he calls the "Dream (or Divine Comedy) Quest," and in so doing, describes the positive version of the quest of the seven stages. He says (pp. 48–49): "The purpose of the journey is no object but spiritual knowledge, a vision of the reality behind appearances, while the dreamer, when he wakes, can henceforth live his life on earth. The dreamer is, theoretically, everyman, i.e., it is not by any act or virtue of his that he attains this vision, for the vision is a gift of Divine Grace. It does not necessarily follow that the vision will change his life, but if he does not change, his responsibility is greater than that of those who have never been granted his vision."

[From *Man's Place: An Essay on Auden* ("In Praise of Limestone" and "Bucolics")]

RICHARD JOHNSON

. . . The comic perspective is more fully realized in another perspective poem, "In Praise of Limestone" (*CSP*, p. 238; *SP*, p. 114), which discusses, among other matters, the "worldly duty" of a fantasy Eden imagined as a limestone landscape. Here again, the poem gives explicit directions for viewing. . . .

> Mark these rounded slopes
> With their surface fragrance of thyme and, beneath,
> A secret system of caves and conduits; hear the springs
> That spurt out everywhere with a chuckle,
> Each filling a private pool for its fish and carving
> Its own little ravine whose cliffs entertain
> The butterfly and the lizard; examine this region
> Of short distances and definite places
> [*CSP*, pp. 238–239, *SP*, p. 114]

The scene is both arbitrary—it could be any set of images—and necessary—for each person it can be only one set of images.

Most simply, this is the world of childish fantasy carried into adulthood. There is a gentle irony throughout, beautifully realized in the speaker's voice: limestone is to be praised precisely because it is malleable; it is both definite ("these solid statues") and indefinite ("it dissolves in water"); the definite indefiniteness of our inner fantasy world makes us unique persons.

What we are asked to view and to praise is a fanciful web of not necessarily related images and actions, praiseworthy precisely because innocent, silly, and, in an important sense, unreal. Objects in this world change immediately as the subject wishes; everything is surface and illusion, and, for just this reason, has the pure reality of a child's daydreams; the mirror of art becomes, here, a door to the other side of the looking glass. Thus neither the poet nor the scientist feels at home:

The poet,
Admired for his earnest habit of calling
The sun the sun, his mind Puzzle, is made uneasy
By these marble statues which so obviously doubt
His antimythological myth.

(CSP, p. 240; *SP,* p. 116)

That is, the poet works under the myth that he can bring word and image together, that the sun (thing) is "the sun" (word); this is an antimythological belief in that it supposes a wedding of fact and fiction that we do not ordinarily ask of myth; it is still myth because it is, for the poet, more a matter of faith than fact. . . .

The importance of this Arcadian daydream world rests in its apparent frivolity, triviality, unpredictability, and outlandishness. The point, which Auden argues in many places in many ways, is that the uniqueness of each person, and his capacity for loving, are based, at least in part, on his internal landscape. This landscape, far from reflecting, as it does in so much modern literature, depths of impassioned feeling, is nothing very spectacular: "Among the half dozen or so things for which a man of honor should be prepared, if necessary, to die, the right to play, the right to frivolity, is not the least" (*DH,* p. 89).

Frivolity, because it is unpredictable and irresponsible, reminds man that there exists no facsimile of himself, and that what the world may well regard as his weaknesses are the bases of his uniqueness. "A sense of humor develops in a society to the degree that its members are simultaneously conscious of being each a unique person and of being all in common subjection to unalterable laws" (*DH,* p. 372). At the end of "In Praise of Limestone," frivolity has modulated into a quixotic, religious playfulness:

. . . if
Sins can be forgiven, if bodies rise from the dead,
  These modifications of matter into
Innocent athletes and gesticulating fountains,
  Made solely for pleasure, make a further point:
The blessed will not care what angle they are regarded from,
  Having nothing to hide.

(CSP, p. 241; *SP,* p. 117)

Characteristically, Auden makes his point in terms of perspective: the blessed will not care what angle they are regarded from. Blessedness, forgiveness, love, resurrection: these are not matters of looking at things in a certain way; each is *sui generis,* and the closest we can come to imagining what they are like is to send our imaginations back to the world of psychomythic Eden. Blessedness, pure innocence, by definition needs no proper perspective, but, since we do not live in a world of essences, we must still look at things from some place.

Perhaps the best way to describe the total perspective of "In Praise of Limestone" is to say that it probes, and accepts, the disproportions and surprises in the relations between the busy world and the fantasy world, the relations among the various functions of the fantasy world, and the relationship between its apparent unimportance and its actual service. Such probing uncovers both political and religious ramifications. And it tells something about the importance of distinguishing between what is serious and what is not: . . . "Christianity draws a distinction between what is frivolous and what is serious, but allows the former its place. What it condemns is not frivolity but idolatry, that is to say, taking the frivolous seriously" (*DH*, p. 430). "In Praise of Limestone" has a shifting perspective, one that surveys the landscape, sorting out what is serious from what is not. It shows the landscape as a pure fantasy world, then as a slightly salacious land of wish projection, then as the abode of the ordinary, then as a backward, seedy province, then as the bulwark of individuality against the encroachment of the Great Powers, and finally as our best image of ideal love and the forgiveness of sins. Limestone is the correct image because it can represent all of these things; its virtue is that the imagination can shape it as it pleases. Thus we see another characteristic strategy of the comic artist: he lets the imagination run wild. Rather than seeking an accommodation between reality and the imagination, he grants the imagination hegemony within its proper realm (as Prospero frees Ariel) in order to keep the distinction between illusion and reality clear, in order to ridicule the pomposities of overseriousness, and in order to let it give us images of what we might be.

. . . .

By its title, *Bucolics* claims kinship with a complicated literary tradition. The pastoral mode involves the sophisticated adoption of a conventionalized innocence, and thus creates a complex interplay between artifice and simplicity. As a long-developing tradition, it carries with it considerable luggage of conventionalized attitudes and techniques, and yet it is always applied to defining the simple, natural, and unadorned; every new use of the tradition both restates the element of simplicity and adds to the accumulation of convention.

Teasing combinations of simplicity and high artifice are so general and pervasive in Auden's work as to need little mention. He has always been interested in "worlds imaginary, but real" (to use his characterization of Tolkien's works), in "secondary worlds." A characteristic pattern of his work is that of going into a world of fantasy and illusion to discover "where we really are," just as, in *The Sea and the Mirror,* a set of multiple actions is based on the original pattern from *The Tempest* of the courtly parties going into the half-natural, half-artificial world of the enchanted island to discover the "actual" relationships usable and desirable in the courtly world. . . .

Pastoral brings all these concerns into a complex artistic form, but the central question concerns the meaning of the word *natural*. For Auden, this question demands that particular attention be given to man's simultaneous existence in and out of nature, as a being who has evolved out of a purely natural existence and who no longer directly *perceives* himself as such a creature (since the immediate data of his consciousness are those of his existential freedom as a historical being) yet at the same time *knows* that he is a natural being. Paradoxically, perhaps, the further he "evolves" away from nature, the more he discovers that both he and the natural world are evolving things and that their evolutionary stories are interdependent. At an advanced state *of* evolution, man begins to be able *to trace* evolution. Thus, just as the light, playful, and at times apparently frivolous manner of *Bucolics* is akin to the pastoral mode, so also is their serious attention to man's nature and his art.

It is possible to identify specifically at least one source of the ideas and language of *Bucolics*. The first stanza of the second poem, "Woods," reads as follows:

> Sylvan meant savage in those primal woods
> Piero di Cosimo so loved to draw,
> Where nudes, bears, lions, sows with women's heads,
> Mounted and murdered and ate each other raw,
> Nor thought the lightning-kindled bush to tame
> But, flabbergasted, fled the useful flame.
> (*CSP*, p. 257; *SP*, p. 145)

The stanza clearly echoes several passages from Erwin Panofsky's essay, "The Early History of Man in Two Cycles of Paintings by Piero di Cosimo," especially one in which Panofsky discusses Piero the man: "But one of Vasari's expressions furnishes a key to the nature of the man: '*si contentava di veder salvatico ogni cosa, come la sua natura.*' This word *salvatico,* derived from *silva* like our 'savage,' explains in a flash both Piero's obsession with primitivistic notions and his magic power in bringing them to life by his brush." Earlier, Panofsky quotes Boccaccio, who, to demonstrate that Vulcan is the "very founder of human civilization," quotes Vitruvius' account of the origins of building: " 'In the olden days men were born like wild beasts in woods and caves and groves, and kept alive by eating raw food. Somewhere, meanwhile, the close-grown trees, tossed by storms and winds, and rubbing their branches together, caught fire. Terrified by the flames, those who were near the spot fled.' " Later in the essay, discussing two Pieros in the Metropolitan Museum in New York, "Hunting Scene" and "Return from the Hunt," Panofsky says: "As there is no real separation between mankind and animals on the one hand, mankind and half-beasts such as satyrs and centaurs on the other, all these creatures love and mate, or fight and kill, indiscriminately, without paying any attention whatever to their common enemy, the forest fire. . . . [It is] a jungle fight of all against all (for instance, a lion attacking a bear but at the same time being attacked by a man)." And, discussing still another Piero, "Landscape with Animals," he notes:

> The woods are still haunted by the strange creatures which resulted from the promiscuous mating of men and animals, for the sow with the face of a woman and the goat with the face of a man are by no means Bosch-like phantasms. . . . These strange creatures seem peacefully to share the woods and fields with lions, deer, cranes, cows, and an enticing family of bears. . . . [But] these beasts and half-beasts are not so much peaceful as exhausted by flight and stunned by terror of the forest fire. Man, too, is now aware of this fire, but instead of being frightened he seizes his chance to catch some of the cows and oxen that have fled from the burning woods; their future yoke he carries providently on his shoulder.[1]

It should be clear that when Auden wrote *Bucolics* he was not only aware of the Panofsky essay but very thoroughly acquainted with it: the language of the first stanza of "Woods" is a thorough mixture of the language of several different passages from the essay. Indeed, the texture of the stanza, with its scrambled images and actions, recreates the quality both of the paintings referred to and of Panofsky's descriptions of them.

"Influences," "sources," and "echoes" are tricky matters in Auden's poetry. Even when we have established that Auden knew at a particular time a given source, we can never with complete assurance establish a connection between general views in the source and general views in Auden's work. Everything we know about Auden suggests that his habit is to refashion materials from "sources" to make them serve his own purpose. Auden's critics have often confused a name with a field of interest; for instance, Freudianism, Marxism, or Darwinism with interest in psychology, society, or evolution. Nonetheless, with these caveats in mind, I would like to suggest that Panofsky's essay indicates much about the themes, methods, and structure not only of "Woods," but also of the whole of *Bucolics*. To demonstrate this point, it is necessary to return to the essay.

Panofsky attempts, primarily by iconographical identification and analysis, to establish the thematic unity of two groups of superficially unrelated Pieros, as "one comprehensive cycle which, in a rich and persuasive manner, would have represented the two earliest phases of human history as described in classical writing . . . . : 'Vulcanus,' raging in the woods, while man, not yet befriended by him, shares the excitements and fears of animals and hybrid monsters; and 'Vulcanus' again, descending upon the earth in human form and pointing the path towards civilization" (p. 57). Panofsky wants not only to establish thematic connections among the now scattered paintings, but also to argue that the two series were "executed for the same employer" as a grand design for a small anteroom and a grand *salone,* and further to suggest that Piero's much later depictions of Prometheus "might be considered a belated postscript to the Vulcan epic," with Prometheus as a kind of successor to Vulcan, bringing not the physical fire of Vulcan but a celestial light of knowledge, though "at the expense of happiness and peace of mind."

Behind this argument about the composition, arrangement, and mythography of the paintings lies Panofsky's larger concern—more fully developed in his more famous essay, *"Et in Arcadia Ego:* Poussin and the Elegiac Tradition"—with the humanistic implications of two conflicting notions of the nature of man's early history:

> There had been from the very beginning of classical speculation two contrasting opinions about the primeval life of man: The "soft" or positivistic primitivism as formulated by Hesiod depicted the primitive form of existence as a "golden age," in comparison with which the subsequent phases were nothing but successive stages of one prolonged Fall from Grace; whereas the "hard," or negativistic, primitivism imagined the primitive form of existence as a truly bestial state, from which mankind had fortunately escaped through technical and intellectual progress.
>
> Both these conceptions were reached by a mental abstraction from civilized life. But while "soft" primitivism imagines a civilized life cleansed of everything abhorrent and problematic, "hard" primitivism imagines a civilized life deprived of all comforts and cultural achievements. "Soft" primitivism idealizes the initial condition of the world, and is therefore in harmony with a religious interpretation of human life and destiny, particularly with the various doctrines of Original Sin. "Hard" primitivism, on the other hand, sought to be realistic in its reconstruction of the initial state of the world, and therefore fitted nicely into the scheme of a rationalistic, or even materialistic, philosophy. This philosophy imagines the rise of humanity as an entirely natural process, exclusively due to the innate gifts of the human race, whose civilization began with the discovery of fire, all ensuing developments being accounted for in a perfectly logical way.

Piero, as Panofsky presents him, is not a philosopher, but his treatment of images puts him clearly if unconsciously into the camp of the "hard" primitivists. Indeed, part of Panofsky's argument is that Piero, whom Vasari and everyone else thought of as rather an odd fish, so to speak, arrived at a sophisticated evolutionism not through theory but through his own atavistic experiences:

> Like Lucretius, Piero conceived of human evolution as a process due to the inborn faculties and talents of the race. . . . But like Lucretius, Piero was sadly aware of the dangers entailed by this development. He joyfully sympathized with the rise of humanity beyond the bestial hardships of the stone age, but he regretted any step beyond the unsophisticated phase which he would have termed the reign of Vulcan and Dionysos. To him civilization meant a realm of beauty and happiness as long as man kept in close contact with

Nature, but a nightmare of oppression, ugliness and distress as soon as man became estranged from her.[2]

As in the essay on Poussin, Panofsky concludes that the true Arcadian spirit more closely approximates "hard" primitivism, with its evolutionist and progressive affinities, than it does the "soft" primitivism of sentimental arcadianism.

With this summary of Panofsky's essay in mind, I would suggest that *Bucolics* is closely related to the paintings of Piero as described by Panofsky; that the poems address themselves to questions connected with the categories of "hard" and "soft" primitivism and hence with the relation of art and civilization to man's origins; that the seven poems can be thought of as a grouping similar to that which Panofsky postulates for Piero's paintings. Since the essay is Auden's direct source, it does not really matter whether Panofsky's speculation is right; what matters is only that Auden found it useful. The series is not a narrative of the prehistory and history of man but a series of *paysages moralisés* whose iconography suggests successive stages in man's development: Auden's treatment of images is somewhat similar to Panofsky's treatment of iconography.

Auden's decision to construct iconographic landscapes rather than narrative allegories probably has two origins. One probable source is the apparent failure of *The Age of Anxiety,* which attempts to treat the phylogenic and ontogenic history of man both as a series of landscapes and as a series of narratives growing out of a dramatized situation; the work suffers, I think, from a confusion of spatial and temporal form.[3] A more positive source is Auden's long-standing interest in allegorical landscape as a method of presentation, evidenced not only in Auden's reading of such essays as Panofsky's, but also, and more important, in his own superb essay, *The Enchafèd Flood, or, The Romantic Iconography of the Sea,* first delivered as lectures in 1949 and published in 1950.

The speaker of *Bucolics* is not a shepherd; but if we accept as pastoral Marvell's "The Mower against Gardens," we certainly can also accept *Bucolics,* noting that its speaker, with his fine mixture of naiveté and sophistication, is a fair modern rendering of the traditional shepherd-poet. Although the play of language and reference is very much alive to the incongruities between hard and soft primitivism, the poems ultimately use the two "modes" or "concepts" as the components of a multiple perspective on man, whom Auden conceives as both a fallen and an evolved being (fallen insofar as he is a historical and history-making being, evolved insofar as he is a creature). But his status as a historical being can be defined as a part of his evolution, and he now exists with mnemonic traces of both atavistic primitivism and Edenic simplicity. Although there are substantial contradictions between hard and soft primitivism, the contradictions are necessary to define the state of man. The poems are finally as much about art as they are about nature, but especially about art as a part of the evolutionary development of man and as an instance of those impulses towards speech and making that define man's "fall" into humanity. Auden, like Piero, might well celebrate Vulcan—"the only ungentlemanly workman . . . in the Olympian leisure class"[4]—as he does Hephaestos, Vulcan's Greek prototype.

"Winds," the opening poem, brings together and compares three acts of creation: of *Homo sapiens,* of civil life, and of poetry. In the first stanza, we sense both festivity and stateliness, the serious purpose as well as the playful means of the verbal rites being undertaken:

> Deep, deep below our violences,
> Quite still, lie our First Dad, his watch
>   And many little maids,
> But the boneless winds that blow
>   Round law-court and temple
> Recall to Metropolis
>   That Pliocene Friday when,
> At His holy insufflation
>   (Had he picked a teleost
> Or an arthropod to inspire,
>   Would our death also have come?)
> One bubble-brained creature said;—
>   'I am loved, therefore I am'—:
> And well by now might the lion
>   Be lying down with the kid,
> Had he stuck to that logic.
>   (*CSP,* p. 255; *SP,* p. 143)

[The] lines suggest an archaeological find and, at the same time, a causal relation, as if our violences were connected to what lies deep below them. The sudden shift in diction, from the stately opening to "First Dad," introduces the kind of riddle that dominates the surface of the whole series: First Dad is both Adam and that primate from whom we evolved, a prehistoric ancestor; his watch and the many little maids suggest a primitive burial grounds, the geological strata in which fossils are found, and perhaps also a biological clock and the daughter cells that lead down to, and determine in part, the character of our present existence. In spite of the fact that our origins are buried, hence skeletons, "boneless winds" recall (jiggle the memory, are an image of) those origins. Pliocene Friday is a runic mixture of Darwinian and biblical accounts of creation, compressed in a phrase: Pliocene is the geological age of the evolution of man; Friday, if we use the Christian rather than the Jewish calendar, is the fifth day of creation, the day of man's creation; the hint of Good Friday is appropriate because, as the parenthetical phrase in the middle of the stanza suggests, death is implicit in creation. "Insufflation" continues the mixture of connotations, being a medical practice (one insufflates an organ, like the lungs or the fallopian tubes, by blowing a gas into it to discover patency), a religious ritual (one insufflates holy water to symbolize the presence of the Holy Spirit, a priest breathes on catechumens, presumably as a rite of initiation into belief), and the image of God's creation of man. The play of words telescopes accounts of creation and views of man as a spiritual and biological creature. Far from being an attempt to reconcile points of view, it works like the principle of complementarity: we understand man, necessarily, only if we understand him simultaneously as both spiritual being and biological creature: the word games create the necessary double focus.

The stanza is exactly dissected by the quirkish question that, once again, mixes religious and biological terminology, and further compounds the perspective by the double sense of inspire and the homonymic pun on anthropoid. The question is doubly a riddle: it might mean, had another species been given consciousness, would we know ourselves as dying creatures? It might also mean, had we, the inspired ones, been another species, would we still have been fallen creatures? And there is also the riddle of what the answer to either question is. The bubble-brained creature is the primate who, at the moment of the evolutionary jump, suddenly "fell into consciousness," that is, had a brain capable of attaining self-awareness. He is bubble-brained in the sense of having a small brain, in the slang sense of "stupid," and in the sense, biologically crucial and accurate, of having a hollow brain. Here, as often, Auden disguises a very precise idea by using a flippant term.

.   .   .   .

The final lines are also playfully riddling: the reference to Isaiah is mixed since the original biblical reference has the leopard lying down with the kid and the calf and the young lion and the fatling together; the mixture is in keeping with the image of a potential peaceable kingdom. More puzzling is the use of an image of the coming of the Lord as something that might be precipitated by sticking to the logic of love. We quickly see that there is a sense, for Auden, in which redemption is accelerated by following the gospel of love, but there is also a witty point in the formulation: Auden uses the animals of the Bible to figure the peace of redemption, to describe the hypothetical consequences of man's sticking to the logic that marked his emergence from the strictly animal world. Wind serves as an image both of memory (by which we recall our creaturely origins) and of the giving of life. . . . The sentence traces a journey backward to origins and forward to the possible consequences of following the doctrine of love; its playful dignity, fusing the divine and the human, is thus a figure for the divinity of human creation.

The first stanza suggests the compatibility of several accounts of man's creation; the second suggests that man's worldly goal, "the Authentic City," will also be reached by evolutionary processes:

> (Across what brigs of dread,
> Down what gloomy galleries,
> Must we stagger or crawl
> Before we may cry—O look!?)
> (*CSP*, p. 255; *SP*, p. 143)

The third stanza aligns the act of poetry with the other two acts of creation (of man and of the authentic city) and places both the poet and the reader between the origin and the goal. The poet, in a sense, prays that he may celebrate both man's origins and his direction:

> That every verbal rite
> May be fittingly done,
> And done in anamnesis
> Of what is excellent
> Yet a visible creature,
> Earth, Sky, a few dear names.
> (*CSP*, p. 256, *SP*, p. 144)

Man is an excellent creation, a miraculous one, and yet a creature, a being with a body who is visible to us and subject to biological law, and he is placed between earth and sky, his humanity manifest in his ability to name. . . .

"Woods" contains the specific references to the Pieros that depict man "ante Vulcanum" and "sub Vulcano"; it, too, covers a whole historical development, presented as a series of antitheses between "sylvan" and "savage," between soft and hard primitivism. The woods themselves are a device of perspective. They establish human scale, both in time, since the woods reach back into prehistory and will continue beyond the lifetime of living men, and in space, since they dwarf men. The poem is not so much about woods as about our continuing double attitude toward them, and indicates that there is psychological truth in both the "sylvan" and the "savage" views.

The poem takes the form of an extemporaneous discussion of its subject, an all-purpose description of the features and uses of woods; it makes apparently gratuitous references and takes tangents that, once mentioned, define the basic themes. It continually focuses attention on the way the meanings of words change and interact. The opening line draws attention to lexical changes, and the reference to the scene depicted by Piero suggests a connection between woods and the origin of speech: the fire in the woods brought the "savages" together for warmth, whence, grouped together, they invented speech as a means of mutual understanding. Separated from nature by our powers of speech, we continually return to nature and reinvolve ourselves with it; word play is both the method and, in part, the subject disclosed in the poem.

The playful nature of the poem's surface continually shows the savage within the sylvan: "Reduced to patches, owned by hunting squires, / Of villages with ovens and a stocks, / They whispered still of most unsocial fires" (*CSP*, p. 257; *SP*, p. 145). Civilization is not as civil as it thinks, and those savage woods, made sylvan, are owned by squires who hunt. The villages have ovens in which to cook the animals killed: the advance of civilization is to eat meat cooked rather than raw, as in the woods of the first stanza. They also have a stocks, the instrument of a human but inhumane punishment. The woods' whispering "still of most unsocial fires" recalls the use of winds, woods, and fire to represent stages of savagery and civility in Piero's woods. And the last three lines of the stanza specifically mock "soft" pastoral, by juxtaposing the synecdochical "Crown and Mitre" against the meiotic "silly flocks," by the play on the archaic ("worthy") and modern ("foolish") sense of "silly," and by the intentionally bad, but still revealing, pun on "flocks" (the "Mitre" warns its "flocks" to approve "the pasture's humdrum rhythms"). The reversals of meaning, the canny misuses, and the mocking metaphors work back to the central formulation: man is a natural creature who transcends, but never abandons, his natural origins. Every time he returns to nature, whether for a picinc or a pastoral poem, he replays the drama of his evolution.

. . . .

"Mountains," both the poem and the image, suggests much sharper divisions between natural and civil man and between man and nature than either of the first two poems. Like the solid, craggy stanza form, and like the mountains themselves, the poem builds an image of a severe hiatus between civil and precivil man. The poem takes us into the mountains, and, iconographically, back to ages of ice, stone, and bronze:

> Tunnels begin, red farms disappear
>   Hedges turn to walls,
> Cows become sheep, you smell peat or pinewood, you hear
>   Your first waterfalls,
>
> And what looked like a wall turns out to be a world
>   With measurements of its own
> And style of gossip. To manage the Flesh,
>   When angels of ice and stone
> Stand over her day and night who make it so plain
> They detest any kind of growth, does not encourage
> Euphemisms for the effort: here wayside crucifixes
>   Bear witness to a physical outrage,
>   And serenades too
> Stick to bare fact; 'O my girl has a goitre,
>   I've a hole in my shoe!'

> Dour. Still, a fine refuge. That boy behind his goats
>   Has the round skull of a clan
> That fled with bronze before a tougher metal.
> (CSP, pp. 259–260; SP, pp. 147–148)

The series has moved forward in two senses: the reference in "Mountains" to the Bronze Age indicates a stage in man's early history later than that at the beginning of "Woods"; and the degree of division, the sharpness of the split between civil man and natural man (an internal as well as an external split), has increased. The images of the natural world are more foreboding: "perfect monsters—remember Dracula— / Are bred on crags in castles"; even mountain climbers "are a bit alarming." But the images of civil man are also altered. The poem is full of phrases that suggest an effete civility—"a retired dentist who only paints mountains," "Well, I won't," "I'm nordic myself"— which fully emerges in the final stanza:

> To be sitting in privacy, like a cat
>   On the warm roof of a loft,
> Where the high-spirited son of some gloomy tarn
>   Comes sprinting down through a green croft,
> Bright with flowers laid out in exquisite splodges
> Like a Chinese poem, while, near enough, a real darling
> Is cooking a delicious lunch . . .
> (CSP, p. 260; SP, p. 148)

The language transforms the mountains from the gothic into the precious; the tough, "dour," noneuphemistic style gives way to terms like "exquisite," "delicious," "darling." Mountains, then, come to represent a severity of separation of man and nature and of natural and civil man that turns the human into cloying and the natural into ominous.

The first three poems form a subgroup depicting two parallel movements, from creation to Stone Age, from a balance of Eden, the world, and Paradise, to a comic imbalance, and then to a still comic but slightly ominous separation. The next two poems, "Lakes" and "Islands," are linked as mirror images ("What is cosier than the shore / Of a lake turned inside out?") and show two sides of civil man as well as two further, much later, stages in man's history.

"Lakes," at the center of the cycle, portrays a highly civilized coordination of human and nonhuman scale:

> A lake allows an average father, walking slowly,
>   To circumvent it in an afternoon,
> And any healthy mother to halloo the children
>   Back to her bedtime from their games across.
> (CSP, p. 260; SP, p. 149)

The size of lakes is defined by the rituals and schedules of family life, well regulated in accord with freedom and order: the father's pace and the mother's halloo define a balance of human scale and natural scale. Although the art does not advertise itself, the locutions, the control of vocabulary, the accumulation of images, and the modulations of tone are immensely skilful. The lake "allows" ("is large and small enough" and "permits") like a benign monarch. The father is "average" in the senses of "statistical mean" and "ordinary." The whole clause is a small triumph of phrasing—the precision of usage, so neatly expressing size and motion, is a lexical trope for the orderly view of nature "lakes" represent. The mother's healthy voice, bringing the children from *their* games to *her* bedtime, coordinates the lake's breadth and the human voice with a gracious balance of freedom and discipline, of nature and man.

Out of the deceptively homely descriptions emerge the images of the circle and the cross-lake dialogue as emblems of a proper relation between the patterns of life and the order of nature. These images are then extended. In the second stanza "A month in a lacustrine atmosphere / Would find the fluvial rivals waltzing not exchanging / . . . rhyming insults." In the third, "pensive chiefs" of Christianity converge, "making catholic the figure / Of three small fishes in a triangle." And in the fourth,

> Sly Foreign Ministers should always meet beside one,
>   For, whether they walk widdershins or deasil,
> The path will yoke their shoulders to one liquid centre
>   Like two old donkeys pumping as they plod.
>   (*CSP*, p. 261; *SP*, p. 149)

The image is double: as man is brought into harmony with nature, he opens up the possibility of harmony with other men, and "sly Foreign Ministers" can seem as unprepossessing as old donkeys pushing a yoke, going in opposite directions but working together.

Nonetheless, in the penultimate stanza of "Lakes," something like the tone of "Mountains" begins to emerge:

> Liking one's Nature, as lake-lovers do, benign
>   Goes with a wish for savage dogs and man-traps:
> One Fall, one dispossession, is enough, I'm sorry;
>   Why should I give Lake Eden to the Nation
> Just because every mortal Jack and Jill has been
>   The genius of some amniotic mere?
>   (*CSP*, p. 262; *SP*, p. 150)

The paradox of the poem's generally humane view of Nature is that it brings out much in man that is not humane. The last four lines of the stanza present the reasoning of the lake-lover, who, having found his "Lake Eden," deludes himself into thinking that he can return to a prelapsarian innocence and refuses to let anyone else in. Either allowing or refusing entrance to the Nation would destroy the paradisiacal quality, a paradox that suggests that the Edenic quality is illusory.

A passage from Empson's *Some Versions of Pastoral* clarifies (and is a likely source of) the last two lines of the stanza:

> The only passage that I feel sure involves evolution comes at the beginning of *Wonderland* (the most spontaneous and "subconscious" part of the books) when Alice gets out of the bath of tears that has magically released her from the underground chamber; it is made clear (for instance about watering-places) that the salt water is the sea from which life arose; as a bodily produce it is also the amniotic fluid (there are other forces at work here); ontogeny then repeats phylogeny, and a whole Noah's Ark gets out of the sea with her. In Dodgson's own illustration as well as Tenniel's there is the disturbing head of a monkey and in the text there is an extinct bird. Our minds having thus been forced back onto the history of species there is a reading of history from the period when the Mouse "came over" with the Conqueror. . . .

"Every mortal Jack and Jill" is both a colloquial phrase for "everybody," like "Tom, Dick, and Harry," and a way of saying that everyone who lives and thus will die ("mortal") is a fallen creature (like Jack and Jill, who did indeed fall). Originally, both phylogenically and ontogenically, we all came from water: from the salt water of the sea and from the amniotic fluid of the womb ("mere," in this context, is probably also a translingual pun on mother). It is also worth remembering that Auden is a Lewis Carroll admirer, and that a hint, even indirect, of the Alice books might well serve to exemplify one more comically inverted world in which the physical and psychological status of man is clarified by reversal. In any event, the stanza concludes that the believer in the benignity of nature ignores the truth of man's rise and fall from nature. . . .

"Islands" is a comic rendering of the escape from history to nature and of the fallacious identification of the lonely, isolated self with "natural man":

> Obsession with security
> In Sovereigns prevails;
> His Highness and The People both
> Pick islands for their jails.
>
> Once, where detected worldlings now
> Do penitential jobs,
> Exterminated species played
> Who had not read their Hobbes.
> (*CSP*, p. 262; *SP*, p. 151)

The logic [in the third and fourth stanzas] is comically spurious, and yet it has a point. The reference to Hobbes leads us directly back to arguments concerning civil man and natural man. If those species had read their Hobbes, they might not have "played"; they would have known that they were supposed to be at war. If they had read their Hobbes, they might have learned enough about humans to protect themselves from "extermination," a word that usually refers to the actions of men. Hobbes premised the need for a sovereign on the bestiality of man in a state of nature; that both democratic and monarchical forms of sovereignty perform the inhuman act of returning their enemies—each other—to a Hobbesian state of nature suggests that Hobbes might have been wrong concerning the civility of civil man.

The poem collects, in witty juxtapositions, a congregation of islanders: pirates, deluded saints (whose creaturely nature is perhaps a kind of millstone), criminals, Napoleons, misanthropes, solipsists. All think they are unique, but the very fact of being susceptible to listing ("Sappho, Tiberius and I") and to conjugation ("They go, she goes, thou goest, I go," which also suggests rote learning) indicates they are wrong. The major comment of the poem comes from its tone, which mocks the assumptions about nature and natural man of both Hobbesian "hard" primitivism and Romantic individualism, describing the islander in terms of pride, aloneness, imprisonment, exile, and solipsism, but suggesting, finally, that these characterize "civil" man as well: "Farmer and fisherman complain / The other has it good." The island character, like the island, is only an inside out turn of the lacustrine.

"Lakes" and "Islands," taken together, present as mirror images an overly humanized, rationalized landscape and the consequent exaltation of the self, both one-sided oversimplifications of man and his relation to nature. . . . [W]ith these poems Auden begins a second cycle of man's history, one that corresponds to the conflict he describes as existing between the Newtonian world view and that of the Romantic reaction. The series is not a precise historical sequence, and I do not mean that Auden is dramatizing specifically the historical conflict between the Enlightenment and Romanticism. Rather, the cycle is in the form of Piero's allegorical representations of man's development; the question is not so much *when* a given phase was reached as the order and nature and interrelationships of the various phases.

"Plains," to follow this hypothesis a step further, completes a second triad of poems by presenting the actualities, both natural and psychological, that both the Newtonian and Romantic views ignore. A plain is the raw stuff that each of the other images is a departure from, and ultimately returns to: ". . . a mere substance, a clay that meekly takes / The potter's cuff, a gravel that as concrete / Will unsex any space which it encloses" (*CSP*, p. 264; *SP*, p. 152). Depicted not as landscape but as the absence of landscape, plains have several references that are important to the whole series. Plains are the "neutral passive stuff" of the Newtonian universe, the fundamental material, without embroidery, on which both the Enlightenment and the Romantic reaction to it are based. . . . Like such poems as "The Shield of Achilles" and "Memorial for the City," "Plains" depicts a temporary equation of the historical and natural worlds, imaged by a bleak landscape, identified with, in particular, the modern world, and opposed to sentimental Arcadian wistfulness; at the same time, this is the place of decisive public events, where the strong "chamber with Clio." [John] Fuller suggests that the final phase, "which is not the case," refers to the world, in the sense that Wittgenstein uses the term "the case," and apparently means, "the way things are."[6] But, ironically, "Plains" approaches very closely both the sense of hard primitivism described by Panofsky in his essay on Poussin and the original Arcadian landscape, which Theocritus forsook for Sicily.

Mythification and demythification work in *Bucolics,* as elsewhere in Auden, like Yeatsian gyres, forever interpenetrating, disappearing into, and creating each other. Having arrived at the desolation represented by plains, the poet moves to "Streams," which celebrates water's "pure being, perfect in music and movement," "the most well-spoken of all the older / servants in the household of Mrs. Nature." The poem is perhaps the purest example of a "verbal rite fittingly done" and, in one sense of the term, the purest "pastoral" in the series. The poem has been praised for itself; it also has an important place in the design of the whole. It has no historical reference; that is part of its point. . . . Timeless in two senses, the poem portrays a personal vision of Eden; it is pure pastoral, that is, as Auden has said, a parable of Grace and Innocence. . . . Both the landscape and the dream at the end of "Streams," and hence of the whole series, correspond to the prose description of pretend Eden. . . . The play of language and sound complements the images of dream, play, and fancy in a pure Arcadian landscape. Auden, in his record jacket notes, describes the stanza form and rhyme patterns: "In each quatrain, lines 1 and 2 have twelve syllables each and masculine endings, line 3 has nine syllables and a feminine ending. A syllable within line 1 rhymes with a syllable within line 3, the final syllable of line 2 rhymes with the penultimate syllable of line 4, and the penultimate syllable of line 3 rhymes with a syllable within line 4" (Caedmon recording, TC 1019). . . . What is most impressive about the poem is the way in which all the verbal and tonal elements participate in its total design and that of the series. The verbal games, the dream, the croquet, the hints of polymorphous-perverse sexuality of childhood, the dream time and dream space, the dancing: all are part of a quixotic figure of Grace. What happens in the dream and what happens in the game is also what happens in the poem; and all these actions are analogues of the vocables of "pure water" and of each other. The requirements of the form, the masculine and feminine endings, the syllable count, and the rhyme of the last syllable in line 2 with the penultimate syllable of line 4, are not very strict; and the other two rhymes allow the poet considerable leeway. Thus, in the first line quoted above, the inversion—"in that dale of all Yorkshire's the loveliest"—is not necessary to get a rhyme; rather, the phrasing creates a certain fastidious formality and sentimental archaism. When the rhymes appear, either in expected or unexpected places, we get the feeling of "temporal novelty without anxiety, temporal repetition without boredom," and the feeling of the movement of water through a creek bed, forever repetitious, and forever novel. When "Kisdon Beck / jumps into Swale with a boyish shouting," the completion of the rhyme with "dale" from the first line figures a movement both free and required, as if Swale, the solid place name, were there to receive the jump. The boyish shouting images the innocent play and prefigures the dream. The consonance and internal rhyming, the mixture of colloquial and archaic diction, the falling dactylic rhythm, as well as the lexical sense of line 2 make a sharp contrast with the smoother and speedier line 3; the jump occurs syntactically and aurally just as the actual jump, across the line break, occurs. The whole poem is constructed with just this exactitude: the interaction of the poem's music with the images, the iconic references, and the "action" is as constant as that among words, phrases, syllables, and sounds.

"Streams" stands in juxtaposition to "Plains," its opposite in almost every sense, but yoked to it by the figure of redemption in "Streams," which is the "answer" to the sterility of the isolated ego in "Plains." The two also represent the sharpest contrast of hard and soft primitivism. "Streams" is the third element of another triadic pattern encompassing the whole series. The first three poems represent in part the movement of man from natural to civil being, both serially and within each poem. The second group, "Lakes," "Islands," and "Plains," represents the movement from civil order to civil sterility and the isolation of the self from both society and nature in a modern desert. The third represents a sense at once renewed and eternal of the benignity of nature and of man's contact, through a return to innocence and a sophisticated playing of games, with nature and with his natural origins; the overall pattern corresponds to the theological patterns of *ante legum, sub lege,* and *sub gratia.*

In each poem a different relation between hard and soft primitivism is portrayed, not so much to debate the merits of either view, or even to say that both have merit, but primarily to work toward a definition of man. For Auden, the myth of the historical Fall is, in a sense, a parable of man as simultaneously a creature and a self-aware being, simultaneously a natural, a social, and a spiritual being, simultaneously a part of and separate from nature. The self-qualifying juxtapositions of man, nature, art, and society within the cycle, in continually new combinations, represent and celebrate the multiplicity of man's being. This is the basis of Auden's serious use of the pastoral mode: it allows him to gather together the multiple aspects of man's relation to nature, gives perspective to man's longings to return to a prelapsarian state, celebrates by its artificiality and "unnaturalness" man as a speaking, making, and potentially civil being, mocks his pretensions to be anything else, and draws comic figures of Grace.

No voice in the poem tells us what the relation of the individual poems to each other is. Unlike the two most comparable pieces, *Horae Canonicae* and *Thanksgiving for a Habitat,* there is no occasion or set of events to which we can relate the poems. The poems present themselves as independent, loosely related units that do not specifically comment on each other and that exhibit no overt temporal or narrative form. Even when the underlying structure begins to emerge, we retain the primary sense of seven apparently independent poems arranged in space rather than in time.

This arrangement allows us to look at the individual styles and the individual features of the topography for their own value, even when they refer to a dangerous, foolish, or limited view of the relation of man to nature. It also allows us to separate our evaluations of the several landscapes from our general sense of artistic fullness and topographic variety. This series, like so many of Auden's poems, is full of anachronisms and of suggested correspondences between ontogeny and phylogeny; in its view of time, the Fall is continually reenacted and Paradise continually remembered. We are meant, I believe, to have a sense of the historic as well as the ahistoric character of experience. The poems are exploratory and analytical; almost every view of nature, of man's relation to it, of civility, and of the way art does or does not treat any of these items is present. Hence, the major statement of the poems is the complex conception necessary to a full view of man as a radically multiple being. Finally, as in so much of Auden's art, definition and celebration are carried out simultaneously. The poems, more than anything else, are verbal festivals. Such festivities, one of whose laws of existence is a certain disconnectedness, are in themselves part of the definition of man and the expression of Auden's deepest humanistic impulse.

Notes

1. *Studies in Iconology: Humanistic Themes in the Art of the Renaissance,* 2d ed. (New York: Harper, 1967), pp. 66–67, 39, 53–54, 55; 1st publ., 1939. Miss Janice Carlisle called my attention to this source.

2. Ibid., pp. 40–41, 65.

3. For me, too much happens iconographically to be supported by the narratives and the dramatic situation. Or, perhaps more precisely, to support allegorical expansion through both images and plot one would need a much more complex unit than the alliterative line: a unit, for instance, like the Spenserian stanza, through which each step of narrative can be expanded and analyzed. But I am far from certain *The Age of Anxiety* is a failure.

4. *Studies in Iconology,* p. 58.

5. New York: New Directions, 1968, p. 255; 1st publ., 1950.

6. *A Reader's Guide to W. H. Auden* (New York: Farrar, Straus & Giroux, 1970), pp. 214–215, 221.

[From *The Later Auden* ("Horae Canonicae")]

George W. Bahlke

In the best of Auden's recent poems there is a close relationship between form and content, and the conception of experience underlying these poems is essentially comic. Auden's sequence of seven poems, "Horae Canonicae," from *The Shield of Achilles* (1955),[1] reveals his continuing commitment to the perfect adaptation of form to content at the same time that it stands as a model of his comic vision. The seven poems constitute a meditation on the meaning of the Crucifixion, and the structure of the sequence derives from the use of the canonical hours as the titles of individual poems. Again, the central theme of the sequence is man's relation to history, and the individual poems in the sequence develop the irony inherent in man's continuing involvement in a pattern of violence and consequent guilt in spite of the high order of civilization he has achieved. This theme emerges clearly in "Sext," in which Auden, while he recognizes that we may not entirely like those men who possess authority, points out that they have given us "basilicas, divas, / dictionaries, pastoral verse, / the courtesies of the city," and have saved us from primitivism; in spite of these contributions, however, at the present moment they represent the authority which "command[s] this death" (p. 70).

"Prime," the first poem in the sequence, the title of which comes from the first canonical hour of the day, initiates the pattern which governs the sequence, the establishment of a parallel between the historical movement in Christianity from innocence through the Fall to redemption, and the day in which this same progression is re-enacted. Thus the poet, in "Prime," speaks of himself (and all men) at dawn as a type of Adam, still "sinless in our beginning, / Adam still previous to any act." The body is also seen ironically as a malcontent, a "rebellious fronde," which has lost its rights through the consequence of "an historical mistake," presumably the fall of Adam. To awaken is to be "recalled from the shades," from the underworld of sleep, to the perception of the real world. Most significantly, the individual at dawn is without identity or any relation to history, is suspended between bodiliness and the perceiving mind.

The second stanza anticipates the day in which the operations of the will

Reprinted from *The Later Auden: From "New Year Letter" to* About the House by permission of Rutgers University Press. Copyright © 1970 by Rutgers, the State University of New Jersey.

and the memory are to create a sense of identity and function as a superego. The first breath becomes a sign of man's wish for intelligence, individuation, mortality, the cost of which he knows to be the loss of paradisal innocence and the necessity to owe a death, to owe it in the sense of having to participate in sacrifice as a duty. Just as the landscape perceived is not yet related to the individual, its features merely "things to hand," the flesh, now an accomplice, will become an assassin. Finally, the recognition of one's identity, one's name, is simultaneously the recognition of one's involvement in history and one's responsibility to preserve the city, understood metaphorically as the civilization man has created without, on his part, any sense of the necessity to relate the city of man to the city of God.

In "Terce" (p. 65), the poem which corresponds to the third hour of the canonical day, the hour when "we all might be anyone," the judge, the hangman, the poet, united through their inability to anticipate what the day will bring, are distinguished from those in authority, "the Big Ones / Who can annihilate a city," and the sacrificial victim, Christ, whose complete knowledge of the future is contrasted to the limited human wish that each man's conception of himself will not be undercut. The tone, in the third stanza here, becomes bitterly ironic through the poet's recognition that our prayers for a scapegoat will be answered, "the machinery of our world . . . function / Without a hitch," our wish for a "good" Friday be fulfilled.

Man's limitations are diagnosed in "Terce" through language which is essentially comic in its plethora of social detail; man's "prayer" in the second stanza is a characteristic example:

> Let me get through this coming day
> Without a dressing down from a superior,
>   Being worsted in a repartee,
> Or behaving like an ass in front of the girls;
>   Let something exciting happen,
> Let me find a lucky coin on a sidewalk.
>   Let me hear a new funny story. (p. 65)

Such a passage might be considered satirical, if it were not clear that Auden is not pointing to specific abuses, but rather expressing a universal condition; the apparently objective speaker of the first stanza includes himself among those who pray and the "we" of the third stanza who cannot forgive Christ his foreknowledge: "If he knows the answers, / Then why are we here, why is there even dust?"

It is in "Sext" (p. 67) that Auden develops most clearly the irony underlying the entire sequence, the development of civilization and of man's religious sense, on the one hand, and the consequences of his achievement, the elevation to authority of men who can enact our violences, on the other. Those in authority, of which the examples chosen are generals, bacteriologists, prosecutors, and jurymen, may be repellent to us in their self-satisfaction, their smug sense of their own embodiment of abstract ethical principles, but they are responsible for "the courtesies of the city" and without them our lives would still be primitive, fearful, and our language barely articulate, a "local patois / Of some three hundred words."

The third section of "Sext" is a reflection on mob psychology; the crowd is indifferent, and since it looks at events as if with a single eye it is destructive of all individuality: "the crowd sees only one thing / (which only the crowd can see), / an epiphany of that / which does whatever is done." A crowd permits no distinctions, and only as a result of the crowd's nature, the poet suggests, can man say that all men are his brothers. It is on the basis of the ready acceptance of all men into a crowd that we can argue that we are superior to bees or ants, the "social exoskeletons":

> When
> have they ever ignored their queens,
> for one second stopped work
>
> on their provincial cities, to worship
> The Prince of this world like us,
>
> at this noon, on this hill,
> in the occasion of this dying. (p. 72)

"Nones" (p. 73) represents the ninth canonical hour of the day, and in terms of the parallel between the passion of Christ and the religious offices, the time immediately following the Crucifixion. It is essentially a meditation on the implications of Christ's sacrifice in human life. The first stanza expresses man's surprise that the act which has long been prophesied, the event which is implicit in his very nature, "revealed to a child in some chance rhyme / Like *will* and *kill*," occurs so suddenly that he hardly realizes what has happened. Already the weather is calm once again, the crowd dispersed, the "faceless many" who, as members of that crowd, absolve themselves through freedom from a sense of responsibility; the enactment of violence is still without consequences or implications in individual life.

Nevertheless, the poet makes it clear that once the Crucifixion has been enacted it becomes an inescapable aspect of our existence: "wherever / The sun shines, brooks run, books are written, / There will also be this death." The Christian pattern of sin and redemption lies behind all individual action:

> Soon cool tramontana will stir the leaves,
> The shops will re-open at four,
> The empty blue bus in the empty pink square
> Fill up and depart: we have time

To misrepresent, excuse, deny,
  Mythify, use this event
While, under a hotel bed, in prison,
  Down wrong turnings, its meaning
Waits for our lives: sooner then we would choose,
  Bread will melt, water will burn,
And the great quell begin, Abaddon
  Set up his triple gallows
At our seven gates, fat Belial make
  Our wives waltz naked; meanwhile
It would be best to go home, if we have a home,
  In any case good to rest. (p. 75)

The stanza above is a superb example of the kind of imagery that appears in all of Auden's poetry, from his first schoolboy exercises to the poems in *The Shield of Achilles*. At its best, as here, those images which refer to the modern world, "shops," "bus," "hotel bed," and "prison" are generalized, and their use is not merely a matter of virtuosity. Here the effect depends upon the implicit contrast between activity and inactivity. The fact that the shops reopen, that the bus and square are now empty, introduces an irony; the images have nonnatural, social referents, but for the moment these objects are not connected with man. The juxtaposition of such imagery with allusions to Abaddon and Belial dissolves the differences between present and past; the nonnatural, social images are evidence of Auden's ability to employ comic incongruities in language even in a poem whose subject matter is profoundly serious.

The last two stanzas in "Nones" return to the distinction made in "Prime" between the will and the flesh, as the poet anticipates the will's attempt to escape through dreams, only to encounter within the Kafkan world of those dreams, man's double; the body, "our own wronged flesh," will restore in sleep the order and rhythm of physiological process without having achieved any understanding of the implications of the Christian sacrifice. Man may be awed, like all other animals, by death, but he cannot make any sense of it.

"Vespers" (p. 77) abandons the careful stanzaic form of the other poems for a conversational series of lines of differing lengths. At the hour of sundown, when "all must wear their own faces," two men of opposing masks meet below the hill in their city. One is an Arcadian, the other a Utopian. In the introductory paragraphs in his essay on Dickens' *Pickwick Papers,* Auden distinguishes between the Arcadian and Utopian characters on the basis of their favorite daydream; the Arcadian's daydream is Eden, the Utopian's New Jerusalem, and between the Arcadian and the Utopian "there is a characterological gulf as unbridgeable as that between Blake's Prolifics and Devourers. . . . Eden is a past world in which the contradictions of the present world have not yet arisen; New Jerusalem is a future world in which they have at last been resolved. . . . the motto over [Eden's] gate is, 'Do what thou wilt is here the Law.' New Jerusalem is a place where its inhabitants like to do whatever they ought to do, and its motto is, 'In His will is our peace.' "² The "characterological gulf" is present in "Vespers" itself. The Arcadian's Eden is incompatible with the Utopian's New Jerusalem: "In my Eden a person who dislikes Bellini has the good manners not to get born: In his New Jerusalem a person who dislikes work will be very sorry he was born" (p. 78). The poem proceeds through a number of contrasts similar to the one above to the conclusion that their differences only conceal their common fear of the fact which unites them: both are responsible for sacrificial acts, the continuing presence of which underlies all secular forms of existence.

In "Compline" (p. 81), the title of which refers to the last canonical hour and service of the day, the poet, as he falls asleep to enter the world of dreams out of which he awoke in "Prime," the body escaping "to join / Plants in their chaster peace which is more / To its real taste," cannot piece together any meaning for the events of the day: "I fail to see either plot / Or meaning; I cannot remember / A thing between noon and three." The rhythm of the heart and the movement of the stars across the night sky express for him a motion which may be measured but not interpreted, although he recognizes that the heart may be "confessing" its involvement in the events of the day and the constellations may celebrate an order beyond the desires of man in a time-bound world. The poet blesses both heart and stars, while recognizing that he and all men are separated by their limited nature from the ultimate significance heart and stars possess.

The dreams he anticipates entering, their embodiment of his wishes, will remain, he knows, without significance for him, in spite of their propitiatory powers; the dreams are defined as "untruth," only slightly removed from nothingness. The attitude here, in the third stanza, becomes a double one, because man moves daily from absence of mind to awareness and the acting out of awareness and again to absence; the movement is seen as part of an equity and rhythm that man cannot understand. The words with which Auden defines the equity and rhythm are "dance" and "perichoresis," the former metaphorical and used in more or less the same sense as in the second section of Eliot's "Burnt Norton," the latter a synonym for circumincession, the theological doctrine of the "reciprocal existence of the persons of the Trinity in one another."³ These words are a part of the prayer in the final stanza, a prayer preceded by the poet's recognition that prayer is difficult in the face of a divine justice which man cannot know, and by love for God, a love whose name has been lost. The meaning of the day's events, the reenactment of Christ's passion, will be known only at the Last Judgment:

> spare
> Us in the youngest day when all are
> Shaken awake, facts are facts

> (And I shall know exactly what happened
> Today between noon and three)
> That we, too, may come to the picnic
> With nothing to hide, join the dance
> As it moves in perichoresis,
> Turns about the abiding tree. (pp. 82–83)

The final poem of the "Horae Canonicae," "Lauds" (p. 84), anticipates the continual renewal of life with the dawn of each day; Lauds, of course, is the last nocturnal liturgical office and hence precedes Prime. The form of the poem is intricate; Monroe Spears has pointed out that it is that of the medieval Spanish *cossante*,[4] and Auden strictly adheres to this form. The line, "*In solitude, for company*," which follows each couplet points to the simultaneous individual and social life which every man must lead, a life in which the city, the individual, and the natural world itself are renewed through the acceptance of the Christian way: "God bless the Realm, God bless the People; / God bless this green world temporal: *In solitude, for company*."

The "Horae Canonicae" may be read best against the background of those shorter poems of Auden's in which he implicitly evaluates Graeco-Roman as opposed to Christian civilization ("Under Sirius" and "The Fall of Rome" in *Nones,* and "Secondary Epic" and "The Epigoni" in *Homage to Clio*). While these poems are related to Auden's earlier interpretation of the Kierkegaardian categories in historical terms, they also imply a comic awareness of the contradictions in human activity "as facts of life against which it is useless to rebel."[5] The poems in "Horae Canonicae" not only point to the ironies inherent in the development of civilization, but also continually dramatize the disparity between man's limited understanding of the degree of his involvement in acts of violence and the infliction of suffering, his inability to understand the ultimate significance of the Crucifixion—things as they are—and the eternal pattern within which men's actions have meaning and all contradictions are resolved.

Notes

1. *The Shield of Achilles* (New York: Random House, 1955), pp. 61–84. The Latin epigraph (p. 61), "Immolatus vicerit," means, "He who has suffered will conquer."

2. *The Dyer's Hand* (New York: Random House, 1962), p. 409.

3. *The Shorter Oxford English Dictionary on Historical Principles,* 3d ed., prep. William Little, H. W. Fowler, J. Coulson, rev. and ed. C. T. Onions (Oxford: Oxford University Press, 1962), definition of "circumincession," p. 315.

4. *The Poetry of W. H. Auden: The Disenchanted Island* (New York: Oxford University Press, 1962), pp. 320–21.

5. *The Dyer's Hand,* p. 388.

[From *W. H. Auden* (*About the House, City without Walls, Epistle to a Godson,* and *Thank You, Fog*)]

Stan Smith

It is in . . . class terms that Auden defines comedy in the essay "The Globe" (*DH,* p. 177):

> [C]lassical comedy is based upon the division of mankind into two classes, those who have *arete* and those who do not, and only the second class, fools, shameless rascals, slaves, are fit subject for comedy. But Christian comedy is based upon the belief that all men are sinners; no one, therefore, whatever his rank or talents, can claim immunity from the comic exposure and, indeed, the more virtuous, in the Greek sense, a man is, the more he realises that he deserves to be exposed.

In all great drama, the essay concludes, "we can feel the tension of this ambivalent attitude, torn between reverence and contempt, of the maker towards the doer" (p. 181). This is the tone of Auden's late poetry. That radically estranging look, which in the thirties had led him to despise a venal society, is now transformed into the comic perspective of the anthropologist who knows that all cultures are historical artefacts but who can nevertheless admire, respect or forgive the diversity of forms they take.

In these late poems, the defamiliarizing gaze serves only to endear. In "Whitsunday in Kirchstetten" (*AH*), for example, the poem bounces various idioms off each other in a way which relativizes them all, translating them into the new polyglot English of the "metic" (an alien resident in a Greek city with some of the privileges of citizens). But while Babel still rules in this world, such "tribal formulae" are merely local dialects of a single, levelling truth. Sacred and profane rituals can, to the anthropologizing outsider, share the same comical patterns: while the church "quietly gets on with the Sacrifice / as Rome does it," outside the "car-worshippers enact / the ritual exodus from Vienna / their successful cult demands."

Economic change has translated this culture into new modes. The "sons

Reprinted from *W. H. Auden* (Oxford: Basil Blackwood, 1985) by permission of Basil Blackwell, Inc.

of the menalty" no longer have to choose their careers only from Army, Navy, Law or Church. If this culture is a product of military or fiscal contingencies, not manifest destiny ("If the Allies had not / conquered the Ost-Mark, if the dollar fell, / the *Gemütlichkeit* would be less"), it is none the less real and tangible for that. Yet ninety kilometres away as the crow flies is the Iron Curtain where "our habits end, / where minefield and watchtower say NO EXIT / from peace-loving Crimtartary, except for crows." This is a complex and comic deposition of absolutes—the archaic name for Russia, the crow's-eye view, the deadpan slogans, reinforced by the wide sweep of the next remark, which reflects adversely on the values of both blocs: "from Loipersbach / to the Bering Sea not a living stockbroker." Is the Cold War, then, really simply a matter of making the world safe for stockbrokers?

Even here, the stranger's look can suddenly turn withering. In "The Poet and the City" Auden wrote that "Today, there is only one genuine world-wide revolutionary issue, racial equality. The debate between capitalism, socialism and communism is really a party issue" about how best to distribute the grub. In the poem the priest's elevation of the host leads him to put East and West in their place in the name of a Third World which turns the lunch tables on them both:

> But to most people
> I'm the wrong colour: it could be the looter's turn
>   for latrine duty and the flogging block,
> my kin who trousered Africa, carried our smell
>   to germless poles.

With a little aftershock, we realize that it is the poet's kin who are the looters, that "civilising" Africa meant introducing the flogging block. Yet it is all said with such old-world charm that it cannot offend. The very ease with which he gets away with such wicked innuendoes means we can easily miss the link between this image of imperialism, in its strangely affectionate dismissiveness, and "the Body of the Second Adam / . . . shown to some of his torturers" just before. These evasions are those of a language which lacks certain resonances: "There is no Queen's English / in any context for *Geist* or *Esprit*." And this encourages a larger evasion, that of the final lines: "about catastrophe or how to behave in one / what do I know, except what everyone knows— / if there when Grace dances, I should dance."

That catastrophe lurks everywhere in this last decade. If translation is a recurrent theme of the poems, it is not simply translation from one language or idiom into another. For over all presides that death which is the ultimate translation: "What is Death?" asks a "Short," "A life / disintegrating into / smaller simpler ones." In this secular, death-defined world Godhead challenges all temporal powers:

He appears in this world, not as Apollo or Aphrodite might appear, disguised as a man so that no mortal should recognize his divinity, but as a real man who openly claims to be God. And the consequence is inevitable. The highest religious and temporal authorities condemn Him as a blasphemer and a Lord of Misrule, as a Bad Companion for mankind. Inevitable because, as Richelieu said, "The salvation of States is in this world," and history has not yet provided us with any evidence that the prince of this world has changed his character. (*DH,* pp. 207–8)

. . . .

[W]hen [Auden] reverts to the idea of the Incarnation in these later poems, he is making a radical correlation. The named historical subject is not a transcendent being, any more than the Christian God. Rather Auden's God is that material ground of being from which the particular creature emerges, deriving its local powers from a source which remains inscribed in all its manifestations. The place of the Incarnation is also that of Carnival, that farewell to the Flesh which is the repeated loving, affectionate and regretful tone of all the last volumes. As he wrote in "Concerning the Unpredictable" in 1970, discussing the evolutionary view of a universe of choice and chance depicted by Loren Eiseley, in a study which is a pervasive influence on these poems:

Carnival celebrates the unity of our human race as mortal creatures, who come into this world and depart from it without our consent, who must eat, drink, defecate, belch, and break wind in order to live, and procreate if our species is to survive. Our feelings about this are ambiguous. To us as individuals, it is a cause for rejoicing to know that we are not alone, that all of us, irrespective of age or sex or rank or talent, are in the same boat. As unique persons, on the other hand, all of us are resentful that an exception cannot be made in our own case. We oscillate between wishing we were unreflective animals and wishing we were disembodied spirits, for in either case we should not be problematic to ourselves. The Carnival solution of this ambiguity is to laugh, for laughter is simultaneously a protest and an acceptance. During Carnival, all social distinctions are suspended, even that of sex. (*FA,* p. 471)

. . . .

There is an interesting corrective to the image of Auden as a grouchy conservative in his old age in those remarks on Carnival. A satisfactory human life requires paying respect to Prayer, Work and Laughter, he says. Those who try to live by prayer alone become pharisaic, those by work alone, "insane lovers of power, tyrants who would enslave Nature to their immediate desires—an attempt which can only end in utter catastrophe" (p. 473)— a catastrophe which in several of these poems Auden equates with nuclear war. Against them, Auden gestures positively to those who lack only one of the triad: "The hippies, it appears to me, are trying to recover the sense of Carnival which is so conspicuously absent in this age, but so long as they reject Work they are unlikely to succeed." The qualified approval is reiterated

in "Prologue at Sixty" where Auden throws in his lot with a younger generation against the "Cosmocrats" jumbo-jetting through time-zones, heads of
state "who are not all there" signing secret treaties, a world of "bugged
phones, sophisticated / weapon-systems and sick jokes."

The accidents of evolution and history have deposited him by "chance
and my own choice" in "this unenglish tract" of Austria which has seen many
successive violations, Turks, Boney's legions, Germans, Russians. No more
than the place can the subject rest assured in a fixed, continuous identity:
"Who am I now?" he asks, "An American? No, a New Yorker, / who opens
his *Times* at the obit. page, / whose dream images date him already, whose
day turned out torturers / who read *Rilke* in their rest periods." . . .

[I]n the title poem of *Epistle to a Godson,* he delights in the accolade of
"boozy godfather," making connections between his generation and that of
the sixties. Asking who he is to "offer ghostly platitudes / to a young man" he
distinguishes between now and "yester times" when the old

> could nicely envisage the future
> as a named and settled landscape their children
> would make the same sense of as they did,
> laughing and weeping at the same stories.

There is a double-take here, for if it is no longer possible to do this it is only
because that earlier generation has been proved wrong in such confidence.
Such stories were always lying pastorals, cast in bourgeois terms as tales of
honest cobblers and evil counts, actually presuming a world where "the poor
were what they were used to being, / the creators of wealth not, as now they
are, / an expensive nuisance." That this is Auden's sly parody of middle-class
selfishness and not his own opinion is confirmed by the parenthesis that
follows: "Nobody / has dared suggest gassing them, but someone / surely
will." . . .

The paradox which opens an ironic gap between "poor" and "creators of
wealth" is the key. The future which has us "gallowed shitless" still has its
origins in the disparities of political power: "global Archons" would be

> figures of fun, if
> very clever little boys had not found it amusing to build devices for them more
> apt at disassembly than any
> old fire-spewing theogonic monster.

These nuclear devices can disassemble all political assemblies and their fables
of democratic involvement. If what is to happen "occurs according to what
Thucydides / defined as 'human,' we've had it." But Thucydides, describing
the degenerations of Greek society brought about by the Peloponnesian War,
wrote as an aristocratic pessimist whose culture's fables assumed the unchang-

ingness of human nature. As "The Greeks and Us" reveals and his contrasts between classical and Christian drama take for granted, Auden assumed no such thing. He starts from an assumption of the transformative character of "human nature," which has converted a paleocene pseudo-rat into the named and bourgeois creatures at a wedding, flakers of flint into Homer's heroes and then into spacemen. The tongue-in-cheek Jeremiads of this poem are counter-balanced by the witty parentheses which disown them. But power remains a serious business, and "To be responsible for the happiness / of the Universe is not a sinecure." On the contrary, the future for the "elite lands" of the First World may hold a Way of poverty.

It is "only / the unscarred overfed enjoy Calvary / as a verbal event." The well-fed pride themselves on their aesthetic refinement, like those torturers who read Rilke in their rest periods. Neither satire nor shoddy workmanship will shame them. The only way to challenge them is to show that we, who care about hunger, also have the best tunes. The impish invocation of his godson's own father's revolutionary past, in the allusion to *The Destructive Element,* suggests that Uncle Wiz is here more subversive than he appears. The utopian dimension of art still holds out the possibility of a reclaimed world, where freedom and order are consonant, not at odds. . . .

The poem plays with a paradox only half redeemed by Marx's remark that history repeats itself as farce. Auden had begun by saying that, unlike previous generations, he neither can nor will offer paradigms or advice for the future. He warns against listening to fairy tales—and then tells one. But history is not simply endless novelty. If it were, no tale could outlive its generation. His godson's generation are now repeating the serio-comic follies of Auden's own. Auden's contemporaries are complaining about them in the way Auden's parents did, and this only echoes the patrician grumbling of Thucydides two millennia ago. If all pleasures come from God, Auden goes on, then no individual life is necessary, all are expendable. Nobody owns himself. But in this case, in a happy pun, the expendable is also the spender. Accidentally interpellated to his patronym, young Philip Spender, like all of us, experiences nevertheless that flavour of uniqueness that goes with particular being. Living is a matter of repeatedly reinscribing ourselves in the discourse which names and gives roles. As Auden has to remind himself "I *am* your godfather," so Philip is advised: "Be glad your being is unnecessary, / then turn your toes out as you walk, dear, / and remember who you are, a Spender." . . .

If the pleasures of the flesh are celebrated in the centre-piece of *About the House,* "Thanksgiving for a Habitat," what endows them with value is the certainty that we must lose them. From the very first poem, "The Birth of Architecture," we are within that shadow: the birth being, ironically, the prehistoric "gallery grave" which records too the birth of a culture-making species. Every poem is an epitaph—in this one, quite literally, "The Cave of Making," which records an imaginary conversation with the shade of Louis

MacNeice. The transit between then and now is "hardly a tick by the carbon clock, but I / don't count that way nor do you." The ambiguous colloquialism links human time-scales to humane scales of importance.

For the experiencing individual, there is only the "still prehistoric *Once*" before experience, and the historical "*After*" which creates its own myths of origin and destination. In that *Once,* all the once-actual moments of living time are condensed into a single compact stratum of pastness, like coal under the immense pressure of the present, the product of a collective patriarch whose whole historical function, it seems to those two foregrounded pronouns, was to produce them:

> to you, to me,
> Stonehenge and Chartres Cathedral,
> the Acropolis, Blenheim, the Albert Memorial
> are works by the same Old Man
> under different names: we know what He did,
> what, even, He thought He thought,
> but we don't see why.

The "Immortal Commonwealth" of the natural world is a conditioned one; by contrast, the human world is a conditional realm, constituted in discourse, taking umbrage at death and constructing a "second nature of tomb and temple" only possible to lives that "know the meaning of *If.*" In the second poem of the sequence that conditional imagining brings the anthropologist's gaze to bear in a double deconstruction. For if the burial rites and codes of honour of the past are disclosed in all their puzzling difference, our own preoccupations are equally estranged:

> Nobody I know would like to be buried
> with a silver cocktail shaker,
> a transistor radio and a strangled
> daily help, or keep his word because
>
> of a great-great-grandmother who got laid
> by a sacred beast.

The irreverent demotic devalues the once authoritative myths and ritual. All ages live on the assumption that they are keeping their word, and all alike break it. For it is in the very nature of the human to act askew to its self-definitions, to be other than it claims, constantly betraying the very words it uses to justify itself. A world "has still to be built," the first poem had said. This second poem raises doubts about the status of the concept of building itself, for if "Only a press lord / could have built San Simeon," we need to ask in what sense that building can be attributed to Randolph Hearst rather than to those unnamed workers who actually put bricks to mortar.

Class as a discourse of exclusions runs through the sequence. In the first poem, masons and carpenters—the actual makers—were seen as belonging to nature, but architects, the conceivers and commissioners, to the realm of the human. Yet "no unearned income," the poem says, subverting its own privilege, "can buy us back . . . / . . . the art / of believing footmen don't hear / human speech." The language, shifting, labile, in turn betrays all our hierarchies of rank and meaning into a common fallibility.

"The Cave of Making" recalls how Auden and MacNeice "once collaborated, once at a weird Symposium / exchanged winks as a juggins / went on about Alienation." Turning an objective process into a subjective one enacts the very alienation of which it speaks. A fact about exploitation in a class society—the alienation of labour into capital, "unearned income"—becomes a vogue word with which intellectuals make their careers and conceptualize their fashionable despair. But if the poet as "maker" seems outside this money economy, there is a residual guilt, surfacing in the reproachful unintended ambiguity of the word "collaborated." For this is not an innocent context. Auden has just spoken of how "we shan't, not since Stalin and Hitler, / trust ourselves ever again: we know that, subjectively, / all is possible." The "subjective" is constituted only as the reflex of a discourse which carries power in every instance of its utterance, subjecting them to its meanings: their "ancestors probably / were among those plentiful subjects / it cost less money to murder." Auden and MacNeice themselves, in a poem which plays off "good mongrel barbarian English" and "Roman rhetoric" as systems of power, became self-conscious at a moment when the idiom of chivalry, by Tennyson out of Malory, still held power, and "the Manor was still politically numinous." Both experienced those social transformations which emptied the churches, made the cavalry redundant, and offered a new language for interpreting the "real" ("the Cosmic Model / became German"). In an earlier age, both would have filled a different slot in the social formation, bards to some tribal chief or Baroque Prince. Even now, it would be an illusion to imagine themselves outside the money economy. It may be a "privilege" to "serve this unpopular art which cannot be . . . / . . . hung as a status trophy by rising executives," but as the connotations of "privilege" and "serve" both indicate, autonomy is merely relative. Even here such affluence and privilege as they have is built upon exploitation coyly evoked, to be ostensibly dismissed, in a parenthesis: "(It's heartless to forget about / the underdeveloped countries / but a starving ear is as deaf as a suburban optimist's . . .)." The starving are not good "clients."

That other form of subjection returns to haunt the feast in "Grub First, Then Ethics." The poet may be able to point to the latest democratic American cooker, blue-printed for a world "where royalty would be incognito" and all cooks are equal. It may no longer be possible to tell "who is to give the orders" from a person's hands; now only the host at a dinner-party, not some

objective hierarchy of precedent, decides who is to be "put below the salt."
Such democratic dining is still a privilege, however, "for the subject of the
verb / to-hunger is never a name" but an animal creature excluded from the
discourse of subjects. "Where the / power lies remains to be seen, / the force,
though, is clearly with them"—that is, with those tyrants whose language
rides the most apparently innocuous words, even "chefs" and "master-dish."
The Third World realm upon which this thoroughly modern, "polite" and
"liberal" kitchen depends for its privileges is still repressed, the theme only
of well-fed fantasies about starvation. Everywhere, Auden's poem subverts its
own satisfactions. This is the meaning of that ghostly intrusion that repeatedly disturbs the feast, even when, like MacNeice or Plato (the enquirer
here), it is welcome.

If death is outside the language, it infiltrates everywhere in this sequence as the sign of a larger guilt, revealed in those fantasies of global
extermination for which the speaking subject in some way feels responsible
while he casts himself as mere victim. For in whatever language he inscribes
himself, he persists hubristically in seeing himself as "Adam's sovereign
clone," a self-sufficient individual, deludedly believing himself "dominant /
over three acres of a blooming / conurbation of country lives." That this is the
hubris of usurpation is disclosed by a wider web of relations. The poem is full
of the language of consanguinity, from "great-great-grandmother," through
"the flesh / Mum formulated," to the "water-brethren" with whom he recognizes affinity. To wipe away a spider's web is a denial of creatureliness which
reveals another aspect of kinship: "fools / who deface their emblem of guilt /
are germane to Hitler." There is a scale of genocide, in a world whose very
vitality is founded in death and, the voice of carnival proclaims, there is no
way of quitting the feast.

A culture "in whose creed / God is edible" must acknowledge its foundation in guilt, as "Tonight at Seven-Thirty" admits. So, in section II, the food
chain is only another aspect of the Chain of Being, where extinction (euphe-
mistically translated as "translation") is the name of everybody's game:

> I ought
> to outlast the limber dragonflies
>
> as the muscle-bound firs are certainly
>   going to outlast me: I shall not end
> down any esophagus, though I may succumb
>   to a filter-passing predator,
>
> shall, anyhow, stop eating, surrender my smidge
>   of nitrogen to the World Fund
> with a drawn-out *Oh* (unless at the nod
>   of some jittery commander

> I be translated in a nano-second
>   to a c.c. of poisonous nothing
> in a giga-death).

As so frequently in these late poems, the apparently casual parenthesis contains the real anxiety, complicity in a world of power that is the obverse of all that festive eating. Chronos who devours his children still presides over these poems, displaced, repressed, evaded in all those euphemisms with which death is denied in the elegy for MacNeice, or translated into the icy evasions of military verbal overkill.

"Geography of the House" reminds of our common fleshiness with a euphemistic joke: the lavatory is what "Arabs call *the House where / Everybody goes.*" Its primal pleasures again recall the common fact of mortality, figured by the morning visit in which "we / Leave the dead concerns of / Yesterday behind us." Far from being a whimsical moment out of the general argument, this poem reminds us, like the bedroom in "The Cave of Nakedness," that we are "corporal contraptions"; and that our "verbal contraptions," whether of poetry or politics, emerge from and dissemble this material base. The prayer in the bog to "Keep us in our station: / When we get pound-noteish" is thus an apposite one.

The last poem in the sequence spells out that creaturely communism at the bottom of all Auden's late verse, the "Common Life" which, in spite of murder, makes us inhabitants of "a common world." Chronos still presides over history:

>   It's a wonder that neither
> has been butchered by accident,
>
> or, as lots have, silently vanished into
>   History's criminal noise
> unmourned for . . .

It is Hermes who is set against Chronos. For "the sacred spells are secret to the kind," "and if power is what we wish / they won't work." Nevertheless, "*The ogre will come in any case:* / so Joyce has warned us." If this final Hermetic secret were acknowledged, those jittery commanders, gallowed shitless with their phallic missiles, might think twice before pulling the chain of being while sitting in their station.

. . . .

Auden's notorious intellectual eclecticism is not a weakness. Like his macaronic style, his deliberate collisions of idiom and image, his frequent metonymies and puns, it points to the artifice of language, reminds us of what is left out, left over, in every utterance. Comprehensiveness and coherence can, as he proposed in *New Year Letter,* be the clearest sign of that absolutist fore-closure which is the enemy of truth. It is in the provisional and speculative, the play of signifiers that constantly subvert their own tendency to settle into platitude, that the unicorn of meaning, that mythical beast on which we found all our projects, may flash whitely among the cedars. The very disparity and incongruity of Auden's "influences" have this function. For it is where Marx and Freud, Christianity and Nietzsche do not fit, where the congruence slides under the smoothing hand and the soothing tongue of language, that an insight hides. The punning correspondences between overlaid systems of thought only expose more clearly the residual differences where meaning loiters. The uncontainable surplus always runs ahead of any movement to closure, inviting us to begin again, read of our losses. . . .

[From *The Poetry of W. H. Auden: The Disenchanted Island* (*The Rake's Progress*)]

Monroe K. Spears

. . . During the last decade Auden has written a number of exceptionally interesting critical and speculative pieces dealing with music. Music, he suggests, imitates or is about *choice:* "a successful melody is a self-determined history; it is freely what it intends to be, yet is a meaningful whole not an arbitrary succession of notes."[1] In a later statement he says that music "presents a virtual image of our experience of living as temporal, with its double aspect of recurrence and becoming."[2] He continues: "If music in general is an imitation of history, opera in particular is an imitation of human willfulness"; the great operatic roles are all passionate and willful states of being (that in real life would all be bores) and the crowning glory of opera is the big ensemble, which presents them in immediate and simultaneous relation to each other (p. 470). Comparing the libretto with the play, he observes that in some respects the librettist is more limited than the dramatist: "The dramatist, for instance, procures some of his finest effects from showing how people deceive themselves. Self-deception is impossible in opera because music is immediate not reflective; whatever is sung is the case. At most self-deception can be suggested by having the orchestral accompaniment at variance with the singer. . . ." While in drama the discovery of the mistake (upon which, says Auden, all drama is based) can be a slow process, in the libretto it must be abrupt, "for music cannot exist in an atmosphere of uncertainty; song cannot walk, it can only jump." On the other hand, the librettist has the great advantage of not needing to worry about probability: "No good opera plot can be sensible for people do not sing when they are feeling sensible." A good libretto is melodramatic; it "offers as many opportunities as possible for the characters to be swept off their feet by placing them in situations which are too tragic or too fantastic for 'words' " (pp. 471–72). Finally, Auden makes a sharp distinction between the libretto and the lyric: in the libretto the verses are really a private letter to the composer; their purpose is to suggest a melody to him, after which they are expendable. They cannot and should not be poetry; one trouble with the *Rosenkavalier,* for instance, is that it is too close to real poetry. (Like many other distinctions in this essay, this one seems too black and white, too absolutely antithetical; but it makes clear Auden's conviction that the libretto must be emphatically subordinate to the musical necessities of the opera.) . . . [T]he operas are, in a sense, a fulfillment of Auden's impulse towards fantasy; they provide an opportunity and justification for transcending the limits of the "normal," common-sense world and representing instead the world of myth, fairy tale, magic, the supernatural—the inner world that has always fascinated Auden, in which the shapes of things are bent to the desires of the mind.[3] This is plain in Auden's first experiment in writing a libretto, though *Paul Bunyan* is in most other respects different from the later operas.

. . . It is perhaps not impertinent to speculate that one of the numerous difficulties under which *Paul Bunyan* labored was this: the librettist should be subordinate to the composer of an opera, but Auden was older, much more famous, and no doubt a more dominant personality than Britten. No such problem could arise in Auden's collaboration with Stravinsky.

The story of the genesis of *The Rake's Progress* is told in full in *Memories and Commentaries,* by Igor Stravinsky and Robert Craft (New York, 1960), in which Auden's letters to Stravinsky and their first scenario for the opera are also printed. As the intimate record of a collaboration, the material is of exceptional interest. To summarize the essentials briefly, the idea of basing an opera on Hogarth's *Rake's Progress* occurred to Stravinsky in 1947. He chose Auden as librettist on the recommendation of Aldous Huxley, knowing of his work only the commentary for the documentary film, "Night Mail." In October Auden accepted the invitation, making his position clear immediately: "it is the librettist's job to satisfy the composer, not the other way round . . ." (p. 145). In November 1947 he visited Stravinsky in California; they agreed on a "Mozart-Italian" type of opera, embodying a moral fable, and together they worked out a complete scenario. Stravinsky says, "Mother Goose and the Ugly Duchess [i.e., Baba] were Auden's contributions, of course, but the plot and the scheme of action were worked out by the two of us together, step by step. We also tried to co-ordinate the plan of action with a provisional plan of musical pieces, arias, ensembles, and choruses" (p. 146). After returning to New York Auden began work on the libretto, and on January 16 wrote to Stravinsky that he had taken as collaborator Chester Kallman, "an old friend of mine in whose talents I have the greatest confidence," and had finished Act I. Act II was finished by January 28, and the whole by March 31, when Auden and Stravinsky spent a day working together in Washington. Stravinsky then composed the music, taking about a year for each act, and finishing early in 1951; he conducted, and Auden and Kallman were present for, the premiere at Teatro La Fenice, Venice, in September 1951. Auden had expressed the wish that he and Kallman might advise during rehearsals, and presumably they did so. This first production was unfortunately not a very good one, according to report (several competent critics feel that the best of all the numerous productions the work has had in Europe was that directed by Ingmar Bergman in Stockholm in the summer of 1961). Of some 200 performances of the work in the first two years, only seven were in the United States;[4] the Metropolitan Opera's production in 1953 was dropped from the repertory the next year.

Since Chester Kallman was Auden's collaborator not only in the *Rake* but in the two later libretti, as well as in the "Englishings" of *The Magic Flute, Don Giovanni,* and Brecht's *Seven Deadly Sins,* and in the editing of the *Elizabethan Song Book,* we should consider his function as collaborator before proceeding with the discussion of the *Rake.* The friendship is of long standing: Auden dedicated *Another Time* to him in 1940 and the *Collected Poetry* of 1945 to him and Isherwood. Kallman was born in Brooklyn in 1921 and educated at Brooklyn College and the University of Michigan. In addition to the collaborations with Auden, he wrote the libretto for *The Tuscan Players,* an opera by the Mexican composer Carlos Chavez, and has translated the libretti of several operas, among them Verdi's *Falstaff,* Monteverdi's *Coronation of Poppea,* and Bartók's *Bluebeard's Castle.* In 1945–46 he reviewed the opera season for *Commonweal.* He has published one book of poems, *Storm at Castelfranco* (New York: Grove Press, 1956); a second, *Absent and Present,* is to appear in 1963. Kallman, Auden has said, "was the person who was responsible for arousing my interest in opera, about which previously, as you can see from *Paul Bunyan,* I knew little or nothing. . . ."[5]

Apparently Kallman does his full share in all the collaborations. We know specifically which parts of the *Rake* he wrote;[6] they constitute a good half, and include some of the most admired passages. Auden has ascribed the larger share of their latest opera, *Elegy for Young Lovers,* to Kallman.[7] Since the whole point of a successful collaboration is that it is more than and different from what each collaborator could do separately, there seems little point in trying to disentangle their respective contributions. . . .

The Rake's Progress is subtitled, "A Fable"; it follows Hogarth's tableaux only partially and generally, transposing the story into modern religious and psychological terms, while brilliantly maintaining the "period" quality. Three primary myths are employed: Eden (with variant forms: the Golden Age, pastoral innocence, and the location of evil in economic problems), Venus and Adonis, and Faust-Mephistopheles; from the world of fairy tale and nursery rhyme there are the three wishes, the Ugly Duchess, and a depraved Mother Goose. To show how these are reinterpreted and fused together, a brief analysis of the libretto will be necessary.[9]

The opening duet of the lovers, Anne Trulove and Tom Rakewell, at Trulove's home in the country, suggests the first two of these myths immediately. They describe spring in ritual terms, "this festival of May," when the "pious earth observes the solemn year," and refer to it as the work of the "Cyprian Queen." Through love, they say, the lost innocence and joy of Eden is restored: in neoclassical terms, "swains their nymphs in fervent arms enfold / And with a kiss restore the Age of Gold." Trulove, in contrast, voices "a father's prudent fears," justified immediately by Tom's refusal to work; instead, he will trust to Fortune, saying "Come, wishes, be horses; / This beggar shall ride." When he makes his first wish, for money, Nick Shadow promptly appears to tell him of a legacy and take him to London. (Nick is both Mephistopheles, to be paid in a year and a day, and, psychologically, "your shadow," given power by Tom's wishes.) Scene Two, set in Mother Goose's brothel in London, presents the whores and roaring boys celebrating the rites of Venus and of Mars. Tom recites the catechism that Shadow, as godfather, has taught him: to do his duty to himself and "follow Nature as my teacher." But he balks at the word "love," and in his cavatina "Renews the vow he did not keep, / Weeping, weeping, / He kneels before thy wounded shade." (The second stanza directly prepares for the ending, as Tom prays "Though thou daily be forgot, / Goddess, O forget me not" and asks her to "be nigh / In my darkest hour that I, / Dying, dying, / May call upon thy sacred name.") He is then initiated by Mother Goose herself, in the long Lanterloo chorus that is a sinister parody of nursery rhymes and children's games; it begins:

> The sun is bright, the grass is green:
> *Lanterloo, lanterloo.*
> The King is courting his young Queen.
> *Lanterloo, my lady.*

At the end, the question "What will he do when they lie in bed?" is answered, "Draw his sword and chop off her head." And Shadow toasts Tom ironically, "Sweet dreams, my master. Dreams may lie, / But dream. For when you wake, you die." A brief third scene shows Anne deciding to go to London; she knows that Tom needs her help. "Love hears, Love knows, / Love answers him across the silent miles, and goes."

Act Two presents Tom in his London house, bored with following Nature ("O Nature, green unnatural mother, how I have followed where you led") and disgusted with pleasure. He makes his second wish, "I wish I were happy." Shadow appears and proposes that he demonstrate his freedom by marrying the bearded Baba the Turk, precisely because there is no reason to do so: true freedom is to ignore the twin tyrants of pleasure and duty, appetite and conscience, passion and reason:

> . . . he alone is free
> Who chooses what to will, and wills
> His choice as destiny
> . . . Whom neither Passion may compel
> Nor Reason can restrain.

Tom laughs (for the proposal is absurd) and agrees. (In a letter to Stravinsky Auden calls Baba "L'acte gratuit," and this notion, so prominent in Gide and later in Camus and other French writers of atheist-existentialist tendency, is clearly what is represented here: it is one form of freedom and one form of the absurd.) Scene Two shows Anne in front of Tom's house, where she confronts him as he brings Baba home after marrying her. She has sung, foreshadowing the denouement, "A love / That is sworn before Thee can plunder Hell of its prey" as she waits for Tom. To Tom's protestations of unworthiness she has said, "Let worthiness, / So you still love, reside in that"; but upon discovering the marriage she leaves, after she and Tom have recalled in their parting songs the springtime Venus-Adonis imagery of the first scene, now transformed to winter as Adonis goes to the underworld. "O bury the heart," Tom sings,

> And should it, dreaming love, ask—When
> Shall I awaken once again?
> Say—Never, never, never;
> We shall this wint'ry promise keep—
> Obey thy exile, honour sleep
> Forever.

In Scene Three Baba and Tom are revealed at home, Tom bored and sulking, Baba prattling in her patter aria, then appealing in her song, then furious; Tom finally cuts her off by plopping a wig on her head backwards, which reduces her to a state of suspended animation. Shadow appears while Tom sleeps and in pantomime demonstrates a fake machine for converting stones into bread; Tom, awaking, says he has dreamed of the machine and makes his third wish, "I wish it were true." When Shadow shows him the machine he hopes that it will enable him to regain Anne through his own merit: "O may I not, forgiven all my past / For one good deed, deserve dear Anne at last?" The machine, abolishing need, will make earth "an Eden of good will":

> Thanks to this excellent device
> Man shall re-enter Paradise
>   From which he once was driven.
> Secure from want, the cause of crime,
> The world shall for the second time
>   Be similar to heaven.

Shadow, in ironic counterpoint to Tom's rejoicing, comments on how easy it is to swindle people, and urges the "men of sense" to invest and make money. (In his letter to Stravinsky, Auden interpreted the incident: "Il désire devenir Dieu.")

Act Three begins with the same scene, with everything, including

Baba, covered with cobwebs and dust; citizens are examining Tom's goods which are to be sold at auction, now that the swindle has been exposed. Sellem auctions off Baba as an "unknown object"; when he snatches the wig off her head she comes back to life and finishes her interrupted speech. Tom and Shadow sing off-stage, "Old wives for sale." Anne and Baba sing a duet in which Baba tells Anne that Tom still loves her and urges her to go to him; Baba will go back to the stage. Tom and Shadow are again heard singing off-stage, and Anne rushes after them. In Scene Two Tom and Shadow are seen in a churchyard, where Shadow claims his wages after serving Tom for a year and a day. He tells Tom to look in his eyes "and recognize / Whom—Fool! you chose to hire"; Tom's soul is forfeit, and he must kill himself on the stroke of twelve. As the clock is striking, however, Nick suspends it and offers Tom escape if he can name three cards; he explains to the audience that this adds to the sport: "To win at once in love or cards is dull." Tom guesses two, and Shadow tricks him by repeating the first card, the Queen of Hearts, for the third, commenting:

> The simpler the trick, the simpler the deceit;
> That there is no return, I've taught him well,
>   And repetition palls him:
> The Queen of Hearts again shall be for him the Queen of Hell.

But Tom, hearing Anne sing off-stage her arioso from II. ii, "A love / That is sworn before Thee can plunder hell of its prey," chooses the Queen of Hearts again, however "absurd" this may appear. (This is the true Absurd, as against the false Absurd of the *acte gratuit;* it is an act of faith, the Pascalian "wager" or Kierkegaardian "leap.") Shadow, balked of his prey, makes Tom insane, and the scene closes with Tom sitting on the grave in spring once more, believing he is Adonis. The final scene reveals Tom in Bedlam as Adonis (to be mad is to be simultaneously on earth and in hell, rather than alternately as in the classical myth), with Anne visiting him as Venus. He repents, begs forgiveness, and she says, "Thy ravishing penitence / Blesses me, dear heart, and brightens all the past. / Kiss me Adonis: the wild boar is vanquished." In a duet they rejoice in their love, then Anne sings him to sleep in a lullaby (the only lyric Auden preserved separately from this libretto; it is called "Barcarolle" in *The Shield of Achilles*), describing Eden, "paradise regained." Trulove appears to take Anne home; she tells Tom, "In this earthly city we / Shall not meet again, love, yet / Never think that I forget." After they leave, Tom wakes, seeks Venus, and dies, while the chorus sings "Mourn for Adonis. . . ." In the epilogue, the characters each draw a moral: Anne says,

> Not every rake is rescued
> At the last by Love and Beauty;

> Not every man
> Is given an Anne
> To take the place of Duty.

Baba warns that all men are mad; "All they say or do is theatre"; Tom warns young men "who fancy / You are Virgil or Julius Caesar" lest they find they are only rakes; Shadow laments that he "Must do as he is bidden"; "Many insist / I do not exist. / At times I wish I didn't." Together, they sing that the Devil finds work for idle hands "And hearts and minds" to do.

The epilogue has been criticized as an overly abrupt return to the mood of Hogarthian comedy and moral platitude, and as nervously mocking the moral tale. But it seems plain enough that, though the obvious meaning of the proverb is certainly not denied, the "idle hands" for which the Devil finds work are those of seekers after freedom in the atheist-existentialist sense, followers of the false absurd, shown in Tom's *acte gratuit* of marrying Baba, rather than of the true absurd, shown in his act of faith in the card game, when he chooses Anne's card for the second time in defiance of reason and common sense. Similarly, the ending has been criticized as ineffectively rendering the theme of redemption since Tom, being mad, dies without understanding. But Tom's crucial act of faith has already shown the fullest understanding and most complete surrender to love ("I wish for nothing else. / Love, first and last, assume eternal reign; / Renew my life, O Queen of Hearts, again"), and his madness merely translates him to literal acceptance of the role of Adonis, in which he repents and regains innocence, Eden, before he dies. This state, being out of time, may well be represented by madness. Anne is a kind of Venus Urania, Heavenly Aphrodite, symbol and bearer of divine grace—like Dante's Beatrice; without her aid, Tom could not have been saved. In human terms, she embodies Agape, unselfish love; it is not Tom's merits but his need that sends her to his rescue. As the epilogue gives a deeper meaning to one familiar proverb, so it might be said that the role of Anne rehabilitates and makes significant the sentimental platitude about the redeeming influence of the love of a good woman.[10] . . .

Kerman calls the *Rake* "the most genuine and the most delightful work for the theatre in years, to say nothing of its being an operatic masterpiece on almost any terms"; the librettists' contribution he describes as "only slightly less brilliant than Stravinsky's," and he says that the work "offers a unique delight to the combined musical and poetic sensibilities. . . . It is faintest praise to observe that no other opera has been written in English with anything like the same effect." And he goes so far as to wonder "whether there ever has been an opera with so elegant-sounding a libretto."[11]

. . . .

Finally, let us recur briefly to the question of the quality *as poetry* of the opera libretti which have been Auden's only long works (except for the groups of companion-poems) in recent years. We have considered their merits as libretti, and we have seen that Auden says flatly that the libretto must not only be subordinate to the musical demands of the opera, but that it should not be poetry. Let us consider the beginning of *The Rake's Progress,* where Anne sings.

> The woods are green and bird and beast at play
> For all things keep this festival of May;
> With fragrant odours and with notes of cheer
> The pious earth observes the solemn year.

Rakewell answers,

> Now is the season when the Cyprian Queen
> With genial charm translates our mortal scene,
> When swains their nymphs in fervent arms enfold
> And with a kiss restore the Age of Gold.

This is pleasant, admirably calculated for singing, sufficiently but not artificially "period" in diction, and full of simple conventional properties for the composer to work with. It introduces the opera's central themes: the quest for lost innocence, Eden; Venus-Adonis, both as the universal power of love in the biological sense of Venus, and the redeeming and transforming effect of Christian love as Anne will embody it. But the texture is strikingly different from that of Auden's non-operatic songs, much thinner and more open and much more conventional. To say, as Auden suggests, that it is not poetry[12] is to make the distinction too black-and-white, too nearly absolute; it is perhaps better to say that this is a highly specialized form of poetry— like that of Eliot's later plays, and for similar reasons. Its interest is, considered simply as verse, very limited; it is not intended to stand alone, but exists as framework or vehicle for the music, is a deflated balloon until the music blows it up. Or we may say that it is poetry with most of the irony, ambiguity, tension, and other elements of inherent verbal interest carefully removed, so that the words will not call attention to themselves as words, but be absorbed into the music. It is probably significant that Auden preserved three songs from *Paul Bunyan,* written before he had mastered the art of the libretto, in *Collected Poetry;* but in later volumes he has thought only one lyric from *Delia* and one from *The Rake's Progress* ("Lauds" and "Barcarolle," respectively) worth collecting. To recapitulate, we may say that Auden writes three distinct varieties of verse for music. The first is the opera libretto, in which the verbal texture is subordinate to larger musical and dramatic necessities, so that the libretto is an extremely important but inseparable element in a unified whole, not to be judged independently. The second is the song, which is a genuine poem that also, by intention or chance, fits the composer's requirements or desiderata. Even when songs are

written with the intention of being suitable for musical setting, they are
written to be the dominant partner; or so I should argue. The third type is
the self-sufficient or literary song, that is, the song which produces the
illusion that it can be set, but which, in fact, has its own built-in verbal
rhythm too complex and powerful to be adaptable to music. "Look, stranger"
is a good example.

About the musical aspect of Auden's achievement we may say, against
the condescending reviewer who called him the "Da Ponte of our time," that
he has rehabilitated the art of the libretto, that he has in his critical writings
clarified some of the perennial questions about the relation of music and
poetry, and that he has written a large number and variety of great songs.

Notes

1. *The Dyer's Hand*, p. 466; originally published in *Tempo*, 1951, as "Some Reflections
on Opera as a Medium."

2. *Ibid.*, p. 504; originally published in *Encounter*, 1957.

3. In his introduction to *Visionary Novels of George Macdonald* (1954) he includes opera
libretti in the category of Dream Literature.

4. Joseph Kerman, in *Hudson Review*, Summer 1954 (pp. 436–44), reviewing the
Columbia recording of the *Rake*.

5. Letter to M.K.S., April 10, 1963.

6. Alan Ansen, who was Auden's secretary 1948–53 (*The Enchafèd Flood*, 1950, is
dedicated to him), and who has recently published a book of poems, *Disorderly Houses*,
Wesleyan University Press, 1962, gave this information in a letter to the *Hudson Review*
(Summer 1956, p. 319), as an authorized corrective to critics who ignored Kallman's contribution. Kallman wrote, he says, the second half of I,i, all of I,iii, the first half of II,i, and all of
II,ii, all of III,i, and the middle part of III,ii (including the recitativo secco). Stravinsky and
Craft (*Memories and Commentaries*, 1960 [p. 150n]) also specify Kallman's contribution: they
attribute to him the second rather than the third scene of I and only the first aria in II,i. Since
they quote a letter from Auden revising part of I,ii (p. 152) and their statement about II,i
looks confused as it covers only one aria but seems intended to cover more, while Ansen states
specifically that Kallman wrote the next passage ("O Nature, green unnatural mother"), it
appears that Ansen's account is the more reliable. It is easy to see how Stravinsky could be
confused on such points since the order of scenes was changed in the process of composition.

7. Letter to M.K.S., Feb. 19, 1962: "about 75% is by Mr. Kallman."

8. The only scenes that bear much resemblance to Hogarth are the brothel, the auction,
and Bedlam. Anne is very different from, but probably suggested by, the milkmaid in
Hogarth who, seduced and deserted, nevertheless repeatedly tries to save the Rake; but there
is little resemblance between Baba and Hogarth's rich old maid. There is, of course, no
suggestion of any mythical level in Hogarth.

9. I am much indebted to Joseph Kerman's excellent anaslysis, published in the *Hudson
Review*, 1954, and then included in his *Opera as Drama* (New York, 1956). I have taken some
points also from George MacFadden's interpretation in the *Hudson Review*, Spring 1955, and
from Robert Craft's annotations to the Columbia recording.

10. My interpretation of the epilogue owes much to MacFadden (see note 9); but I have
freely changed and revised his suggestions.

11. Kerman in the *Hudson Review*, 1954; Kerman does not include these comments in

Opera as Drama, but he calls *Wozzeck* and the *Rake* the "major operas of this century" (p. 247) and suggests that "in dramatic conception *The Rake* is finer and more meaningful than *Wozzeck*, even though it fails at the end" (p. 248). The libretto, he says, "is indeed unusually subtle for an opera book—though I should certainly not say unduly subtle" (p. 240).

12. I did say this at the English Institute meeting in New York in September 1962 and provoked much indignation from the audience—with which, on further reflection, I found myself in agreement.

Auden as a Literary Critic

CLEANTH BROOKS

Auden is pre-eminently the poet of civilization. He loves landscapes, to be sure, and confesses that his favourite is the rather austere landscape of the north of England, but over and over he has told us that the prime task of our time is to rebuild the *city,* to restore community, to help re-establish the just society. Even a cursory glance over his poetry confirms this view. Who else would have written on Voltaire, E. M. Forster, Matthew Arnold, Pascal, Montaigne, Henry James, Melville, and Sigmund Freud? On any one of them, yes, any poet might. But only a poet of civilization would write poems about them all. If one looks through the reviews and the criticism that he has published during the last thirty years, the case for calling Auden the poet of civilization becomes abundantly clear.

A great deal of this criticism is non-literary or only partially literary. Characteristically, it has to do with the problems of modern man seen in an economic or sociological or psychological context. Auden is everywhere interested in the relation of the individual to society, in the metaphysical assumptions implied by the various societies that have existed in history, and in the claims of history and of nature as they exert themselves upon the human being. What constitutes a society and what holds it together? What is an individual and how is he related to society? What makes a hero and from what does his authority over his fellows derive? How do the differences between Greek tragedy and Elizabethan tragedy reflect differences in the civilization that produced them? What basic changes of sensibility have occurred during the history of Western civilization?

To his interest in cultural patterns and to basic psychological patterns, Auden brings a real zest for classification. In view of such interests and aptitudes, it is not surprising that much of his criticism deals with genres. He devotes a great deal of attention to such topics as the theory of comedy or the kinds of tragedy or the modes of the romantic hero. "Notes on the Comic," an essay published in 1952 in *Thought,* is typical. The tone and general arrangement of the essay remind one a little of the *Poetics*—but

Reprinted from *A Shaping Joy: Studies in the Writer's Craft* by permission of Harcourt Brace Jovanovich and Methuen & Co. Copyright © 1971 by Cleanth Brooks.

Auden is not consciously trudging after either the Stagirite himself or the critics of the Chicago School. He is simply very much interested in his subject, there is a great deal that he wants to make clear to the reader, and he prefers to work systematically.

Genre criticism is closely related to the explorations of the psychological categories of character and action. In this area, Auden has done some of his most brilliant work. A masterpiece of this kind of criticism is his elaborate discussion of the master-servant relationship in literature. The title of the essay is "Balaam and the Ass." It was published in 1954 in *Thought*. Auden begins by defining the master-servant relationship in almost pedantically exact terms. It is not a relationship given by nature but comes into being through an act of conscious volition. It is not an erotic relationship. It is a contractual relationship. (Auden even takes care to tell his reader precisely what a contract is.) Finally, the master-servant relationship is a relation between real persons. (The employees of a factory, for example, are not servants because the master they serve is the factory, a fictitious and not a real person.)

And what, we may ask, has all of this to do with literature? Because the soliloquy, useful though it is, is not enough. In order to present "artistically a human personality in its full depth," we need dialogue and the requisite dialogue demands a special pair. The two people must be similar in certain respects, but in others polar opposites. They must be inseparable—that is, the relationship must not be the kind that is affected by the passage of time or the fluctuations of passion. There is, Auden tells us, "only one relationship which satisfies all those conditions, that between master and personal servant."

The neat click of the logic here may remind us of Edgar Allan Poe, in his "Philosophy of Composition," reasoning his way to the most poetic of all possible topics, the death of a beautiful woman. The apparatus assembled by Auden is, in all conscience, formidable, so much so as to create some anxiety in the reader as to what of value the writer can possibly say after such a prologue. What follows, however, fully vindicates him.

The essay is too long and too richly packed for me to do more than suggest some of the matters treated. There is a very interesting account of the master-servant relationship between lovers, with observations on chivalrous service for the sake of the master-mistress of one's passion. There is a very interesting discussion of Faust and Mephistopheles, and of Don Giovanni, and of Tristan and Isolde. How does the master-servant relation bear upon these characters? Because Don Giovanni's pleasure in seducing women is not sensual but arithmetical. He simply wants or make his list as long as possible, and, since his servant Leporello keeps the list, Leporello in effect becomes the master.

Auden goes on to say that "Just as . . . Don Giovanni might have chosen to collect stamps instead of women, so . . . Tristan and Isolde might have fallen in love with two other people; they are so indifferent to each other as persons . . . that they might just as well—and this is one significance of the love potion—have drawn each other's names out of a hat." A romantic idolatry can be maintained through a lifetime only if the romance is one-sided and one party plays the Cruel Fair. In spite of their declarations of love for each other, Tristan and Isolde in fact "both play the Cruel Fair and withhold themselves." Their passion is not for each other—here Auden is in basic agreement with Denis de Rougemont—but for the Nirvana that each hopes to obtain by means of the other. They do not know each other *as persons* at all; they are really insubstantial, and it is the servants, Kurvenal and Brangaene, who make their decisions and finally control the action.

The next two sections of "Balaam and the Ass" deal with Shakespearian plays, *King Lear* and *The Tempest*. Lear as master and the Fool as servant provide the occasion for some familiar observations upon their relationship but also for much fresh and exciting commentary. A hint of its quality is given in Auden's comment that in an ideal stage production "Lear and the fool should be of the same physical type; they should be athletic meso-morphs. The difference should be in their respective sizes. Lear should be as huge as possible, the fool as tiny." Shakespeare's *Tempest* apparently exercises a peculiar fascination upon Auden. He has discussed it on a number of occa-sions. His *The Sea and the Mirror* carries as its subtitle "A Commentary on Shakespeare's *The Tempest*," and its long prose third section, spoken by Caliban to the Audience, has to do with the nature of art and its function in the human economy.

In "Balaam and the Ass," Auden says of *The Tempest* that he frankly finds it "a disquieting work." Auden cannot really approve of Prospero, who is guilty of—though Auden does not use the term—what would be called today colonialism. Caliban loses much more than he gains under Prospero's domination of the island. If Prospero is master and Ariel a servant who is under proper contractual relation, Caliban is simply a slave. Auden sums up his sense of disquiet by saying that *"The Tempest* is overpessimistic and manichean." On the other hand, *The Magic Flute,* one of Auden's favourite works of art, is, he concedes, "overoptimistic and pelagian."

The most orthodox, as well as the greatest of the spirit-nature pairs in the master-servant relation is that of Don Quixote and Sancho Panza. "Unlike Prospero and Caliban," Auden observes, "their relationship is harmonious and happy; unlike [that of] Tamino and Papageno [in *The Magic Flute*], it is dialectical; each affects the other." But Don Quixote is one of Auden's favourite characters and of him he always writes *con amore.*

The concluding section of this highly interesting and highly speculative essay has to do with the master-servant relationship in Jules Verne's *Around the World in Eighty Days* and in the novels of P. G. Wodehouse. At the opening of Verne's novel Mr. Fogg, Auden tells us, is a kind of stoic and his servant Passepartout a kind of mercurial spirit. But, as the novel goes on, man and master transcend the merely contractual relationship: each ceases to be impersonal to the other, and finally each is willing to sacrifice himself for the other.

In the final paragraph of "Balaam and the Ass" the discussion is connected with another one of Auden's favourite themes, that of the quest and the actions of the quest hero. Wodehouse's Bertie Wooster becomes a kind of inverted quest hero. Through the voices of Bertie Wooster and his incomparable servant, the godlike Jeeves, Auden is able to hear, in spite of their comic intonations, "the voice of Agapé, of Holy Love."

The last comment is calculated to leave the reader gasping. Even the reader sympathetic with Auden's religious position may feel that this essay contains more stimulation than nourishment and constitutes a diet much too rich for his blood. But I shall not say this for myself. With particular aspects of the discussion, I have my own quarrels. I am at odds with Auden's reading of *The Tempest,* for example. I have certain reservations about the kind of criticism exhibited in "Balaam and the Ass." Discussion of ideas and psychological patterns, I would observe, always tends to move away from specifically *literary* criticism. It seems to me significant that Auden can illustrate some of the relationships that interest him most from second- and third-rate artists like Verne and Wodehouse as well as from first-rate artists like Shakespeare and Cervantes. But I go on to reflect that such observations need not, and would not, disconcert Auden. On the whole, I must say that I find "Balaam and the Ass" a remarkable document: the author is sensitive, intelligent, resourceful, quick to discern analogies and linkages where most of us, left to our own devices, would see nothing at all.

In view of his general interest in psychology and the recurrent psychological patterns that underlie the literary genres, it is apparent that Auden is also to be regarded as an archetypal critic. It is true, of course, that he does not often use the term "archetype." I recall only one instance of it in my recent reading of his critical essays and reviews. In his first volume of criticism, *The Enchafèd Flood,* he usually employs the term "symbol" or "symbolic cluster," but his discussion of the images used by the Romantics— the desert and the sea, the paradisaical island and the magical garden, the stone and the shell carried by the Arab in Wordsworth's vision—constitutes what is frequently called archetypal criticism. His interest in symbolic clusters, especially in those that relate to recurrent psychological situations, goes far back in his literary career. That interest was well developed as early as 1940 when he published "The Quest." The psychological situations dramatized in these sonnets receive a full-scale elaboration in the essay titled "K's Quest," which was published in *The Kafka Problem* in 1946. There Auden distinguishes seven kinds of quest, beginning with the fairy story which typically has for its goal "either some sacred object which endows its possessor with magical powers . . . or marriage with a beautiful princess, or both. . . ." One of the more curious versions of the quest is the one that Auden calls the "quest for innocence." It is exemplified in the typical detective story.

In the typical detective story one finds, according to Auden, "a group of people . . . living in what appears to be a state of innocence and grace, where there is no law since there is no need for it. A corpse is found under conditions which make it certain that one of the group must be the murderer, i.e., that state of innocence is lost and the law enters. All fall under suspicion but the hero-detective who identifies and arrests the guilty one and innocence is restored to the rest. . . ."

To apply terms like "state of innocence and grace" to the detective story will seem to many addicts pretentious; but a year or two later in "The Guilty Vicarage: Notes on the Detective Story, by an Addict," Auden was to take the whole thing up another notch. There, for example, he writes: "There are three classes of crime: (a) offences against God and one's neighbor or neighbors; (b) offences against God and society; (c) offences against God."

Now Auden becomes very specific: "Murder," he writes, "is a member and the only member of Class B. The character common to all crimes in Class A is that it is possible, at least theoretically, either that restitution can be made to the injured party . . . or that the injured party can forgive the criminal. . . . Consequently, society as a whole is only indirectly involved; directly, its representatives (the police, etc.) act in the interests of the injured party. Murder is unique in that it abolishes the party it injures, so that society has to take the place of the victim and on his behalf demand restitution or grant forgiveness; it is the one crime in which society has a direct interest." But this is so legalistic, so hairsplittingly precise, that to many readers it will sound like an embarrassing self-parody. People who are bored by detective stories and resent Auden's Christianity will see in this essay Auden at his weakest and most absurd. I should prefer to regard portions of "The Guilty Vicarage" as representing Auden at his most special, limited, and eccentric.

Where is he at his best as a critic? I have already praised the quality of discussion in "Balaam and the Ass" and in *The Enchafèd Flood*. If asked for a shorter example and one more directly concerned with literature as such, I think that I should suggest Auden's introduction to *A Selection from the Poems of Alfred, Lord Tennyson* (1947). It is brief—about 4,000 words—but very much to the point, distinctly a professional job, the work of a practicing man of letters. In the first place, it is characteristic of Auden in its systematic arrangement. Auden defines three kinds of bad poetry. . . .

Next Auden lists—system again, though useful in this brief note—five elements that are found over and over again in Tennyson's poetry. He comments that "In no other English poet of comparable rank does the bulk of his work seem so clearly to be inspired by some single and probably very early experience." Then comes the shocker: "If Wordsworth is the great English poet of Nature, then Tennyson is the great English poet of the Nursery . . . i.e., his poems deal with human emotions in their most primitive states, uncomplicated by conscious sexuality or intellectual rationalization." Here again the reader may or may not be convinced, but he will find Auden's judgement plausible, at least partially true, and, in any case, one that will force him to consider from a new angle Tennyson's special preoccupation with numbed sadness.

In order to "place" Tennyson in his cultural scene, Auden invokes Nietzsche's description of Wagner, Kierkegaard on the subject of his own childhood, a passage from Saint Augustine's *Confessions,* and some quotations from Baudelaire—the reflections, as Auden terms them, of a "cosmopolitan satanic dandy." The range of reference is, again, characteristic of Auden's criticism. The allusion to Baudelaire develops into an extended series of parallels and contrasts with Tennyson, a series which occupies the last several pages of the introduction. . . .

I find these parallels and contrasts highly interesting. It is, in the best sense, an act of the imagination to relate two such poets so as to make each reflect light upon the other. But the confrontation is not arbitrary and mechanical: the perception of a meaningful relation between them derives from a coherent theory of poetry, including the limitations of poetry as well as its powers, together with specific notions about the function of the poet and his proper role in a society. To see this, one need only extract from the concluding pages of Auden's introduction such suggestive phrases as "a first-rate critical intelligence" as a prime resource of a poet, "the error of making a religion of the aesthetic" as a modern misconception of the poet's role, the lack of any "sense of a historical relation between individuals"—this said of Tennyson—and, finally, the attempt (Auden regards it as a mistaken one) "to evade the need for a religious faith by finding some form of magical certainty."

"The error of making a religion of the aesthetic" constitutes much of the substance of Caliban's speech to the audience in Auden's *The Sea and the Mirror.* Auden takes this error very seriously, but he is in no sense a didactic poet who demands that poetry should propagandize for Christianity or any other faith. Indeed, for a man so deeply engrossed in the political problems of our day, for a person who is so serious a moralist and so keen a psychologist, Auden's conception of poetry may seem startling in the limited role which he assigns it. What that role is, what the structure of poetry is, and what the relation of poetry to truth is in Auden's account—these are matters which will occupy most of the space remaining to me in this paper.

The indirect relation of poetry to the world of fact and action is not an idea which came to Auden rather late in his career. It occurs in the well-known and often anthologized poem, "In Memory of W. B. Yeats," where the poet says, "For poetry makes nothing happen: it survives / In the valley of its saying where executives / Would never want to tamper. . . ." But though poetry makes nothing happen, the poet evidently has a role of some importance and a duty, for he is urged, in the perilous times of 1939 when the poem appeared, to make a vineyard "of the curse" and, though he must sing of human unsuccess "in a rapture of distress," he should "teach the free man how to praise. . . ."

The first of Auden's essays that reveals his fully developed theory of poetry is "Squares and Oblongs." Though it appears to be no more than a collection of scattered observations on the poet and poetry and his audience, a very coherent and self-consistent pattern emerges. For example, Auden's earlier observation that the poet is a man of action in one field only, that of language, here becomes the statement that the poet is "before anything else, a person who is passionately in love with language." And Auden illustrates this notion by proposing a test: Ask a young man why he wants to write poetry; if his answer is, "I have important things I want to say," one can conclude that he is not a poet. But if he answers, "I like hanging around words listening to what they say," then maybe he is going to be a poet. So much for the stigmata of the poet. Now for a concise definition of poetry: there are, Auden says, "two theories of poetry. Poetry as a magical means for inducing desirable emotions and repelling undesirable emotions in oneself and others, or Poetry as a game of knowledge, a bringing to consciousness, by naming them, of emotions and their hidden relationships. The first view was held by the Greeks, and is now," Auden remarks, "held by MGM, Agit-Prop, and the collective public of the world. They are wrong."

Auden's characterization of poetry "as a magical means for inducing desirable emotions and repelling undesirable emotions in oneself and others" is derived from R. G. Collingwood's *Principles of Art,* a book published in 1938. In his chapter titled "Art as Magic," Collingwood argues that the primary function of all magical acts is "to generate in the agent or agents certain emotions that are considered necessary or useful. . . ." Magic usually works through artistic or quasi-artistic means, but its aim is not that of art: magic works up the emotions to release them for the sake of a particular practical act.

In "Henry James and the Artist in America" (1948), Auden writes about the temptation to the artist to become "an official magician, who uses his talents to arouse in the inert masses the passions which the authorities consider socially desirable and necessary." But the artist, Auden says, must never have "any truck with magic, whether in its politer forms like diplomatic cultural missions, or in its more virulent varieties. . . ." This is not, however, because art is of sacred importance but on the contrary because it is, as Auden puts it, "in the profoundest sense, frivolous. For one thing, and one thing only is serious: loving one's neighbor as one's self."

Collingwood also makes a sharp distinction between magic and religion, and between art and religion. Here the influence of Collingwood—if I am right in supposing that it is behind much of Auden's theory—would corroborate the much more powerful and pervasive influence of Kierkegaard.

Art, Auden tells us in "Squares and Oblongs," is not a religion. He has to concede that the Greeks did produce some great works of art in spite of the fact that they "confused art with religion." This could happen, Auden tells us—rather consciously riding his high horse here—because the Greeks were, "in reality, like all pagans . . . frivolous people who took nothing seriously."

Auden is willing to follow this anti-emotive view of poetry right on through. He rejects, for example, in Aristotle's *Poetics* the one main deviation into emotive theory, saying that if he understands what Aristotle means when he speaks of "catharsis, [he] can only say he is wrong." You do get a purgation of the emotions from witnessing a bullfight or a professional football match, but not from a work of art. Moreover, poetry is not prophecy. Shelley's claim for the poets that they are "the unacknowledged legislators of the world" is, says Auden, "the silliest remark ever made about poets. . . ."

That the present state of the world is parlous, Auden agrees. Indeed, that state of the world is "so miserable and degraded that if anyone were to say to the poet: 'For God's sake, stop humming and put the kettle on or fetch bandages. The patient's dying,' I do not know how he could justifiably refuse." Unfortunately, no one ever asks the poet to carry out some useful and practical action. What the self-appointed, unqualified Nurse typically says to the poet is this: "Stop humming this instant and sing the Patient a song which will make him fall in love with me. In return I'll give you extra ration-cards and a passport"; and the poor delirious patient cries (out to the poet): "Please stop humming and sing me a song which will make me believe I am free from pain and perfectly well." But the poet, though he ought to be willing to mop the floor or carry bedpans or do any other useful task, must have the courage to deny all such requests and the bribes that go with them.

Does the poet, then, have no responsibility to society? Auden would, I believe, answer that he does, but he would insist that the poet cannot allow a Stalin or a Goebbels or even a President Hoover—I believe I remember Hoover's asking in 1931 for the production of a good poem that would restore our confidence and end the depression—to tell him how to discharge that responsibility, nor can the poet allow the public to tell him how to discharge it. If he has a specific responsibility *as poet,* that responsibility can be discharged only through his being the best poet that he knows how to be.

In "Nature, History, and Poetry" (1950) appeared Auden's most fully matured statement of his conception of poetry. As the title would suggest, nature and history are the co-ordinates for a whole series of definitions and observations about man and his experience. Auden distinguishes, for example, between natural events, which are related by the principle of Identity, and historical events, which are related by the principle of Analogy. He also distinguishes between laws that apply to natural events and those that apply to historical events, "laws-of" and "laws-for." As for man's social life, there are crowds, societies, and communities—among which Auden draws a very careful distinction. Crowds are simply happen-so; societies have a definitive size and specific structure. (Elsewhere, Auden tells us a "society is a group of rational beings united by a common function.") A community, on the other hand, is bound together by a common love. "It is only in history that one can speak of communities as well as societies. . . ."

Man exists "as a unity in tension of four modes of being, Soul, Body, Mind and Spirit. . . . As body and mind, man is a natural creature; as soul and spirit, an historical creature." Auden then works out the implications of this dual position for man's consciousness of himself in relation to the world about him.

Nature and history provide the distinction between science and art. The subject matter of the natural scientist "is a crowd of natural events at all times. He assumes this crowd to be not real but apparent and attempts to discover the true system concealed under its appearances. The subject matter of the poet is a crowd of historic occasions of feeling in the past. He accepts this crowd as real and attempts to transform it into a community. . . ." The implications for poetry of this last comment are immense. Because the subject matter of the poet consists of occasions of *past* feeling, in poetry "desire is seen, as it were, in a mirror, detached from its roots in appetite and passion. . . ." Auden agrees heartily with Wordsworth in thinking that in poetry the emotion must indeed be "recollected in tranquillity." Language, to be sure, can be used to introduce "emotion into the present," for example, in propaganda or pornography; but, Auden says, "such use is magical, not poetical." Elsewhere in this essay he defines propaganda as "the employment of magic by those who do not believe in it over against those who do."

In order to define a poem, Auden invokes an analogy from the social context in which men live. A poem, he says, is a linguistic society or verbal system. But a poem differs from many other "verbal societies" in that "meaning and being are identical." Thus, it is not quite accurate to say that "a poem should not mean but be." On the other hand, a poem differs from a human society in the fact that it has natural being and not historical being. "Like an image in the mirror, a poem might be called a pseudo person"; that is, the poem has "uniqueness and addresses the reader as person to person but like all natural beings and unlike historical persons, it cannot lie."

Auden thus makes Philip Sidney's famous point very adroitly but in his own way. He writes that "it is not possible to say of a poem that it is true or false[,] for one does not have to go to anything except [the poem] itself to discover whether or not it is in fact . . . a community of feelings truly embodied in a verbal society. If it is not, if unfreedom or disorder is present, the poem itself reveals this on inspection." That is, if I may be allowed to make my own comment here, the problem is not one of discovering whether some proposition made by the poem is true or false; it is rather that of discovering whether the poem is truly unified or chaotic, whether its parts are related or unrelated, whether it embodies order or is rent apart by disorder.

How does the poet go about transforming the two "crowds" at his disposal—the words in his vocabulary and the feelings of past occasions that he can recall—into a verbal society in which the feelings form a community? Through a dialectical struggle. For the verbal system is "actively coercive upon the feelings it is attempting to embody" and, Auden admits, what it "cannot embody truthfully it excludes." On the other hand, "the feelings are passively resistant to all claims of the system to embody them [all claims, that is] which they do not recognize as just. . . ."

This recognition of resistances to be overcome, as feeling competes with feeling, and as word exerts its pressure on feeling and feeling exerts its pressure on the choice of word, is reminiscent of a considerable body of critical opinion in our day. I am thinking of Yeats, Nietzsche, I. A. Richards, John Crowe Ransom, and others; but I am not concerned here to trace Auden to a particular set of sources or to impugn his originality. In discussing the resistances to be adjusted and the conflicting claims to be reconciled, Auden writes that "every feeling competes with every other demanding inclusion and a dominant position to which they are not necessarily entitled, and every word demands that the system shall modify itself in its case. . . ." Like a human society, the poem embodies tensions and achieves its unity, when it achieves it, through tensions. Since this is the way in which a poem is organized, it may fail in either of two ways: it may exclude too much and thus fall into banality, or it may "attempt to embody more than one community at once" and thus fall into disorder.

Naturally, my own ears perk up at Auden's use of terms like "inclusion" and phrases like "exclude too much." Let me attempt, then, my own summary of what Auden is saying in this highly condensed essay. Throughout the essay, Auden sees the basic poetic problem as the problem of securing unity. He takes into account the resistances which any poet must acknowledge and reconcile if his poem is to become a poem at all—resistances which he cannot deny if he is to hope to produce a mature and an honest poem. In any poem unity is secured by means of two basic principles. The first involves trimming off the contradictions and irrelevances—that is, *excluding* what cannot be honestly embodied in the poem. The second involves a procession of *inclusion* in which the disparate and recalcitrant are fitted into the poem by a deepening and widening of the imaginative context. The poem which is overambitious in its attempt to include the jarring and the difficult may, of course, fail to achieve unity and remain incoherent. But too much reliance on exclusion carries its risks, too: the poem may be robbed of depth and richness.

Auden concludes his essay with a series of analogies drawn from Christianity. Every poet, he writes, consciously or unconsciously holds the following "absolute presuppositions, as the dogmas of his art: (1) An historical world exists, a world of unique events and unique persons. . . . (2) The historical world is a fallen world. . . . (3) The historical world is a redeemable world. The unfreedom and disorder of the past can be reconciled in the future." That is, any poet at work on a poem finds himself trying to put in order, and thus into meaningful relationship, experiences which demand to be redeemed in knowledge.

As he pursues this analogy, Auden may be said to present a parallel to Eliot's view of the impersonality of art: "In poetry as in other matters," Auden says, "the law holds good that he who would save his life must lose it; unless the poet sacrifices his feelings completely to the poem, so that they are no longer his but the poem's, he fails." Whether borrowed from Eliot or not, the basic conception is the same: the poem is not primarily the poet's expression of personal feelings; it is not the expression of the poet that counts but the organization of the thing that he is making. The poem, then, according to Auden, is "beautiful or ugly to the degree that it succeeds or fails in reconciling *contradictory* feelings in an order of mutual propriety."

Why contradictory, someone will ask; and Auden's implied answer surely would run something like this: because the material with which he works involves unfreedom and disorder. Poetry which systematically ignores contradiction and disorder and evil is banal, if not lying. In the end, I suppose that Auden would finally simply appeal to the facts. The great poems, not merely the great tragedies but even lyrics that possess depth and resonance, are not really "simple" but exhibit in their very make-up a triumph won over confusion, disharmony, and disorder. Auden continues his comment by saying that "Every beautiful poem presents an analogy to the forgiveness of sins, an analogy, not an imitation, because it is not evil intentions which are repented of and pardoned but contradictory feelings which the poet surrenders to the poem in which they are reconciled."

Auden obviously values his analogy and presumably would be reluctant to surrender it. But to people who are ruffled by the Christian association, Auden could, without giving up his essential point, offer the testimony of Nietzsche. I am thinking of such of Nietzsche's statements as "contrasts are . . . the highest sign of [artistic] power . . . manifesting itself in the conquest of opposites"; or his remark that the greatest artists are those "who make harmony ring out of every discord." The genuine artist does not narrow his poetry to express one or the other of the contradictory feelings. He fashions a poem in which they are reconciled and unified.

That Auden, the poet of civilization, the student of cultural history, the serious moralist, should hold what amounts to a formalist conception of poetry may come as a shock. Yet it is plainly a fact, and a little reflection will indicate that no contradiction is involved. Auden's position may disturb some of our conventional notions and habitual associations, but the conventional notions of most of us usually profit from being shaken up. The assumption that poetry must be either an escape from life or else the blueprint for a better life is obviously oversimple.

I shall not, however, be content to argue that Auden's critical position is self-consistent and tenable for a man who is deeply concerned with the problems of civilization. I propose that Auden's special position is a positive source of strength. It has enabled him to avoid most of the traps laid for the historical critic, the moralistic critic, and the archetypal critic. Auden's respect for the autonomy of art has forbidden him to consider it as merely the handmaiden of a religion or of a political party. On the other hand, his sense of the limitations of art—he is willing to call it in final terms *frivolous*—prevents his turning it into a kind of *ersatz* religion.

Auden is not only aware of the relation of art to religion and to science. He knows how the various kinds of criticism are related to the literary work and to each other. Indeed, he practices several kinds of criticism with equal competence—not, surely, as a virtuoso display and not because one kind of criticism is as good as another or because any old criticism will do, but rather because an expert craftsman possesses specialized tools and knows what each is good for.

Auden's virtues as a critic obviously spring from his intelligence, sensitivity, power of imagination, and depth of insight. These qualities are primary: no literary theory could possibly provide a substitute for them. But a sound theory does allow the critic to make the best use of his natural endowment, and his possession of a coherent and responsible theory accounts for Auden's having become one of the soundest as well as one of the most exciting critics of our day.

[From *W. H. Auden*]

GEORGE T. WRIGHT

As critics study Auden more fully in years to come, I suspect we shall see more clearly not only his psychological penetration but the force of his delicate poetic strategies, his superb balances, his unprecedented uses of the comic, his careful arrangements of surprises that disturb our expectations and yet fulfill them, the harmonies that are at once resolved and disconcerting. He disconcerts us so oddly that we think he must be at fault. We have hardly any previous experience with literary irony pushed so far, made to do so many things, in single poems and throughout a long career. But we ought by now to guess that the reason a poet like Auden puzzles is that we have not yet understood him and to think it likely, as in similar past cases, that as the world we live in grows clearer to us, these intricate ironies will seem more and more appropriate to it.

. . . .

Since 1969, when the first edition of this book was published, many books and articles have appeared, and they tend, on the whole, to support the prediction in the final paragraph of the previous chapter. Scholars are clearer now about the meanings and contexts of the early work of Auden, and the later poetry is beginning to be better understood and appreciated, as a result of studies by Replogle, Johnson, and others. . . . Anthologists still suffer from the lazy habit of using only early poems to give students an idea of Auden's work. Occasionally, they include "In Praise of Limestone" (1948) or "The Shield of Achilles" (1952) but almost never a syllabic poem written by Auden during his last quarter-century as an active poet. Until they begin to do so, new readers of Auden will continue to get a distorted notion of what his work is like.

We now know much more, too, about Auden's personal life, and his death in 1973 permits us to begin to see his life and poetic career as a whole. One question bound to be debated is whether Auden was happy. In his last years he certainly became very lonely in his New York apartment during the half-years that Chester Kallman spent in Greece. Still, he could write in 1965 that the three months he had traveled in Iceland in 1936 were "among the happiest in a life which has, so far, been unusually happy."[1] He appears to have thought of himself as having been blessed in his life and in his talent, and he appreciated, as most of us do not, what a privilege it is to lead a comfortable life unmarked by personal catastrophe.

Yet many of his friends report his closing years to have been increasingly lonely. At one point in the early 1970s, Auden proposed to his younger friend Orlan Fox, with whom he had been dining on Friday nights for years, that they should share an apartment. Fox declined but realized later that "it was a cry for help, for companionship."[2] Finding his isolation unbearable, and physically threatening (he told reporters: "If I should have a coronary, friends may not find me for days"[3]), he decided, after more than thirty years, to give up his residence in New York and to spend his winters instead at his old college at Oxford, Christ Church. He had taught for five seasons at Oxford (1956–61) as Professor of Poetry and hoped to find there a more companionable setting for his winter months. In December 1972 he accordingly left New York, spent the next few months at Oxford, where, it appears, he was too old and formidable a lion to get close to,[4] and in the spring moved on to the little house in Kirchstetten, Austria, which he and Kallman had shared during springs and summers since 1957.

Although Auden's health in these years is often described as failing— his corns had long required him to wear house slippers everywhere and to walk with a shuffling gait, his "breathing was labored and he was blue around the lips," his heart was "playing up a little," and he had had "an attack of severe vertigo"[5]—at least one visitor to Kirchstetten in the summer of 1973 found him lively, "rejuvenated," talkative, and charming.[6] In late September, having closed up the house for the season, he was preparing to return to England after spending the weekend in Vienna. There he gave a poetry reading on September 29, retired to his hotel room, and was found dead the next morning. He had evidently suffered a heart attack. "I shall probably die in a hotel to the great annoyance of the management," he had written to Ursula Niebuhr in 1947.[7] He was buried in Kirchstetten, but a plaque in the Poet's Corner of Westminster Abbey also commemorates his life. Whether Kallman had any intention of writing at length about his famous life-companion is not known; but he, too, died of a heart attack in Athens less than two years later.

I AUDEN'S INFLUENCE

The influence of Auden on contemporary American poetry has still to be studied in detail. Hardly any poet in English history has been so intensely admired as Auden in the early part of his career, and even in 1956 Allen Ginsberg and Gregory Corso on meeting him tried to kiss "the turn-ups of his trousers."[8] But as early as 1941 Randall Jarrell was shocked by Auden's changes in style, which he anatomized in two brilliant essays, . . . and in later years Auden's reputation among poets was mixed. He continued to be admired for his prodigious craftsmanship, but as more young writers learned to write free verse or to explore what came to be known as deep-image poetry, they found more congenial models in Pound, Williams, and others. For some time Auden's easy conversational style—the classic example is "Musée des Beaux Arts"—was much praised and imitated by poets eager to avoid the hyper-Romantic bardic chanting of Dylan Thomas, but only a few American poets have found it possible or desirable to mix that easy style with formal verse. Similarly, although Auden, following Eliot's lead, showed later poets with what strong ironic effect ordinary phrases and slang could be used in modern poems, it was the Beat poets, not Auden, who extended the principle so far as to make available to contemporary poets any English words or locutions, no matter how obscene they might have been thought by earlier writers.

Even relatively traditional poets, such as Adrienne Rich, James Wright, W. S. Merwin, and John Ashbery—all chosen by Auden as winners in the Yale Series of Younger Poets—in time moved away from stricter to freer styles. On the other hand, Richard Wilbur, Anthony Hecht, John Hollander, James Merrill, and other poets influenced by Auden have continued to explore the possibilities of metrical verse and regular stanzaic forms. Merrill's allegiance has been carried even further: mainly in iambic pentameter lines, often in rhymed couplets, he has made Auden one of the chief characters in an elaborate three-volume account of his experiences with the Ouija board.[9]

It is still too early to tell whether free verse will become the characteristic mode of American poetry in the future, or whether formal verse—iambic, accentual, or syllabic—will continue to be composed by our chief poets. In England the question is, if anything, even more open. In any event, the formality of Auden's verse is less and less likely to be considered a ground for reproach as his life recedes further into the past, for to write a formal poem in an age of free verse is to make a polemical statement; twenty years later all that matters is whether the poem is, of its kind, as good as it might be. If poets do continue at all to write in formal verse, they are bound to pay homage to Auden, who is one of the art's great practitioners.

In addition to assisting contemporary poets to develop more conversational styles in their verse, Auden also helped them to feel more at home with symbolism. He is, from first to last, a symbolist poet who in his own way carries on the tradition of the great modernist writers Yeats, Joyce, and Eliot. But, unlike them, he repudiated the idea that symbolist poetry must be portentous in manner, grandiose in scale and design. Whereas they saw in symbols a means of transcending or aggrandizing commonplace reality, Auden succeeded, as it were, in domesticating symbolism. His way of seeing everything in our lives, no matter how trivial, as symbolic—streams, waking up, the bathroom, killing mice—implies, and is meant to imply, that our symbolic habits are themselves commonplace, that symbolism, far from justifying flights of romantic emotion, is merely part of the ordinary furniture of our lives. It has been exciting, even fun, to become aware of it; we need to understand how it works; we need, especially, to see how largely it figures in our lives, and how necessary to us are the "secondary worlds" (like poetry or opera) that we construct with our symbolic imaginations. But our aim is to understand, not to be transported out of time, not to seek those eternal moments so valued by Yeats and Eliot, but to develop an accurate understanding of the conditions, both inner and outer, under which we live and the behavior we characteristically use to cope with those conditions.

Although Auden's almost nonchalant use of symbolism has undoubtedly helped make it easier for some contemporary poets to incorporate it without fuss into their own work, it is still uncertain what influence Auden's later, less resonant poetry may have. For if Auden was at all a revolutionary poet, this well-made comic verse of his mature period was his most revolutionary work. It goes against a two-hundred-year-old tradition of Romantic verse, in which we expect a poet to lift us out of ourselves, to offer archetypal sufferers and symbolic experiences with which we can deeply identify, to present human life essentially through images of successful or failed transcendence. Auden's highly original later poetry goes counter to this whole tradition, and most other poets have not yet become aware of its force, its meaning, and its possibilities. In time we can reasonably expect that other poets of merit will find in his work a classic model of a poetry strong in feeling, large in scope, but centered in the perception of truth rather than in the emotional transport.

II   ANTI-ROMANTIC HYPERBOLE

In declining to overstate the importance of our passionate moments, and in turning an essentially comic glance on our most intense feelings, Auden in his later years incurred the doubt and even the hostility of many writers and readers of poetry. Often committed to fuzzy ideas about myth, religion, or mystical sources of self, or at least convinced of the primacy of personal or political feeling in any account of human values, they sometimes found Auden's subjects trivial, his manner frivolous, his concern with forms mere playing. And it is difficult still for many readers to go all the way with Auden in his views of life and art. Refusing to exaggerate the role of poetry in the world, recognizing that it can have almost no political impact and is enjoyable simply for its own sake, content to have been fortunate enough to excel at it and to have spent his life as a maker of poems, Auden has seemed to some to be concerned with a poetry whose passional center is missing. The *angst* is gone, and what remains is a brilliant but fussy verse-maker: Hans Sachs has turned into Beckmesser.

Poets who felt this way became increasingly aware that Auden's way of producing poetry was radically different from theirs. The visionary poetry of his early phase gave way to a verse of intellectual insight in which ideas—often comically presented, and always with panache—are central. Although it is hard to imagine a poet without an idea, there are many contemporary poets who hold a much more organic theory of poetry. For them the poem is likely to begin with an image or a rhythm which serves as a kind of mystical vortex around which the poem in all its phrases gathers like a thunderstorm. Or, in more moderate versions, the poem should at least confess its origins in some more passionate center than the brain. If Auden would regard all such views as fatally Romantic ("The romantic lie in the brain / Of the sensual man-in-the-street"—EA, 246), his own later poetry has seemed to many readers too directly concerned with ideas, and its whimsical or even at times its precious tone has been heard as a ghastly thinning of the prophetic voice that rang out so impressively in his youth.

The figure Auden cut in his last years in literary circles contributed something to this picture. A great, aging presence in American poetry, Auden had brought many younger poets into prominence when, as editor of the Yale Series of Younger Poets from 1947 to 1958, he had chosen to publish their first volumes. By 1972, however, he had stopped reading the new poets. "One hasn't the time!" he said in an interview,[10] and it is clear that as he grew older his ideas became codified, his receptiveness to new ones diminished. Again and again in interviews, lectures, readings, conversations, and letters the same formulated convictions, the same canonical examples, are trotted out, almost verbatim. When interviewers continually ask Auden the expected questions, he provides the expected answers. More and more, too, those formulations—often phrased with beautiful clarity and conciseness, and proceeding out of extremely intelligent observation of people and life—are disturbingly systematic: there are only two ways of doing this, or three ways of doing that. All life is analyzed schematically, and sometimes one senses that the beauty of the scheme has been more important to Auden than the accuracy of the observation.

In *Secondary Worlds,* for example, Auden makes the point that statements in poems, as opposed to statements in life, are neither true nor false:

> Similarly, if a boy says to a girl "I love you," she may with good reason wonder if he really means what he says, or is only pretending in order to seduce her, but if I read the lines

> My dear and only love, I pray
> That little world of thee . . .

I cannot raise the question of sincerity: the words mean neither more nor less than they say.[11]

But, like many statements in the later criticism of Auden, the conclusion is too downright. Such lines as Auden quotes may be ironic or insincere, and we regularly raise questions about the sincerity of speakers in poems. Or again, he writes: "In a secondary world [art, as opposed to life], we are omniscient, aware of everything which exists and happens in it, and understanding exactly why."[12] But this is obviously not true: we value some works for their ambiguity, for their being open to different readings, and after several hundred years we are still not sure why Hamlet acts as he does. When he makes such statements, Auden seems to have mainly in mind the lucid, unambiguous poetry that he himself came to write in his later years.

But if such statements suffer from an exaggerated lucidity, an overstatement of what is generally the case, it is exactly this quality that readers have often found most exciting in Auden's early poetry. His art strangely mixes crisp, logical statement with hyperbole; its discourse constantly proceeds as if something were literally true that can only be understood as metaphor. Throughout his career, from the spy-imagery of the early poems to the quest of *The Age of Anxiety,* from the notion that Yeats, as his body breaks up, *becomes* his admirers to the transformation of Caliban into our most sophisticated fleshly selves, from the exegetical reading of desolate early landscapes to that of "Streams" and "Islands," Auden's technique has been to overstate his insights. That his prose, that his talk, often did the same—" 'Only the "Hitlers of the world" work at night; no honest artist does' "[13]—serves to remind us how deeply the habit was ingrained and how inseparable it was from his quest for truth. Truth hides in our lies; lies peep out at us from behind our truths. In an odd way, Auden's finished work stands as an express, and also as an implicit, warning against the excessive claims of any abstract system.[14] The most uncanny strength of his hyperbolic art is that it warns us against hyperbole.

III   YES, LOVE, YOU HAVE BEEN LUCKY

For many British critics, Auden's apostasy has seemed of several kinds—the abandoner of his country in time of crisis, and of his commitment to politics in a troubled age. As expatriate, Anglican, and homosexual, he appears to have made all the wrong choices; at the very least, everyone can accuse him on *some* score. Radical enough to begin with, and always at odds in some ways with traditional measures of respectability, he nevertheless traveled his own odd path toward a modified *rapprochement* with conventional good behavior. As François Duchene puts it:

> Yet, for all his cosmopolitan activity and catholic interests he has, in his attitudes, seemed more and more a caricature of an Edwardian upper-middle-class Englishman of his year of birth. His clerihews, his whimsy, his faintly

stiff-upper-lip emphasis on the decencies . . . his nonsense rhymes, his daydreams of lawns and rain-gauges, his dislike of ash in teacups or his assumption that a *nurse* will first point out the moon to the infant poet-to-be, have
vanishing English privilege written all over them. To emerge as a posthumous
Victorian is a curious consummation for the marxist *enfant terrible* of the
Thirties and naturalised postwar American. It is a distinguished and well-
earned retirement, but a kind of retirement all the same.[15]

Most writers, as they grow older, lose some of their creative energy, and
their imaginative work falls increasingly into a familiar mold. Some go on
writing, but their novels and poems repeat each other; they have trouble
finding anything new to say. Shakespeare retired before he was fifty; Wordsworth was not quite forty when his verse began to cool; when Eliot gave up
poetry (for verse plays), he was fifty-five. The contrary example of Yeats in
our century has perhaps led us to expect too much of our poets' stamina. But
those who are disappointed by Auden's later career are probably troubled not
merely because a fine poet abandoned a successful early style or the right
views, but because his whole later life was a deliberate repudiation of his
earlier position as a poetic *leader,* not merely one of many admired young
writers but the poet who established the tone, the idioms, the imagery, of a
whole generation of poets and fiction writers, or at least of many among
them. (No one has cared very much when Robert Lowell took up, or put
down, his religion.) Probably no poet since Wordsworth, not even Eliot to
the same degree, has been regarded in this way, as the poet who could show
the way to new modes of writing. What becomes increasingly clear in
retrospect, and increasingly remarkable, is that Auden deliberately resigned
this position at the age of thirty-two, and that he did so out of profound
conviction. Always interested in leadership, both personally and as a subject
to explore in poems and plays, he was never really comfortable with it, and
he writes most often about the inadequacy of leaders. He came to feel, with
the help of Kierkegaard, that the single ordinary man is a better subject, and
that is what, in his gifted way, he tried to become. In the private world,
where everyone is alone, there are no leaders. Every poet must write his own
poems, not those that belong to another's style or thought, so that to be a
poetic leader is really to falsify the whole enterprise. Honesty, in poetry as in
life, is the best policy.

To be gifted and ordinary at once may seem a paradox, but it is a
paradox at the very heart of Auden's view of life. Every human being is
special, but no one is heroic in all respects, and Auden from the beginning is
fascinated by the coexistence in the same person of remarkable and commonplace qualities—to cite one example, the great writer of "Who's Who," full
of "honours" but "Love made him weep his pints like you and me" (*EA,* 150).
For Auden, being human means being divided, and among the divisions that
count in his work is that between having great talent and being an ordinary

muddled mortal. "The Arts? Well, FLAUBERT didn't say / Of artists: '*Ils sont dans le vrai*' " (*CP* [1976], 171). The maker of poems is also a liver of life, and no better than most at that. Auden seems to have known that in his own life he never quite got over being a precocious boy, slovenly in his habits, inordinately fond of jokes, and caustically critical of obtuse people: "I was . . . insufferably superior with anybody who, when speaking about matters in which I was interested, said something I thought stupid."[16] Contempt for stupidity goes along with cleverness, the character fault with the intellectual virtue. And one of Auden's recurrent themes (notably in *Elegy for Young Lovers*) is the knowledge that to be brighter than everyone else is not at all to be better.

Auden's work is divided in other ways, too. It is a strange mixture, for example, of the caustic and the bland, of satire and praise. It seems to go in for praise on principle, not by nature, and this is partly what irritates critics—that his gift for the absurd detail, the comic instance, should have been used, finally, in the service of relatively bland statements about the nature of man, or even of more trivial notions, instead of in the service of some overwhelming tragic or Swiftian vision of twentieth-century life. We keep asking Auden to have been some other kind of poet, instead of noticing exactly the kind of poet he was. For Auden's own nature appears to have been divided along lines that his poems reflect, between personal disorder and an exaggerated intellectual clarity, between a neurotic untidiness in the spaces where he lived and a compulsive punctuality, between his sense of himself as quicker and cleverer than almost anyone else in the world and his sense of himself as unloved, unattractive, lonely, fat, faulty. There are other oppositions—between the one-night sexual stand and his enduring life with Chester Kallman, in the division of his life into a European spring and summer and an American autumn and winter, between his English youth and his American maturity, between a professional fame that enabled him to meet and influence great numbers of the world's, and especially New York's, artists and intellectuals and a personal life of sordid encounters with barmen, drifters, and call-boys. His firm intellectual control of abstract ideas and formal structures seems clearly to have been Auden's way of coping magisterially with elements in his nature that remained perpetually adolescent; his insight into secondary worlds at once brilliantly clarifies the role they play in everyone's life and confesses the miseries of his own primary world.

Yet even those miseries were the limited ones of loneliness and isolation, and critics who discuss his personal foibles as if they could constitute a convincing moral case against Auden have been beautifully answered by Elizabeth Hardwick: "Auden's eccentricities were harmless and had the good fortune to be predictable, sparing his conduct thereby from rushes of paranoia, violence, and pettiness. If he knocked off at nine, his example was not of sufficient tyranny to drag anyone else along with him. His mind, his loneliness, his ability to love, his uncompetitive sweetness of character survived his ragged bedroom slippers and egg-spotted tie. And his genius, the high seriousness of his life, survived his death."[17]

If Auden failed to develop the promise of his numinous early poetry into a later work of great power and presence, he did so out of conviction that to write such a poetry in our age was, at least for him and probably for everyone, a dishonest act. The best poetry he wrote after 1940 is certainly stunning and impressive; it glows with insight and intelligence, and its forms and rhythms are richly inventive. He managed to survive his own divided life and to make its disorder into art, to turn Caliban (Wystan) into Ariel (W. H. Auden). From his own art, as well as from the reminiscences of others, the picture we get of Auden's own life is of a brilliant, only fitfully happy boy turning gradually into a world-weary roué, his growing irritation with the world relieved only by bouts of elegant mischief and cleverly phrased *aperçus*. For many readers this vision seems insufficiently large: too little of the inner man, the sufferer, appears, too much of the comic diminisher. The imposing art which his early poetry promised, a poetry which would provide a ringing appraisal of an age, of our public as well as our private problems, never materialized, or not in the looked-for guise. In the early 1940s Auden's verse ceased to refer to current public events, and a generation of readers that had hoped to find in him a continuing commentator on political events was disappointed.

Their expectations, of course, were unrealistic, even Romantic. Auden knew that he could not continue as a cultural spokesman, that his insight into day-by-day or year-by-year political affairs was that of an amateur, and that his continuing to claim to have more than a distant general perception of the cultural anxieties of his time would be dishonest. Looking at Europe in the 1930s, Auden could see an Inferno of damned leaders, driving their peoples blindly to war or stumbling stupidly in ignorance of what to do: "And still all over Europe stood the horrible nurses / Itching to boil their children" (*EA*, 240). Unlike Voltaire, the subject of this poem, Auden was wise enough not to think that "Only his verses / Perhaps could stop them." But if a poet could not change the world, if he could not even, in conscience, lead a poetic revolution, he could still tell the truth in his poems.

We can now begin to see Auden's whole career in perspective, and it is his whole career that will have to be understood if we are to judge his achievement. This is still not easy to do, and most critical studies have concentrated either on the poetry before 1940 or on the poetry after, on the English Auden or the American, or have seen these phases as deeply opposed and inconsistent. What we may come to see in his whole career is a powerful but erratic imaginative talent scattering its striking images of inner and European life but gradually corrected and controlled by an art that regularly exchanges mythic power for intelligence, elegance, comedy, and truth. If Auden was not happy in his life, he was happy in his art: he achieved what he wanted to achieve.[18] Over nearly half a century he composed an impressive array of masterful poems and other writings, and these should assure him a prominent place among the great poets who have written in English.

Notes

1. "Foreword," *Letters from Iceland,* by W. H. Auden and Louis MacNeice (New York: Random House, 1969), p. 9.
2. Orlan Fox, "Friday Nights," in *W. H. Auden: A Tribute,* ed. Stephen Spender (New York: Macmillan, 1975), p. 174.
3. *Minneapolis Tribune,* February 19, 1972, pp. 1A, 8A.
4. David Luke, "Homing to Oxford," in *W. H. Auden: A Tribute,* pp. 202–17.
5. Dr. Oliver Sacks, "Dear Mr. A . . . ," in *W. H. Auden: A Tribute,* pp. 192–93.
6. Anon., "Auden at Kirchstetten," *South Atlantic Quarterly* 75 (Winter 1976): 12.
7. Ursula Niebuhr, "Memories of the 1940s," in *W. H. Auden: A Tribute,* p. 118.
8. Charles Osborne, *W. H. Auden: The Life of a Poet* (New York and London: Harcourt Brace Jovanovich, 1979), p. 246.
9. See "The Book of Ephraim" in *Divine Comedies* (New York: Atheneum, 1977), pp. 47–136; *Mirabell: Books of Number* (New York: Atheneum, 1978); and *Scripts for the Pageant* (New York: Atheneum, 1980).
10. Daniel Halpern, "Interview with W. H. Auden," *Antaeus* 5 (1972): 139.
11. *Secondary Worlds* (New York: Random House, 1969), p. 50.
12. Ibid., p. 52.
13. Fox, p. 173.
14. As Hannah Arendt summed up his thoughts, in words quoted earlier: "The main thing was to have no illusions and to accept no thoughts, no theoretical systems that would blind you against reality" ("Remembering Wystan H. Auden," in *W. H. Auden: A Tribute,* pp. 184–85).
15. François Duchene, *The Case of the Helmeted Airman: A Study of W. H. Auden's Poetry* (London: Chatto and Windus, 1972), pp. 179–80.
16. "As It Seemed to Us," in *Forewords and Afterwords,* ed. Edward Mendelson (New York: Random House, 1973), p. 508.
17. Elizabeth Hardwick, "Love It or Leave It!" (review of Peter Conrad, *Imagining America*), *New York Review of Books* 27 (April 3, 1980): 27.
18. I owe this assessment to Stephen Spender, who ventured it during a visit to the University of Minnesota some years ago.

[From *Lions and Shadows*]

CHRISTOPHER ISHERWOOD

. . . Weston and I met again, by purest chance, seven years later. Just before Christmas, 1925, a mutual acquaintance brought him in to tea. I found him very little changed. True, he had grown enormously; but his small pale yellow eyes were still screwed painfully together in the same short-sighted scowl and his stumpy immature fingers were still nail-bitten and stained— nicotine was now mixed with the ink. He was expensively but untidily dressed in a chocolate-brown suit which needed pressing, complete with one of the new fashionable double-breasted waistcoats. His coarse woollen socks were tumbled, all anyhow, around his babyishly shapeless naked ankles. One of the laces was broken in his elegant brown shoes. While I and his intro-ducer talked he sat silent, aggressively smoking a large pipe with a severe childish frown. Clumsy and severe, he hooked a blunt dirty finger round the tops of several of the books in my shelves, over-balancing them on to his lap and then, when his casual curiosity was satisfied, dropping them face down-wards open on the floor—serenely unconscious of my outraged glances.

But when my acquaintance, who had another engagement, had gone, Weston dropped some of his aggressive academic gaucherie: we began to chatter and gossip: the preparatory school atmosphere reasserted itself. We revived the old jokes; we imitated Pillar cutting bread at supper: ("Here you are! Here you are! Help coming, Waters! Pang-slayers coming! Only one more moment before that terrible hunger is satisfied! Fight it down, Waters! Fight it down!") We remembered how Spem used to pinch our arms for not knowing the irregular verbs and punish us with compulsory fir-cone gather-ing. We tried to reconstruct the big scene from Reggy's drama, *The Waves,* in which the villain is confronted by the ghost of the murdered boy, seated in the opposite chair: ("The waves . . . the waves . . . can't you hear them calling? Get down, *carrse* you, get down! Ha, ha—I'm not afraid! Who says I'm afraid? Don't stare at me, *carrse* you, with those great eyes of yours. . . . I never feared you living; and I'm demned if I fear you now you're—*dead!* Ha, ha! Ha, ha! Ha ha ha ha ha ha ha!") Weston was brilliant at doing one of Pa's sermons: how he wiped his glasses, how he coughed, how he clicked his fingers when somebody in chapel fell asleep: ("Sn Edmund's Day. . . . Sn Edmund's Day. . . . Whur ders it *mean?* Nert—whur did it mean to *them, then, theah?* Bert—whur ders it mean to *ers, heah, nerw?*") We laughed so much that I had to lend Weston a handkerchief to dry his eyes.

Just as he was going, we started to talk about writing. Weston told me that he wrote poetry nowadays: he was deliberately a little over-casual in making this announcement. I was very much surprised, even rather disconcerted. That a person like Weston (as I pictured him) should write poems upset my notions of the fitness of things. Deeper than all I. A. Richards' newly implanted theories lay the inveterate prejudices of the classical- against the modern-sider. People who understood machinery, I still secretly felt, were doomed illiterates: I had an instantaneous mental picture of some childish, touchingly crude verses, waveringly inscribed, with frequent blots and spelling mistakes, on a sheet of smudgy graph-paper. A bit patronizingly, I asked if I might see some of them. Weston was pleased, I thought. But he agreed ungraciously—"Right you are, if you really want to"—his bad manners returning at once with his shyness. We parted hastily and curtly, quite as though we might never bother to see each other again.

A big envelope full of manuscript arrived, a few mornings later, by post. The handwriting, certainly, was all I had expected, and worse. Indeed, there were whole lines which I have never been able to decipher, to this day. But the surprise which awaited me was in the poems themselves: they were neither startlingly good nor startlingly bad; they were something much odder—efficient, imitative and extremely competent. Competence was the last quality I had been prepared for in Weston's work: he had struck me as being an essentially slap-dash person. As for the imitation, it needed no expert to detect two major influences: Hardy and Edward Thomas. I might have found Frost there, too; but, in those days, I hadn't read him.

. . . .

Six months later—this was July 1926—Weston came down to stay with me at the seaside. I see him striding towards me, along Yarmouth Pier, a tall figure with loose violent impatient movements, dressed in dirty grey flannels and a black evening bow-tie. On his straw-coloured head was planted a very broad-brimmed black felt hat.

This hat I disliked from the start. It represented, I felt, something self-conscious and sham, something that Oxford had superimposed upon Weston's personality; something which he, in his turn, was trying to impose upon me. He wore it with a certain guilty defiance: he wasn't quite comfortable in it; he wanted me to accept it, with all its implications—and I wouldn't. I will never, as long as I live, accept any of Weston's hats. Since that day, he has tried me with several. There was an opera hat—belonging to the period when he decided that poets ought to dress like bank directors, in morning cut-aways and striped trousers or evening swallow-tails. There was a workman's cap, with a shiny black peak, which he bought while he was living in Berlin, and which had, in the end, to be burnt, because he was sick into it one evening in a cinema. There was, and occasionally still is, a panama with a black ribbon—representing, I think, Weston's conception of himself as a lunatic clergyman; always a favourite role. Also, most insidious of all, there exists, somewhere in the background, a schoolmaster's mortar-board. He has never dared to show me this: but I have seen him wearing it in several photographs.

The black hat caused a considerable sensation in the village where I was staying. The village boys and girls, grouped along the inn wall by the bus stop, sniggered loudly as we got out of the bus. Weston was pleased: "Laughter," he announced, "is the first sign of sexual attraction." Throughout the journey, he had entertained our fellow passengers and embarrassed me furiously by holding forth, in resonant Oxonian tones: "Of course, intellect's the only thing that matters at *all*. . . . Apart from Nature, geometry's all there is. . . . Geometry belongs to man. Man's got to assert himself against Nature, all the *time*. . . . Of course, I've absolutely no use for colour. Only form. The only really exciting things are volumes and *shapes*. . . . Poetry's got to be made up of images of form. I hate sunsets and flowers. And I loathe the *sea*. The sea is formless . . ." [ellipses in original].

But however embarrassing such statements might be to me, when uttered in public vehicles, they never for a moment made me feel—as I should have felt if a Poshocrat had been speaking—that Weston himself was a sham. He was merely experimenting aloud; saying over the latest things he had read in books, to hear how they sounded. Also they were a kind of substitute for small talk: for Weston, in his own peculiar way, made strenuous attempts to be the model guest. He really wanted every minute of his visit to be a success—on the highest intellectual plane. I was touched and flattered to discover, bit by bit, that he admired me; looked up to me, indeed, as a sort of literary elder brother. My own vanity and inexperience propelled me into this role easily enough: nowadays I should think twice about assuming such a responsibility—for Weston, who was as lazy as he was prolific, agreed without hesitation to any suggestion I cared to make; never stopping to ask himself whether my judgment was right or wrong. If I wanted an adjective altered, it was altered then and there. But if I suggested that a passage should be rewritten, Weston would say: "Much better scrap the whole thing," and throw the poem, without a murmur, into the wastepaper basket. If, on the other hand, I had praised a line in a poem otherwise condemned, then that line would reappear in a new poem. And if I didn't like this poem, either, but admired a second line, then both the lines would appear in a third poem, and so on—until a poem had been evolved which was a little anthology of my favourite lines, strung together without even an attempt to make connected sense. For this reason, most of Weston's work at that period was extraordinarily obscure.

Over, in any case, were the days of his pastoral simplicity. Since our meetings at Christmas, Weston's literary tastes had undergone a violent revolution. Hardy and Edward Thomas were forgotten. Eliot was now the master. Quotations and misquotations were allowed, together with bits of foreign languages, proper names and private jokes. Weston was peculiarly well equipped for playing the *Waste Land* game. For Eliot's Dante-quotations and classical learning, he substituted oddments of scientific, medical and psycho-analytical jargon: his magpie brain was a hoard of curious and suggestive phrases from Jung, Rivers, Kretschmer and Freud. He peppered his work liberally with such terms as "eutectic," "sigmoid curve," "Arch-Monad," "ligature," "gastropod"; seeking thereby to produce what he himself described as a "clinical" effect. To be "clinically minded" was, he said, the first duty of a poet. Love wasn't exciting or romantic or even disgusting; it was funny. The poet must handle it and similar themes with a wry, bitter smile and a pair of rubber surgical gloves. Poetry must be classic, clinical and austere.

I got very tired of the word "austere" in the course of the next few days: I began to wonder whether it didn't, as a rule, mean simply "pompous" or "priggish." At this time, Weston was a warm admirer of the works of Edwin Arlington Robinson: Robinson, it appeared, was very austere indeed. We nearly had a serious quarrel over "The forehead and the little ears / Have gone where Saturn keeps the years" [—]a couplet which he particularly liked, but which I thought, and still think, unintentionally very funny.

"Austerity" was also mixed up with Weston's feelings about the heroic Norse literature—his own personal variety of "War"-fixation. Naturally enough, he had been brought up on the Icelandic sagas; for they were the background of his family history. On his recommendation, I now began, for the first time, to read *Grettir* and *Burnt Njal,* which he had with him in his suitcase. The warriors, with their feuds, their practical jokes, their dark threats conveyed in puns and riddles and deliberate understatements ("I think this day will end unluckily for some, but chiefly for those who least expect harm"): they seemed so familiar—where had I met [them] before? Yes, I recognized them now: they were the boys at our preparatory school. Weston was pleased with the idea: we discussed it a good deal, wondering which of our schoolfellows best corresponded to the saga characters. In time, the school-saga world became for us a kind of Mortmere—a Mortmere founded upon our preparatory-school lives, just as the original Mortmere had been founded upon my life with Chalmers at Cambridge. About a year later, I actually tried the experiment of writing a school story in what was a kind of hybrid language composed of saga phraseology and schoolboy slang. And soon after this, Weston produced a short verse play in which the two worlds are so confused that it is almost impossible to say whether the characters are epic heroes or members of a school O.T.C.

In the intervals of all this talk, we bathed, got mildly drunk at the village pub and sang hymns to the accompaniment of Weston's banging on the piano in our lodgings. Weston, despite the apparent clumsiness of his large pudgy hands, was a competent pianist. He could never resist the sight of a piano, no matter whether it was in the refreshment room of a German railway station or the drawing-room of a strange house: down he would sit, without so much as taking off his hat, and begin to play his beloved hymn tunes, psalms and chants—the last remnants of his Anglican upbringing. When he had finished the keyboard would be littered with ash and tobacco from his huge volcano-like pipe. He smoked enormously, insatiably: "Insufficient weaning," he explained. "I must have something to *suck*." And he drank more cups of tea per day than anybody else I have ever known. It was as if his large, white, apparently bloodless body needed continual reinforcements of warmth. Although this was the height of the summer, he insisted, if the day was cloudy, on having a fire in the sitting-room. At night he slept with two thick blankets, an eiderdown, both our overcoats and all the rugs in his bedroom piled upon his bed.

When he had gone, I sat alone in my seaside lodgings and felt sorry: despite the fact that my most precious books were full of nicotine stains and dirty thumb-prints, that a hole had been burnt in my overcoat with a lighted cigar, and that I could hardly venture to show my face in the pub, since Weston had been practically turned out of it for loudly quoting the most lurid lines of Webster and Tourneur. With or without his hat, Weston was a most stimulating companion; and his short visit had excited and disturbed me profoundly. He had given me a badly needed shaking-up. Inevitably, I compared him with Chalmers. When Chalmers and I were together there were, and had always been, certain reticences between us: parts of our lives were common ground, other parts were not—and these, by mutual consent, we respected and left alone. The same thing was true of my other friends, Philip, the Cheurets, Eric. But Weston left nothing alone and respected nothing: he intruded everywhere; upon my old-maidish tidyness, my intimate little fads, my private ailments, my most secret sexual fears. As mercilessly inquisitive as a child of six, he enquired into the details of my dreams and phantasies, unravelled my complexes and poked, with his blunt finger, the acne on my left shoulder-blade, of which, since the age of eighteen, I had been extravagantly ashamed. I had found myself answering his questions, as one always must answer, when the questioner himself is completely impervious to delicacy or shame. And, after all, when I had finished, the heavens hadn't fallen; and, ah, what a relief to have spoken the words aloud!

[From *Themes and Conclusions*]

IGOR STRAVINSKY

If poets are rare, an all but extinct species, it follows that a great one, who is at the same time a great moralist, is a rarity indeed. Hence at least the public uniqueness of my old friend Wystan Auden, who has visited me more than once of late. Hence, too, my assumption that the reader, if only because of the social facts of this introduction, is naturally as interested in Mr. Auden as I am myself; and that it will not greatly matter to him that I have been unable to make the poet say anything momentous, or even something that one would want to put in a locket and carry away. What the *reader* must assume, on the other hand, or take on my word, is that Mr. Auden's talk is not merely rich but diamantiferous. The loss of sparkle is the price of any attempt to indite it, which I do not say as an attempt to excuse the particular shortcomings of my own retelling.

Yet perhaps not quite all of the glitter depends on precisely *how* he says it, some minute amount just possibly being due, for example, to scenic factors. These are not exotic; in fact, except for fetching, pasha-like felt slippers, themselves remarkable only by contrast with the boots and over-shoes favoured by other people in this season, they are not exotic at all. What one *is* aware of, and above all, are the invisible clocks. The poet's day is so strictly scheduled, his punctuality so tyrannical, that he will depart of an evening at some exactly predetermined hour—9.15, say, and it is seldom later than that—even if this deadline should find him in mid-thesis and only half-way through the consommé. Moreover, he is a man of such firm virtue and fixed habits (if *I* had them I would look like the Dong with the Luminous Nose) that he will forbear even to glance toward the gin-containing fridge before sundown—at which time, however, one imagines him, binoculars up, rather anxiously scanning the western sky. And speaking of gin, both of us, at that first, pre-Christmas, reunion party, let our hair down somewhat (the more he, for reasons of supply), except that in his case the consequences were noticeable only by a certain difficulty in marksmanship as he attempted to reoccupy the sleeves of his overcoat, and a certain tactile dependency on the corridor walls, of a kind employed (one imagines) by spelunkers in very dark caves or by Secret Service agents searching for hidden compartments and trapdoors.

To judge by his conversation, as well as by some recent poems, Wystan is deeply troubled by the generation gap. Whereas the twenty-five-year age difference between the two of us hardly counted (he said), the distance between himself and the very young was unbridgeable. "And the reason is that you and I are makers of objects; a poem is an object just as a table is an object, and one that, like a table, must be able to stand up." He also said that we shared a sense of the continuity of the past, and he contrasted our own state of affairs in this regard with that of the young "for whom, as for anyone else mad enough to suppose that it is possible to write or paint or compose independently of the past," he portended an unhappy denouement. "One finds things in a certain way, and one goes on from there," he said, and with that *he* went on to outline his creed of "work, *carnevale,* and prayer," which is a framework not merely of his intellectual beliefs, I should add, but of the way of life of a profoundly good man. I hardly need to say that it also constitutes a rather formidable obstacle between himself and the super-young.

Seeing the two purple tomes of *Blake and Tradition* on one of my tables, he remarked that he had not read them because "I can't 'take' the Prophetic Books." Then finding a copy of his own *City Without Walls,* in the same pile, he set about correcting misprints: capitalizing the pronoun for the Deity in "Song of Unconditional Surrender"; correcting a German spelling in the "Elegy"; deleting a gratuitous introductory "b" on "oggle." "The proof-reader, poor dear, obviously had never heard of the word, and what else *was* there but 'boggle'?"

He switched to German at one point, wanting to say something personal and probably finding it easier that way. *What* he wanted to say was how much I had meant in his life, beginning as far back as his sixteenth year when he first played my *Huit Pièces faciles.* I was moved by his remarks, of course, though they made me feel posthumous, and no less so by the unspoken thought behind them, though that came out, too, when he noted, near the end of the evening, that "to record an obituary for someone and then have him die a month later—which is what happened to me in the case of T. S. Eliot—makes you feel as if you were in some way responsible."

My wife translated his German into Russian—English accents are difficult for me not only in English—and my Russian back to German, which gave the scene an East-West aura and my wife the aura of the double-agent aware that both parties are only pretending not to speak each other's languages. A similar thought may have occurred to Wystan, for he began to talk about the Soviet poets, saying he had recently introduced an anthology of their work for Penguin and that he now considered Brodsky to be the best of them. Brodsky was to have been invited with Akhmadulina to a poetry conference in London last summer, he told us, but the Soviet official who had been approached to extend the invitation dampened the idea by advising us that "they will probably be ill at that time."

Wystan somehow got on to Goethe, perhaps only because we had been speaking German, but possibly because a thought had crossed his nimble mind about the drawing in of his own *Wanderjahre;* he said, at any rate, that he might soon cease to be a part-time or any-time New Yorker. Then, however, it became clear that the connection was a remark of mine about my dread of being recognized in public. "Goethe," he said, not altogether aptly, "was the first intellectual pin-up, the first culture figure at whom people came to stare in the modern, movie-star sense; and in consequence he may also have been the most conceited writer before Vladimir Nabokov." On the question, still debated in Weimar in my own youth, of whether Goethe "did or didn't" with Frau von Stein, Wystan sided with the "didn'ts." The Stein woman was "Hell," he said, and he gallantly defended Goethe's wife.

Part of our second evening together was spent looking at my manuscript sketches of *The Rake's Progress*—in which, incidentally, he seemed especially interested in my habit of translating syllables to note values before any real notes were composed. When we put the *Rake* aside, he gave me his and Chester Kallman's new libretto after *Love's Labour's Lost*. But about this unique achievement—Boito did not have to contend with Shakespeare's *language,* after all—I will say no more than that I became very envious reading the following exchange, so like the catechism in the *Rake:* "What is the end of study, let me know / To know what else we should not know"— and wanted to compose the music myself. In fact, I *did* compose the song "When daisies pied," with which *L.'s L.'s L.* (the opera) begins, and which the authors could do worse than to borrow.

Mr. Auden's recent thoughts on opera, *Words and Notes* (Festungsverlag Salzburg, 1968), include a number of distinctions between the requirements of libretti and those of spoken drama, all well worth carrying about in that locket, at any rate by aspirants to the librettist's art. Even more valuable, however, is a distinction, expressed in terms of grammatical function, concerning the nature of music itself. Thus he says that in contrast to the actors in a naturalistic stage drama, "the singers in an opera address themselves primarily to the audience." Whether they *do* anymore, on the *surface* level, is of course debatable, but "address" is meant in the largest sense, the sense in which "All musical statements are intransitive, in the First Person, singular or plural, and in the Present Indicative." Music, in other words, is for everyone and no one, and it is always in the Present Tense. And Mr. Auden establishes his grammatical classification by comparing music to poetry, which does not have these limits, and should not, in his opinion, seek them. The attempt of the *Symbolistes* "to make poetry as intransitive as music," could get no farther, he says, than a "narcissistic reflexive."

But music's intransitiveness is also proven by the circumstance that "We may sing a tune without words, or a song where the notes are associated with words, but when we *feel* like singing, the notes will always seem the more important element." (My italics.) And does the qualification, "when we *feel* like singing," not say, as I would say, that the words even of the Ninth Symphony can be reduced to nonsense without affecting the meaning of the music?

The most beautiful of Mr. Auden's operas will be brought to the stage at the Juilliard School this spring, an event that will in turn be brought to the attention of readers of this column, providing *Harper's* and God extend the necessary contracts.

[From *Journals 1939–1983*]

STEPHEN SPENDER

11 April [1979:] Five a.m. Centre College, Kentucky. Met at airport by a genial Southerner. The sort of man who talks about horse racing and Jane Austen in the same breath. He showed me to the campus guest room where I slept for an hour and then worked on my lecture with autobiographical references to Auden. This was better than the one I gave in Indianapolis, but I have the same sensation of not being in touch with the audience, of feeling, and looking, frightfully unhappy. Ended by reading three poems, "The Secret Agent," the first part of "Consider this and in our time," and "Look, Stranger, on this island now." Read not badly, but feel critical of A's early poems if I read them aloud, whereas they give me pleasure if I read them on the printed page. "Financier leaving your little room," etc., seems rather verbose and abstract read aloud, "The Secret Agent" hopelessly obscure and the kind of pleasure I get when I come to the line, "The street music seemed gracious now to one"—difficult to communicate. After lecture one of those faculty parties with a few students.

Someone asked me whether I really liked Wystan. This was a disconcerting question because it seemed to imply that I had drawn a picture of him which was unsympathetic. Thinking it over, I can see that I may have partly done so. I described him seeing his friends one by one in his rooms at hours he had fixed and interviewing, cross-examining them, laying down the law about the poets of whom he approved, the way poetry should be written, the personality of the poet, being very dogmatic about everything. I did insist that he was not a "leader" or authoritarian and that he brought a touch of absurdity to his pronouncements which made them seem jokes. He did not wish to be taken altogether seriously. But this would mean nothing to a member of the audience without a sense of humour. In fact to the American who thinks that when one is serious one should be serious, and when funny, un-serious, this would make A. seem even more unsympathetic. But during sleepless patches of the night I asked myself a question I certainly did not ask at the time—*did* I really like Wystan? To attempt to answer the question I had to recall what Wystan thought of me. He thought I was a wild romantic, rather "mad" (using the word rather loosely). To him I was, I suppose, a kind of Dostoevskian Holy Fool. I was so tall, he once told me, because I wanted to reach heaven ("The heaven-reachers"). I wanted really to be a saint. References to me in *Paid on Both Sides* and the original version of *The Orators* bear this out. He was so contemptuous of my pamphlet *Nine Experiments* (which certainly was very bad) that when this was reported back to me (of course, by Gabriel Carritt) I destroyed every copy of it I could retrieve from friends.[1] On the other hand, there was something about my utter vulnerability and openness which he respected. When I first knew him and told him about my plans for writing (which included writing novels, etc.) he said, "We must save you for poetry" and I was instantly a member of an élite which was headed by Auden and Isherwood but included Day Lewis, Rex Warner and very few others. He said, "You will be a poet because you will always be humiliated" and he felt that I had a kind of truth ("Blurting out the truth"— Isherwood). I imagine he laughed at me a lot behind my back. He also regarded me as a bit paranoid at Oxford (which I was). So, to measure my attitude to Auden, it is that of a somewhat battered observer. Moreover when a friend forms an idea of one when both he and you are very young and retains the same attitude throughout one's life, one feels a bit resentful. Finally, he came to be slightly jealous of me for reasons not indeed to do with talent or success, but because I had a family. When, in May 1945, wearing GI's uniform, Auden arrived at our house in London, the first thing he said when I opened the front door was, "You've got a son."

The lady who asked me whether I liked Auden said I had made him sound a bit inhuman. This did ring a bell, because I remember when we were both young thinking of him as *sui generis,* not at all like other people and of an inhuman cleverness. I did not think of him as having ordinary human feelings and I felt about his early poetry the lack of any "I" at the centre of it. If you appealed to Auden for sympathy or help he would be attentive, kind, but like a benevolent doctor or psychoanalyst whose task it was to provide a diagnosis and prescribe a treatment, more than as a friend who entered imaginatively into your situation as though it might be his own. He seemed also to have this detached "clinical" attitude towards himself even, and this is borne out by some of his early poems. A famous poem called "The Letter" is about the poet walking through a landscape where he takes shelter from a sudden shower by crouching behind a wall where he reads a letter from someone with whom he is in love. The contents of the letter are summed up in a line: "Speaking of much but not to come." The reader scarcely feels the emotion implied. The poet seems consciously to be exploiting it for the purposes of a poem in which he expressed clinical detachment even from his own hurt.

24 April: Nashville. I did not finish the notes above about Auden. And now I don't have the heart to read them.

Note

1. Gabriel Carritt, son of E. F. Carritt, Professor of Aesthetics. Friend of Auden at Oxford, referred to often in his early poems. He became a Communist Party member in the thirties and later a journalist on the *Daily Worker*.

INDEX

Index

◆